A Guide to Oregon South Coast History

Traveling the Jedediah Smith Trail

Books by Nathan Douthit

Uncertain Encounters: Indians and Whites at Peace and War in Southern Oregon, 1820s-1860s (Oregon State University Press, 2002)

The Coos Bay Region 1890-1944: Life on a Coastal Frontier (Coos County Historical Society, 2005)

A Guide to Oregon South Coast History

Traveling the Jedediah Smith Trail

NEW EDITION, REVISED & UPDATED

Nathan Douthit

Oregon State University Press

Corvallis

Publication of this book was made possible in part
by a contribution from

The Delmer Goode Fund

The Oregon State University Press is grateful for this support

The paper in this book meets the guidelines for permanence and durability of the
Committee on Production Guidelines for Book Longevity of the Council on Library
Resources and the minimum requirements of the American National Standard for
Permanence of Paper for Printed Library Materials Z39.48-1984.

Library of Congress Cataloging-in-Publication Data
Douthit, Nathan
A guide to Oregon south coast history : traveling the Jedediah Smith Trail / by
Nathan Douthit
 p. cm.
Includes bibliographical references and index
ISBN 978-0-87071-462-7 (alk. paper)
1. Historic sites—Oregon Guidebooks. 2. Oregon—History, Local. 3. Jedediah Smith
Exploring Expedition (1828). 4. Oregon Guidebooks. 5. Coasts—Oregon—History.
6. Northwest, Pacific—Discovery and exploration. I. Title.
F877.D68 1999
979.5'2—dc21   99-25339
                                                                               CIP

Oregon State University Press
121 The Valley Library
Corvallis OR 97331
541-737-3166 •fax 541-737-3170
http://oregonstate.edu/dept/press

To Eva and her students

Table of Contents

Preface to the New Edition

In the publication of this new edition, I have updated information concerning South Coast historical societies and museums. Several new books and Internet sites will be found in the "Sources of information" section. I also have made minor revisions and corrections of fact throughout the book. Museums change their exhibits from time to time, and therefore my descriptions of them should be taken as suggestive of what a visitor might find on display. In other respects the book stands unchanged from the last edition. It represents a personal perspective on South Coast history and historical landmarks as of the turn of the twenty-first century. Historians and archaeologists will continue to add to our knowledge of particular topics, but it's my hope that this book will provide a reliable intrroduction and guide to the core of the region's history for some years to come.

Nathan Douthit
Portland, Oregon 2006

Preface to the First OSU Press Edition

In the twelve years since publication of the first edition of this book, there have been enough changes in the historic landscape of the South Coast to justify a new edition. The Coquille River Museum has changed location and added to its exhibits. The former coastal steamer, whaler, and later tug, *Mary D. Hume*, is rotting away, half-sunk near the mouth of the Rogue River. The opening of the Cape Blanco Lighthouse to summer visitors has been a great success. The Coos County Logging Museum in Myrtle Point has developed from a collection of artifacts into a museum in its new quarters. The city of Coos Bay has a new boardwalk on its historic wharf-site. The Coos County Historical Society Museum has completely reorganized its exhibits around a new theme, "Tidewater Highways." Reedsport has a new museum called the Umpqua Discovery Center that highlights natural and human history of the lower Umpqua River. And the Siuslaw Pioneer Museum, south of Florence, has become an excellent center for historical and genealogical research for the Siuslaw River area. In general, I am happy to report that historic sites on the South Coast have survived the past decade in better shape than I expected. There seems to be more interest in historic preservation locally and an increase in "heritage tourism."

I want to thank the people who have helped make this new and updated edition possible: George Case, Steve Greif, Ann Koppy, and Frank Walsh for rereading the first edition and not hesitating to recommend changes; museum directors Vern Wimmer (Curry County Historical Society Museum), Ann Koppy (Coos County Historical Society Museum), Judy Knox (Coquille River Museum), Melvin Zumwalt (Coos County Logging Museum), and Louis Campbell (Siuslaw Pioneer Museum) for highlighting museum changes; archaeologists Steve Samuels (Bureau of Land Management, Coos Bay District), and Jon Erlandson and Mark Tveskov (University of Oregon), for archaeological information;

Phyllis Steves and Sue Powell (Siuslaw National Forest, Oregon Dunes National Recreation Area) for Oregon Dunes changes and archaeological information; Elizabeth Potter (National Register Coordinator, State Historic Preservation Office, Oregon Parks and Recreation Department) for National Register information; archivists in the Reference Unit, Oregon State archives for help in finding materials on Oregon State Parks; Jana Doerr for information on plans for a Bal'diyaka interpretive center; Warren Slesinger, Acquiring Editor, Oregon State University Press, for suggested changes to the format of the book; reviewers of the book for Oregon State University Press for their many recommendations for changes in organization, grammar, and subject matter; and Eva for her usual encouragement and critical perspective.

Nathan Douthit
Coos Bay, Oregon 1998

Acknowledgments
From Preface to the First Edition

This book would have been impossible without the research work and inspiration of other historians, archaeologists, library and museum professionals, and friends. My first acknowledgment of assistance must go to the pioneer South Coast historian Orvil Dodge. His "pioneer history," published in 1898, remains a treasure of information, although it is difficult to use and sometimes inaccurate. Emil R. Peterson and Alfred Powers added to Dodge's basic research a little over a half century later. Lewis A. McArthur has been the major source of information on the background of geographic names.

Since 1971, Stephen Dow Beckham has contributed a long list of historical articles, books, and inventories on the South Coast, which have provided me with much useful information. Edward G. Olsen's research on Curry County is the major source after Dodge, Peterson and Powers, and McArthur on the southern end of the region. Victor West has generously contributed the information on shipwrecks that appears in this book. Alice Bay Maloney's careful research in the late 1930s identified the Jedediah Smith expedition's campsites on the South Coast with local landmarks. Her article "Camp Sites of Jedediah Smith on the Oregon Coast" (1940) is the inspiration for my use of Jedediah Smith's exploration of the South Coast as a major structural theme of the book.

Steven Clay's research on the architecture of downtown Coos Bay has gone into that section of the guide. The research and writing of Joanne Metcalfe on the Coos Bay Wagon Road made it much easier to pull together the materials provided to me by Clara Eickworth, a wonderful woman whose life was dedicated to keeping the history of this region alive. Gene Large, resource specialist with the Oregon Dunes National Recreation Area, provided helpful leads to the history of beaches as a transportation route. I am indebted to University of Oregon Institute of Marine Biology (Charleston) students for their research over the years on the history of South Slough. Reg Pullen, Bureau of Land Management archaeologist, generously made available his library of materials on South Coast archaeology and shared with me his extensive knowledge of the region's prehistory.

I want to thank Dwight A. Smith, Cultural Resources Specialist, Oregon State Highway Division, Environmental Section, who made available his files of materials on the history of coastal bridges. He and co-researchers James B. Norman and Maxine Banks shared with me the South Coast bridge information that has gone into the Oregon Department of Transportation's new study, Historic Highway Bridges of Oregon. Their assistance has enabled me to treat South Coast bridges in far greater detail than otherwise would have been possible.

I also am indebted to the following people for their research assistance and their encouragement: Norman L. Stocking, for permission to use quotes from Captain Albert Lyman's journal and a drawing of the Samuel Roberts; Ella Mae Young, Research Librarian, Douglas County Historical Museum, for her help in obtaining use of the Captain Lyman materials; Kevin Kadar, for his skillful drawing of maps and illustrations; Jack Slattery and Victor West, for making available historical photographs from their collections; Pat Masterson, for sharing his knowledge and photographs of Port Orford-Cape Blanco history; Frank Walsh, for his book publishing advice; Rollie Pean, for use of photographs of McCullough and Siuslaw River bridges from his postcard collection; Terry Weaver, for his assistance in photo processing historic illustrations; John Gardner and Mary Enstrom of the South Slough Estuarine Sanctuary, for their help in providing information and photographs about the history of South Slough; Curt Beckham, Robert Bartholomew, George and Elaine Case, Virginia Fendrick, Lola Gardner, Sarah Heigho, Marguerite Metzgus, Erik Muller, Reg Pullen, Walt Schroeder, and Victor West, for reading selected portions of the manuscript for this book and offering many helpful suggestions for its improvement; the readers of my first book about the Coos Bay region and those people who have asked me when this book would be finished, for your much-needed encouragement; and Curt Beckham, Doug Borgard, Robert and Lucille Bartholomew, Ann Collins, Greg Dilkes, Kathy Grossman, Sarah Heigho, and Reg Pullen, with whom I have worked closely on local museum activities in recent years, for your fellowship and support. Finally, thanks to my wife Eva, who has shared in the development of this book through many discussions over the past four years, and who as usual has served as my most devoted critic and weaver of loose ends.

Nathan Douthit
Coos Bay, Oregon 1986

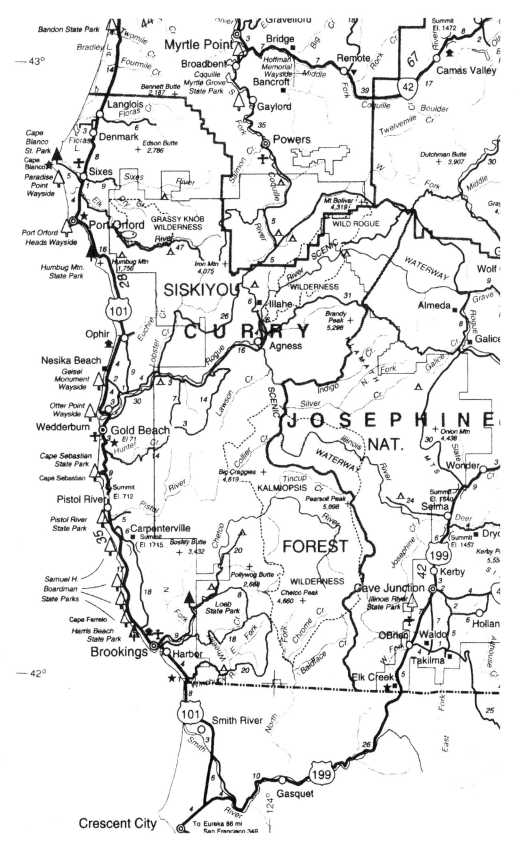

Oregon South Coast/ south half. Courtesy of Oregon Department of Transportation.

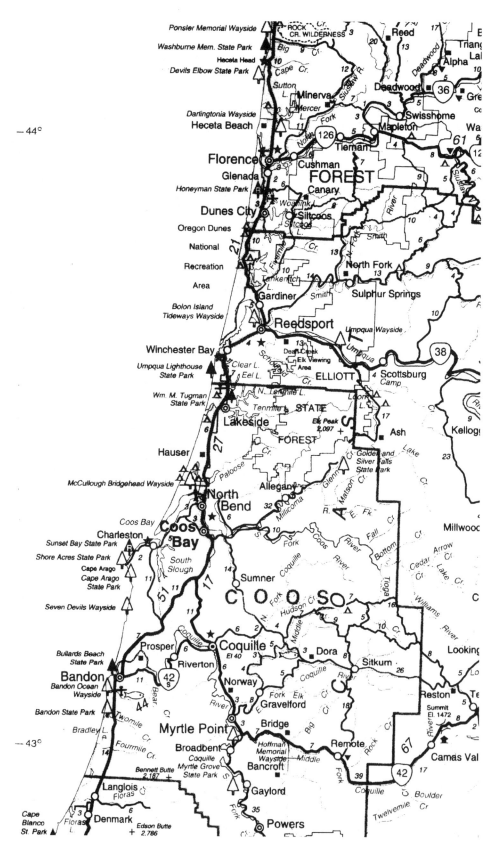

Oregon South Coast/ north half. Courtesy of Oregon Department of Transportation.

Part One
Oregon South Coast History

The Natural Setting and Its Transformation

The natural environment has played a major role in shaping the South Coast's history. The rivers and streams that run west to the sea from coastal mountains have provided rich natural resources, shelter for people to live, and routes of transportation. The major rivers occur at regular intervals along the coast, with the Rogue River, Coquille River, Coos River (and Coos Bay), Umpqua River, and Siuslaw River offering ideal locations for human settlement in ancient and modern times.

It is, most importantly, a coastal marine environment that is remote even today from the inland valleys of Oregon. It takes two to three hours of driving time to get from the inland cities of Eugene, Roseburg, and Medford to the coastal towns of Brookings, Gold Beach, Bandon, Coos Bay, Reedsport, and Florence. The ocean, like coastal rivers and streams, has provided economically important natural resources and a transportation waterway, but it also has contributed to the region's remoteness. The region's offshore waters are treacherous during frequently adverse weather conditions.

Native Americans, who lived in this coastal environment for thousands of years before European-Americans began to explore the coastline and trade for furs in the late eighteenth century, modified it in limited ways. They built villages, used fire in some areas to improve game forage, constructed fish weirs along rivers and streams, and developed trails for moving between villages.

With the arrival of white gold miners and settlers in the mid-nineteenth century, the land underwent substantial change. Farming brought new plant and animal species; cutting down trees for lumber began a process of deforestation, especially near coastal bays and accessible shoreline. White settlements and towns took shape, some on or near the sites of former Indian villages. These were larger in scale than the earlier Indian villages and resulted in the clearing of adjacent forests.

On Coos Bay and the Coquille River, early coal mining resulted in underground tunneling and above-ground excavation and industrial construction. Coal mining brought some of the first industrial technology to the region as early as the 1850s, and it encouraged the use of increasingly larger ships on the rivers and bays for transportation of coal to markets in San Francisco and Portland. Gold mining on coastal beaches and rivers in the 1850s littered the region with placer mining debris. Later, around the turn of the century, hydraulic and lode mining on the Rogue River and elsewhere left behind such remains as old trestles for water carrying flumes, stamp mill machinery, and abandoned mine shafts.

The early impact of settlement and industrial development from 1850 to the early 1900s transformed the natural environment of the South Coast in major ways. However, by comparison with other parts of Oregon and the nation in the twentieth century, Oregon's South Coast continued to be a region of small forest industrial and coastal port towns. As the largest estuary and harbor on the Oregon Coast, Coos Bay experienced the greatest development.

Today, much of the forest industrial economy has been stripped away on Coos Bay and elsewhere, although there are many log and chip trucks on the highways, and logs can be seen on rivers and sloughs or stacked on dry ground awaiting transport abroad. A pattern of small-town rural life along coastal bays and rivers continues, even though the region's people are as much exposed to American commercial and popular culture on the South Coast as anywhere.

In the period of the region's history since the 1930s, the most significant change in land and coastal water use has been the creation of coastal parks and nature preserves, and, quite recently, strict regulation of coastal fisheries. This reflects a new use of South Coast natural resources for tourist, recreational, educational, scientific research, and preservation ends. Effects of long-time forest industrial land use are quite evident in the clearcuts and young stands of recently planted Douglas-fir trees visible from highways and from the air. Climatic and soil conditions make it easy for trees to grow back on South Coast land, and some forest land in the region has been re-harvested several times since the mid-nineteenth century. But the historic forest ecosystem is gone forever. The once-abundant Port-Orford-cedar is nearly extinct. In offshore waters, coastal salmon struggle to survive.

The South Coast natural environment has favored a natural resource industry-based regional economy and a rural way of life. The region is likely to continue to be characterized by small towns and a rural life-style, but with decreasing dependence on natural resource industries. In a predominantly metropolitan, urban America, that is perhaps the region's unique historical value.

Early Coastal Exploration

European explorers approached the Pacific Northwest from the south in the 1500s, some 450 years ago. The Spanish, having conquered Mexico and first laid eyes on the Pacific Ocean in 1522, sent several expeditions northward by ship in the next two decades to search for a water connection between the Atlantic and Pacific oceans. A map of 1562 shows such a connecting waterway called the Strait of Anian. Spanish coastal as well as land explorers also search for a fabled land called Quivera, which mapmakers inconsistently located as far east as the great plains and as far west as Oregon and northern California.

As early as 1565, Spanish galleons sailed south along the north Pacific Coast on their return trip from the Philippines and Moluccas. At least one Manila galleon wrecked on the north coast of Oregon at Nehalem, casting its cargo of beeswax upon the shore.

After the Spanish voyages of exploration northward by Juan Rodriguez Cabrillo and Bartolome Ferrelo in 1542–1543, the next explorer known to have approached the Oregon Coast was the Englishman Francis Drake. In search of Spanish ships to capture, Drake probably entered South Coast waters in 1579. The precise site of Drake's northernmost approach to the Pacific Coast is still disputed. Early accounts of his voyage located it somewhere between 42 and 48 degrees latitude. It is believed by some contemporary students of his voyage that he took shelter briefly in the south cove of Cape Arago at 43 degrees 20 minutes latitude before putting ashore in the lee of Point Reyes in California to repair his ship the *Golden Hind*. The nineteenth-century historian Hubert Howe Bancroft, however, concluded that probably "the truth cannot be known respecting the latitude of the freebooters' landfall." He doubted that Drake went farther north than 42 degrees latitude.

Early maps reflect Drake's contribution of the name "Nova Albion" to the region of northern California and southern Oregon. But accurate information about his places of anchorage and landing is unavailable. Although the name Cape Blanco appeared on a map of 1597, it is not known who sighted it before its existence is believed to have been confirmed by Martín Aguilar in 1603.

Later Spanish Coastal Exploration

Spanish explorers usually found bad weather and heavy seas north of Cape Mendocino in California. Galleons returning from Manila in the Philippines probably passed the South Coast far out to sea. Lacking knowledge of the coastal waters, Spanish sea captains feared wrecking and preferred to sail as quickly as possible to their homeport of Acapulco. On the same voyage that Martín Aguilar claimed to have found Cape Blanco, his commander Sebastián Vizcaíno is believed to have sighted and named Cape Sebastian, but we don't know for certain what headlands the two captains sighted.

Accurate maps of the Pacific Coast shoreline did not become available until after English exploration in the late eighteenth century. As late as 1671, California still was being shown as an island detached from the American continent. But despite their inaccuracies, early maps have familiar place names. Capes Mendocino, Sebastian, and Blanco appear in sequence from south to north on some early maps as they do today. The lack of knowledge about the Pacific Coast of North America was due to the Spanish government's policy of secrecy. The Spanish feared that knowledge of the Pacific Coast region might encourage competition from European rivals.

For almost a century and a half after the expedition of Vizcaíno and Aguilar, the Spanish appear to have lost interest in learning more about the Northwest Coast. No other English explorers followed in the wake of Francis Drake, although English, Dutch, and French corsairs continued to prey on Manila galleons. In the 1600s, exploration of North America focused on the

Atlantic Coast. It took Russian fur trade and exploration along the coast of Alaska in the 1740s to revive Spain's concern with the northern region beyond Alta California.

By 1776, when Americans declared their independence from England, the Spanish had established a permanent settlement at San Francisco Bay. A year earlier, the Spanish sea captains Bruno de Hezeta, Juan Pérez and Juan Francisco de la Bodega y Quadra sailed north from San Blas, stopped briefly near the California-Oregon border, and then sailed as far north as Vancouver Island. The Indians who were visited by the expedition at several points along the coast saw three relatively small ships captained by young men. Hezeta was twenty-four and commander by virtue of seniority, while Bodega was the oldest at thirty-two. Hezeta's ship the *Santiago* was the largest at seventy-seven feet along the keel; it had a twenty-seven-foot beam. The *Santiago* may have carried ninety men. Bodega's ship *Sonora* was barely thirty-eight feet in length, much too small for a comfortable coastal voyage with at least sixteen men on board.

Although the Hezeta-Bodega expedition did not stop along the Oregon Coast, it did make a sighting of the Columbia River on August 17. Hezeta called it the Bay of the Assumption of Our Lady. The outgoing current was too strong to allow the expedition to explore it, but Hezeta guessed that it was "the mouth of some great river, or of some passage to another sea." Heceta Head, north of Florence, was named after Hezeta nearly a century later because of his observations of the shallow water of this coastal headland.

Captain James Cook

News of the Spanish expeditions along the Northwest Coast in the years 1774–1775 soon reached England. It made the English all the more eager to discover a waterway between the Atlantic and Pacific oceans of North America. In 1776, Captain James Cook was appointed commander of an expedition to explore the Northwest Coast. He left England with two ships, the *Discovery* and *Resolution*.

Captain Cook began his navy career in 1755 as a seaman and worked his way up the enlisted ranks until he was selected to command a scientific expedition to the South Pacific and received an officer's commission in 1768. His voyage of 1769–1771, with its objective of observing the transit of Venus between the earth and sun, resulted in a circumnavigation of the globe and established England's claim to New Zealand and Australia in addition to its scientific benefits. A second voyage of discovery in 1772–1775, also to the South Pacific, elevated Cook to the rank of Captain and made him a national hero.

Captain Cook's expedition to the Northwest Coast in 1776 unfolded in a spirit of high drama, nationalism, and international intrigue. Finally England was going to give serious attention to that part of the world which Francis Drake nearly 200 years earlier had called Nova Albion, or New England.

Cook again headed for the South Pacific; then in 1778 headed north to the Hawaiian Islands. By March, his ships lay off the Oregon Coast. The first prominent headland Cook sighted was Cape Foulweather, just north of Yaquina Bay. The coastal weather that prompted that coastal place name must have forced Cook south, because five days later, on March 12, he sighted another headland just south of Coos Bay, which he named Cape Gregory for the saint of the day. This cape later was named Arago after a nineteenth-century French physicist and geographer.

Cook's expedition continued northward along the coast as far as the Arctic Ocean before turning back to the Hawaiian Islands for the winter. At Kealakekua Bay, Cook was slain by native islanders. But Captain Cook's tragic end did nothing to diminish the importance of reports about potential wealth to be gained from trade in furs which his expedition brought back to England in 1780. In 1785, the first of many ships with goods to trade for furs arrived off Nootka Sound on the westside of Vancouver Island where Cook had stopped. It was typical of most fur-trading vessels to pass the coast of Oregon far out to sea. Their principal destination was the large island lying north of the Strait of Juan de Fuca, and the present-day coastline of British Columbia and Alaska.

American Coastal Exploration

Over the next few years, competition between Spanish, English, and Russians intensified from the Strait of Juan de Fuca north to the Bering Strait. The struggle for control of the fur trade passed by the Oregon Coast. But it did lead to circulation of an increasing number of trade goods, some of which were traded southward. This helped to make the Indians of Oregon's South Coast eager for trade when American and British ships appeared in 1788 and 1792.

In 1787 John Kendrick, commander of the *Columbia Rediviva*, and Robert Gray, commander of the *Lady Washington,* set forth from Boston to the Northwest Coast. These were the first American vessels to enter this region's waters. Financed by a group of New England merchants, the ships sailed with goods to trade for furs. In 1788, Robert Gray's ship sailed up the Oregon Coast, finally anchoring in Tillamook Bay, where several days of trading ended in a skirmish with local Indians. The first known contact with South Coast Indians by seaborne fur traders came three years later in 1791, when Captain James Baker's *Jenny* out of Bristol entered Winchester Bay at the mouth of the Umpqua River. A year later, Captain Charles Bishop, commanding the *Ruby*, followed Baker and noted that although Baker had traded with Indians for ten or twelve days, he obtained few furs and found the Indians hostile.

Captain George Vancouver

The next recorded European exploration of the South Coast was by Captain George Vancouver in 1792. At age thirty-four, Vancouver commanded two warships, the *Discovery* and *Chatham*; they mounted thirty cannons and guns in all. Vancouver's orders instructed him not only to show the British flag in northwest waters, but to bring back information about the northwest coastline and to continue the search for a passageway between the Pacific and Atlantic oceans. Based on knowledge of Francis Drake's landing north of San Francisco Bay, Vancouver laid claim for England to the coastline that stretched north to Puget Sound. However, it was Robert Gray who, in 1792, sailed about twelve miles up the Columbia River and thereby helped establish a United States' claim to the Oregon Country.

On April 24, 1792, Captain Vancouver anchored his ships just south of Cape Blanco at present-day Port Orford. Almost immediately, Indians paddled out to the ships in canoes hollowed out of tree trunks that carried about eight men each. Vancouver noted in his journal: "A pleasing and courteous deportment distinguished these people. Their countenances indicated nothing ferocious; their features partook rather of the general European character. . . ." Vancouver also commented on the Indians' desire to barter for "iron and beads."

Vancouver named the cape after his friend, George, the Earl of Orford. He doubted that it could be the Cape Blanco that the Spaniard Aguilar was supposed to have sighted, inasmuch as it did not appear to him to be white in color. Proceeding north along the South Coast, Vancouver confirmed the location of Cape Gregory, later renamed Arago, which Captain Cook had first sighted and named. Vancouver's survey of the South Coast was more precise than Cook's and beyond comparison with earlier Spanish conjectures about the northern coastline.

Later geographers retained the name Cape Blanco and ignored Captain Cook's naming of Cape Gregory, although Gregory Point just north of Cape Arago still remains on the map. North of the Umpqua River, the English left a more lasting imprint. Captain Cook's naming of Cape Perpetua and Cape Foulweather, and John Meares' responsibility for the naming of Cape Meares and Cape Lookout, are still evident on a coastal map of Oregon. Despite the naming of the Columbia River after the American Robert Gray's ship, the British monopolized the place names elsewhere on the northern Oregon Coast.

Early Nineteenth-Century Contacts
with South Coast Indians

In the years that followed Vancouver's voyage of exploration, many ships of European and American fur trading companies passed along the Northwest Coast. Because most of these went unreported, there is no way to know how many contacts were made with Indians on the South Coast. One Englishman wrote in 1792 that "hardly is there a point on the coast from 37 degrees to 60 degrees which is not visited. . . ."

The United States took a bold lead in Pacific Northwest exploration when President Jefferson sent out the Lewis and Clark Expedition in 1804. It reached the mouth of the Columbia River in 1805 after traveling along the Missouri River and then over the Rocky Mountains. Lewis and Clark did not explore southward along the Oregon Coast, but they did hear of a "Cook-koo-oose Nation" that lived far to the south. Clark also noted that he "saw several prisoners from this nation from the Clatsops and Kilamox, they are much fairer than the common Indians of this quarter, and do not flatten their heads."

The next reported contacts with Indians of the South Coast came in the years 1818–1821 when the British North West Company penetrated the Umpqua Valley to trade for furs. The North West Company merged with the Hudson's Bay Company in 1821. James Birnie, a fur trader with the company, may have visited the mouth of the Umpqua River that year.

Contacts with the Umpqua Indians were sporadic over the next decade. In 1826, Alexander Roderick McLeod was sent to explore the lower Umpqua and the region to the south in hopes of finding a large river leading inland. McLeod traveled through the Coos Bay and Coquille River region and south to the Rogue River before returning to the Willamette Valley.

The first expedition to explore the length of Oregon's South Coast by land was led by the young American fur trapper Jedediah Smith, who entered the fur trade at age twenty-three in 1822, just when Americans were beginning to challenge British fur trading interests in the upper Missouri region. In 1826, he led a party of mountain men or fur trappers from an annual summer fur-trading rendezvous in Utah's Cache Valley through the Great Basin and into California. He repeated this trip a year later.

In 1828, instead of crossing eastward over the Sierra Nevada, Smith headed north to Oregon. His expedition eventually reached the Umpqua River, where only Smith and three of his men survived an Indian attack. These explorations made Smith one of this country's most important explorers of the American West, although his achievements were for the most part unknown and unappreciated in his time.

Prehistory

In the past several decades, there has been renewed archaeological research interest in the South Coast. Intermittent archaeological research took place in the 1870s, 1930s, and 1940s. Archaeological research in the 1990s along the Oregon Coast has resulted in the addition of nearly one hundred new Native American sites to the National Register of Historic Places. Many more sites have been inventoried and radiocarbon dated. Among these are seventy-two fish weir sites on coastal estuaries. This research has helped to document the long history and scope of Indian coastal settlement that pre-dates Euro-American arrival. [Para. Break] Radiocarbon dates go back 3,000 years for South coast sites on Myers Creek near Pistol River and Umpqua-Eden near the mouth of the Umpqua River.

Archaeological excavation at Marial on the Rogue River by Oregon State University archaeologists in the summers of 1982 through 1985 yielded an even more surprising radiocarbon date of 8,560 years ago for the deepest layer some fourteen feet below the surface of the ground. Below the material used for dating, artifacts were found. This makes the Marial site the oldest in southwestern Oregon. It lies at the mouth of Mule Creek on what used to be part of the Billings family ranch, now the Bureau of Land Management's Rogue River Ranch. Ranch buildings on the east bank of Mule Creek were acquired by the United States government in 1972 as part of the Wild and Scenic Rivers program. They are on the National Register of Historic Places.

Nearly as old is the Tahkenitch Landing site located on Tahkenitch Lake between Florence and Reedsport. This site also has been dated to some 8,000 years ago. Archaeologist C. Melvin Aikens of the University of Oregon, who has described the site in his book, *Archaeology of Oregon* (1993), highlights an important aspect of some early sites. They existed in a quite different coastal environment:

> *Tahkenitch Lake now fills the old estuary of a small river flowing out of the steep, rugged Coast Range. The Tahkenitch Landing site occurs along the base of a small sandstone knob slightly elevated with respect to the adjacent flats. A shell midden containing artifacts is about 150 feet wide and 500 feet long. The abundant marine shells show unequivocally that the current fresh-water lake did not exist at the time the archaeological deposit was formed; the estuary then was directly open to the sea. The coastline now lies about a mile west of the site, and in early postglacial times, when meltwater from the world's icecaps had not yet brought the global ocean to its present level, the Pacific shore would have been more distant yet.*

In 1993–1994, anthropologists from the University of Oregon conducted a survey and radiocarbon dating program study of archaeological sites on state-owned lands along the South Coast. Professors Madonna L. Moss and Jon M. Erlandson, with the help of graduate students, evaluated fifty-two sites and radiocarbon dated twenty-six sites. Their work documented fifteen previously unrecorded sites. The purpose of the study was not the excavation of sites, but rather the documentation of their location and condition. The radiocarbon dates from this work ranged from historic times to about 8,600 years ago. Most of the sites were identified as less than 1,300 years old. The oldest site dated in the study was one in Samuel H. Boardman State Park, a shell midden like the other sites documented by the study.

One of the most productive archaeological sites on the South Coast has been the Umpqua-Eden site in the vicinity of Reedsport near the mouth of the Umpqua River. A large variety of remains have been found at the Umpqua-Eden site: circular and rectangular house pits; marine and terrestrial mammal remains; fish and bird remains; as well as, at the lowest level, lanceolate projectile points; sunbaked clay pipes; barbed bone harpoon points; and decorated bone ornaments. Charcoal taken from the bottom of the excavation yielded a date of some 3,000 years ago.

A site on Lone Ranch Creek south of Pistol River was worked by archaeologist Joel Berreman in 1936 and 1937. Although this site was not radiocarbon dated, it contained projectile points similar to those found in the Myers Creek site dated to nearly 3,000 years ago. The remains of four houses uncovered at the site included pieces of charred vertical plank walls, indicating the existence of house structures in a very early period similar to those known to exist in more recent historic time. Professor Aikens has suggested that "these houses indicate the permanence of the settlement, as do the 32 human burials encountered at various places during the excavations."

In 2006, Oregon State University archaeologist Roberta Hall and colleagues announced that they had completed research at a coastal bluff site just south of Bandon that is about 10,000 years old. Another site called Indian Sands in Boardman State Park north of Brookings has been radiocarbon dated to about 12,000 years ago. These two sites may be the oldest found in Oregon and on the South Coast thus far, but archaeologists believe that Native Americans lived on the South Coast even earlier.

These are only the most prominent among South Coast archaeological sites. Sites vary widely in size and significance. Some have been excavated to a very limited extent while others have had repeated work. Some sites appear to have been permanent village sites at one time, while others probably were used only as seasonal camps. In the case of both inland and coastal sites, they may not have been occupied through both early and late periods, or by the same people. The Athapaskan-speaking people who occupied the coastal region from the Coquille River southward are believed to be late arrivals. Penutian-speaking Indians from Coos Bay on north are believed to have come earlier.

Indian Linguistic Groups

When White people first came to the South Coast, the region was inhabited by two major Indian linguistic stocks: Penutian and Athapaskan. The languages within these two stocks were as different as German and Chinese. From the California border north to the upper reaches of the Coquille and Umpqua rivers, people spoke Athapaskan languages. The people living on the lower Coquille River northward to the lower Umpqua River and beyond spoke Penutian languages.

Each river valley had its own languages or dialects of the same language. The languages spoken in adjacent river valleys in some instances overlapped. There was language similarity between the Siuslaw and lower Umpqua Indians. Their language characteristics were more like those of tribes to the north than to the south. On Coos Bay there were two language groups: Hanis and Miluk. These languages were as different as some northern European languages of Germanic stock are today. The Coquille River Valley was divided between those people on the upper reaches of the river who spoke an Athaspaskan language and those near the mouth of the river, the Nasomah, who spoke a variation of the Miluk language.

South of the Coquille River to the Pistol River was the land of the Tututni. Although different villages with their own dialects were located along this section of coastline, they were related to the Tututnis, whose villages lay along the lower reaches of the Rogue River. To the south of the Tututnis were the Chetco Indians, and south of them were the Tolowas, who lived in the vicinity of the Winchuck River near the California border.

Anthropologists and historians have had difficulty estimating the South Coast Indian population. Their estimates are based on a combination of the number of village sites identified by older Indian informants and reports by White explorers and early Indian agents. Before the Rogue River Indian War began in 1855, the sub-Indian agent at Port Orford counted 1,311 Indians living from the Coquille River south to the Chetco River and up the Rogue River to the Illinois River. In 1858, the first census of the Siuslaw (95 persons), lower Umpqua (125), and Coos (234) Indians totaled 444. Because of late eighteenth- and early nineteenth-century White-caused smallpox and measles epidemics, demographic historians have recently estimated that the South Coast population prior to White contact may have been five times greater than it was by 1855.

A late nineteenth-century anthropologist who collected information about Siuslaw River Indian villages obtained names of thirty-four villages. Lottie Evanoff, a Coos Indian woman, recalled that there were about forty different village sites around Coos Bay. Villages varied in size, some reported by early Indian agents ranging from 30 to 120 or more people. Village sites named by Indian informants may have included both permanent and semi-permanent sites. In any case, pre-White contact populations far exceeded those enumerated in the 1850s.

Although the Indians living on the South Coast had many cultural traits in common, there were, in addition to language differences, variations in house building techniques, ceremonies, and food sources (depending on proximity to the sea). Indian tribes living south of the Coquille River drew cultural traits from northern California and Rogue Valley Indians. The Coos and lower Umpqua Indians drew upon influences from the north.

Indian Food Resources

South Coast Indians living near the sea relied upon its food resources. Salmon, steelhead, shellfish, and surf fish were staple foods. Sea lions, although prized, were less commonly killed for food. Like deer and elk, they were more difficult to catch without firearms. In addition to fish and animals, coastal Indians used many plants for food: roots (including camas, fern, and skunk cabbage roots), berries of many kinds, green shoots of various plants, seeds, and several kinds of seaweed were used for salt. Certain food resources were taboo. The Tolowa, for example, were forbidden to eat dog, coyote, wildcat, grizzly bear, cougar, birds of prey, seagull, land bird eggs, snakes, frogs, and octopus.

As one moved upriver, food gathered from the sea became less important, and acorns, camas roots, manzanita berries, deer and elk, salmon, and trout were the main foods. However, Indians living near the ocean moved upriver in late summer to gather acorns and to hunt for deer. Upriver Indians, on the other hand, seem to have been less mobile in their search for food, although they made occasional visits to the coast. During the summer months, food was dried for storage through the winter when high water in the rivers and the movement of game into higher country made fishing and hunting more difficult.

By the beginning of winter, a wealthy family would have its house lined with baskets of food for the winter. But although food was hunted and gathered individually as well as in groups, it was shared communally. In 1933, Annie Miner Peterson, age seventy-three and a Coos Indian, gave anthropologist Melville Jacobs this description of food distribution among the Coos Indians: "Whenever a poor person lacked food, he watched for where he saw smoke, and into there he went. He was given food indeed. When he had finished eating he would say, 'I'll take a gift of food.' Then indeed he would be given food, he would be given a lot. He would take them back with him to his own home, he would gather up all the leftovers."

Indian Houses

South Coast Indians built their permanent houses out of cedar planks split from logs with wedges of bone and stone hammers. The planks were stood on end around a rectangular pit dug into the ground. The planks were held in place by corner posts and connecting timbers. Over this rectangular frame they built a pitched plank roof, the planks resting at the peak of the roof on a horizontal beam or ridgepole and at the sides on the horizontal beam supporting the vertical plank walls. A space was left between the center roof planks for a smoke hole. A notched log ladder led down to the pit floor of planks laid at right angles to the long axis of the house. The depth of the pit varied from one foot among the Tolowa to four to five feet among the lower Rogue River Indians. The houses typically were about twelve by sixteen feet square.

South Coast Indians used other kinds of shelter too. The Siuslaw Indians, for example, used the typical South Coast semi-subterranean, plank slab house, a grass-covered summer house, and a sweat lodge. The Coos Indians, according to anthropologist Melville Jacobs, also had ceremonial dance houses, men's communal sweathouses, and several types of dwellings used by particular sex or status groups (e.g., chief's house, hired men's houses, boys' adolescent bunkhouse, and girls' adolescent bunkhouse [names descriptive of use rather than physical appearance]).

Temporary camps built in the summer were built characteristically of grass thatch or brush. Although summer shelters of the Coos were like those of their southern neighbors, their plank houses followed a Lower Columbian style in which the walls were entirely below ground with only the roof rising from ground level. Sweat houses for the men were built in a manner similar to the plank living house except that they had no smoke hole. The roof was covered over with earth and the inside area usually was smaller than a regular plank house.

Indian Wealth and Class Distinctions

Wealth among the South Coast Indians was measured in terms of the primary item of currency in the Pacific Northwest—dentalium shells. These were used like money to buy a canoe, to settle a debt, to pay the price of a bride, or to pay for a shaman or Indian doctor's cure. A rich family passed on its wealth from one generation to the next through the senior male. It was next to impossible for a poor family to become rich. Becoming a shaman was one of the few ways of getting ahead.

Other forms of "money" were scarlet woodpecker scalps, large blades made of black obsidian, and " women's money" (beads and shells used to decorate a woman's ceremonial dress). Families also had hereditary rights to use certain sites for deer hunting, acorn picking, and fishing. Rights to the parts of dead whales were reserved for various members of a village depending on their status. Although less extravagant than the "potlatches" of the British Columbia Indians, display dances were held periodically on the South Coast. These were five- to ten-day events during which there was dancing, feasting, and the display of wealth.

Indian Religious Beliefs

As in other Indian cultures, the Indians of the South Coast believed that the world was filled with supernatural powers. Nearly everything in nature was believed to possess a spirit and power to influence human beings. As young boys and girls, South Coast Indians went on vision quests. The vision quest consisted of a period of several days during which the person went off to a remote spot and, through fasting, lack of sleep, and exposure to the elements, waited for a guardian spirit. The guardian spirit would come in a dream, appearing as a bird or animal in human form and promising to guide the young person through life.

A belief in the sacred quality of things in nature led to many essentially religious rituals. The catching of the first salmon, for example, was always the occasion of an elaborate ritual to ensure the renewal of the salmon run. Among the Tolowa, a priest entered the sacred sweathouse for five days of fasting and repetition of sacred formulas and prayers. When he came out, he would go to the river and spear a salmon. The salmon would be carried to the village ceremonial site. After the salmon had been cooked, each person in the village would be given a bit of salmon rolled into a ball. Each person then would go to the river, dive under the water, and spit out the ball. This ceremony marked the beginning of the salmon season, and then everyone could catch salmon and eat them. There were variations on this ceremony among other South Coast Indian tribes.

Survival of Indian Culture

In the late nineteenth and early twentieth centuries, anthropologists sought out knowledgeable survivors of the reservation period to help them document different aspects of South Coast Indian culture. One of these survivors was Annie Miner Peterson. Her story recently has been told in Lionel Youst's excellent biography, *She's Tricky Like Coyote: Annie Miner Peterson, an Oregon Coast Indian Woman* (1997).

Annie was born in 1860 on Coos Bay, the daughter of a Coos Indian woman and a White man. At the time, Coos Indians were being moved from the reserve at the mouth of the Umpqua River to Yachats, farther north along the coast. Annie's father worked in a sawmill and he was away from home when soldiers came to take Annie and her mother. She recalled that her father wanted to keep her, but that her mother insisted that she belonged to her.

Life was difficult for Indians on the reservation. Annie recalled: "We lived poorly, we had nothing, we had no food, only just some Indian foods. That is how we lived at Yachat[s]. The Indians' head man [Indian agent] did not look after us. We had no clothes, we had to wear any old thing. That is how I grew up." But she lived among her own people, and learned their culture. Lionel Youst has told how Annie learned the two Coos Indian languages: "Annie's mother was bilingual in Hanis and Miluk, but she nearly always spoke Hanis. Annie was also bilingual. She picked up Miluk from her grandmother, her other relatives, and her childhood companions." In the process of learning two Coos Indian languages, she also learned many stories about her people while out "berry picking, root digging, and camping out."

By 1880, Annie had moved back to Empire on Coos Bay with her daughter Nellie. She worked as a live-in housekeeper while her half-sister Fannie, who was married to Coos Indian Chief Jackson, took care of her daughter. It had been five years since the Alsea Subagency at Yachats closed and the Coos and Lower Umpqua Indians who lived there had been forced to decide whether to go north to live at the main Siletz Reservation or to live among Whites. Most decided to return to their former homeland.

Years later, after several difficult marriages, Annie went to Portland, where she met and married a White man by the name of Peterson. The couple eventually moved from Portland to Charleston on Coos Bay because of the 1930s economic depression. It was there, in 1933, that University of Washington anthropologist Melville Jacobs met Annie.

Jacobs wrote in the preface to his book *Coos Narrative and Ethnologic Texts*:

> *In 1933 and 1934 I collected myth, narrative, and ethnologic texts in the two Coos dialects Hanis and Miluk, without preliminary study of the grammar. The informant, one of the last if not the very last of the bilingual speakers of these dialects, was Mrs. Annie Miner Peterson, now of Charleston, Oregon. Aged about 73, she is the oldest Coos survivor since the death of Jim Buchanan in June, 1933. Perhaps only two or three other persons have been able to speak in the Miluk dialect with comparable fluency during the last ten or fifteen years.*

Jacobs noted that Annie had not learned to speak English until she was in her twenties. She helped translate her dictations to him.

Annie's life, for all its hardships, ended in the preservation of the most complete picture of Coos Indian culture that we have. The two volumes of texts that Jacobs recorded were drawn from the memory of a woman whom Jacobs characterized as having remarkable humor, intelligence, and sensitivity to language. The narrative and ethnologic texts contain information on the treatment of children, anxieties and taboos, marriage, social distinctions, food, naming of children, fighting, attitudes toward poor people, and religious beliefs and rituals. The myth texts consist of stories about mythical beings and creatures—moon, crow, coyote the fourth worldmaker-trickster, buzzard, snail, water spider, Blue Crane, and others.

Other Coos Indians survived the period of removal and reservation life and contributed to the perpetuation of Coos Indian political and cultural identity. But thanks to the research work of Melville Jacobs and Lional Youst, Annie Miner Peterson has emerged as the most prominent Native American responsible for the preservation of South Coast Indian culture.

Beginning of White Settlement

The great migration to Oregon began in the 1840s following the westward advance of fur traders in the 1820s and missionaries in the 1830s. The gold rush in California began in 1849. It soon reached northern California and then spilled over into the Rogue Valley of southern Oregon.

In the summer of 1850, a party of men who had formed a joint stock company and called themselves the Klameth Exploring Expedition left San Francisco on the schooner *Samuel Roberts* to investigate the southern Oregon Coast. Their objective was to find a good harbor, lay out town sites, and explore inland along the Rogue River (called the Klameth River on early maps) in search of gold. Not finding the lower Rogue River Indians to their liking, they sailed on to the Umpqua River. On the north spit of the Umpqua River entrance, they laid out the town site of Umpqua City.

By coincidence, the *Samuel Roberts* entered the Umpqua River at the same time as three men who had taken out donation land claims upstream reached the mouth of the river. One of these men was Levi Scott, who had a land claim about twenty-six miles upstream. Scott donated a strip of land along the river to the company, and the town of Scottsburg was born. At first called Myrtle City, then Scottsville, and finally Scottsburg, it was the first White settlement on the South Coast. By 1852, it was a busy little town with some fifteen businesses.

In June 1851, a year after the Umpqua town sites were established, Captain William Tichenor landed a small party of men at Port Orford. The party was attacked by Indians and forced to flee to the Umpqua River. Captain Tichenor, who sailed on to San Francisco for reinforcements, returned in mid-July with sixty-seven men and supplies. The men built two blockhouses that marked the beginning of the town of Port Orford.

Because of the threat of Indian attack and a need to find a route inland, a detachment of soldiers was dispatched to Port Orford. But the new settlement's survival was tenuous until the following year. Captain Tichenor wrote: "It was unsafe to penetrate very far into the interior without sufficient force, as the natives were hostile. Everyone was building shelter for themselves. The quarters of the U.S. troops were incomplete, owing to the continued storms until late in the spring of [1852 when Tichenor's family arrived]."

In December, the small army detachment at Port Orford returned to San Francisco. Its replacement left for Port Orford on the schooner *Captain Lincoln* in January 1852. Due to bad weather, the schooner was blown north of Port Orford to Coos Bay, where it wrecked on the bay's north spit, a thin line of dunes separating the bay from the ocean. Rescue of the soldiers and supplies on north spit by the schooner *Nassau* in the spring made known the potential of Coos Bay as a harbor for ships and as a likely place for White settlement.

In February 1852, gold was discovered on Jackson Creek in the Rogue River Valley. The town of Jacksonville sprang up nearby. Miners from northern California crossed over the Siskiyous to the new diggings. Later that year, gold also was discovered on the beach north of the Coquille River. But it took until the spring of 1853 before miners from Jacksonville worked their way down the Illinois River to the mouth of the Rogue River. In the summer of 1853, miners converged on the mouth of the Rogue River from Crescent City, Port Orford, and Randolph (north of the Coquille River). The town of Ellensburg, later Gold Beach, was one of several clusters of log cabins built on the south shore.

About the same time gold was being discovered on South Coast beaches, twenty men in Jacksonville formed a joint stock company to establish a settlement on Coos Bay. They called themselves the "Coos Bay Commercial Company." Arriving on Coos Bay in the summer of 1853, this group established the town sites of Empire City and Marshfield. At the same time, discovery of gold on the beach just north of the Coquille River brought a rush of miners and the construction of a temporary mining camp called Randolph near a creek the miners named Whiskey Run.

By the fall of 1853, White occupation of the South Coast was well underway. Small towns had appeared overnight at the mouths of the Umpqua and Rogue rivers, on Coos Bay, and at the harbor site of Port Orford. In the years that followed, White settlement grew and spread.

Indian-White Conflict

Gold mining and white settlement in southern Oregon devastated the Indian inhabitants of the region. Between 1852 and 1854, the Rogue River Valley Indian population declined from about 1,154 to about 523 people. The Superintendent of Indian Affairs, Joel Palmer, wrote in 1854: "I found the Indians of the Rogue River Valley excited and unsettled. The hostilities of last summer had prevented the storing of the usual quantities of food; the occupation of their best root-grounds by the whites greatly abridged that resource; their scanty supplies and the unusual severity of the winter had induced disease, and death had swept away nearly one-fifth of those residing on the reserve."

An attack by a group of White "exterminators" against Rogue River Indians, who had agreed to come onto a reservation near lower Table Rock, provoked an uprising among the Rogues in the fall of 1855. After losing eight men and fifteen women and children, the Rogues retaliated by killing neighboring white settlers.

News of events in the Rogue Valley spread across the Coast Range. Indians on the lower Rogue River decided the time had come to make a last stand. In early 1856, they attacked white gold miners and settlers in and around Gold Beach, causing them to take refuge on the north bank of the river in a hastily built fortification called Fort Miner. On his way by ship to Crescent City, Captain Tichenor observed that "all along the coast was nothing but a blaze; wherever there was a hut it was in flames or in smouldering ruins."

In early 1856, most of the surviving Indians in the Rogue Valley were marched north to a reservation on the Yamhill River on the west side of the Willamette Valley. But those who continued fighting had to retreat down the Rogue River with White volunteers and government soldiers soon in pursuit. Other government troops were rushed to the South Coast and they moved east up the Rogue River to close off the Indians' route of escape. One last pitched battle at the Big Bend of the lower Rogue River near Illahee led to the Indians' final defeat.

The Indian warriors and their families who survived the war were marched to Port Orford, where they boarded a coastal steamship that took them part of the way to reservations established on the Yamhill and Siletz rivers. Nearly 1,200 Indians made this trip. Even though they had not participated in the war, Indians on Coos Bay, and on the lower Umpqua and Siuslaw rivers, were forced to leave their homes and to take up residence in the vicinity of Fort Umpqua at the mouth of the Umpqua River. They remained there between 1856 and 1859, then were forced to move again to a sub-agency of the Siletz Reservation at Yachats. By 1859, the South Coast had been cleared of Indians, which allowed White settlement of the region to proceed without interference.

Pioneer Economy

Most of the first White people who came to the South Coast in 1853 were gold miners with an interest in getting rich quick. But in the fall of that year, the families of the men of the Coos Bay Commercial Company arrived on Coos Bay. They took up residence near Empire City and around the bay. In the next few years, fighting between Indians and Whites in southwestern Oregon kept most people from settling very far away from major settlements on the bay. Although Coos Bay Indians didn't participate in the Indian-White conflict of 1855–1856, the upper Coquille Indians held back settlement in the Coquille Valley. The removal of Indians to reservations farther north on the coast ended this threat.

The economic base of settlement on the South Coast in the 1850s–1890s was coal mining, agriculture, logging, shipbuilding, lumber manufacture, and commercial salmon fishing. At the end of this period, the value of agricultural production still was equal to the combined value of logging, coal mining, lumber manufacture, and shipbuilding.

Coal mining began on Coos Bay from the first year of settlement. Members of the Coos Bay Commercial Company discovered coal outcroppings and began digging. The first shipments of coal left Coos Bay for San Francisco in the spring of 1854. At first, early settlers mined for coal on a small scale, but by the 1870s, California capitalists owned the major coal mines in the region. The coal mines provided jobs for hundreds of miners and a livelihood for them and their families. The coal mines in turn contributed to the growth of local towns and businesses. In 1876–1877, coal exports from Coos Bay reached just over $300,000.

Logging and lumber milling on the South Coast also began with early settlement. Lumber was needed to build mining camps and sluice boxes used in placer mining for gold. Small mills were set up to supply this need. The first of these consisted of open pits with two men operating a whipsaw to cut a log into planks. But Port Orford got the machinery for a real mill in 1853 or 1854. About the same time, a water powered mill was set up on a creek running out of Fahy Lake into the Coquille River near the later site of Bullards State Park.

By 1856, Henry H. Luse and Asa M. Simpson had built sawmills on Coos Bay at Empire City and North Bend. Both were cutting about 15,000 board feet a day by 1861. Simpson also established mills at Crescent City, Port Orford, and Gardiner on the South Coast, as well as at Astoria, Knappton, and Grays Harbor, thereby becoming one of the major lumber company owners on the north Pacific Coast.

Lumber milling and shipbuilding went together. Ships were needed to carry lumber in the coastal trade, and lumber was needed to build coastal schooners. Coos Bay and the Coquille River became a major center of shipbuilding activity. Asa M. Simpson was himself a master shipbuilder. By 1902, fifty-eight ships had been built at Simpson's mill and shipyard at North Bend. The most famous of these was the *Western Shore* built to Simpson's specifications by ship builder John Kruse. It was a three-masted ship that classified as a clipper, and in 1876 it made a record run of 101 days from Portland to Liverpool.

While Coos Bay became the center of lumber milling on the South Coast, commercial salmon fishing spurred growth at the mouth of the Rogue River. After the gold rush of the 1850s, the population at the mouth of the Rogue River dwindled. But the arrival of R. D. Hume at the Rogue River in 1876 led to its development as a major commercial salmon-canning site on the Pacific Coast. Hume's cannery output reached three-quarters of a million cans annually from 1880 to 1900.

Further development of settlement at the mouth of the Rogue River was hindered by its coastal isolation. A wagon road connecting Gold Beach with communities to the north and south wasn't completed until 1890. Commercial salmon fishing occurred along the South Coast on all the major streams, and salmon canneries also were built on the Coquille River, Coos Bay, Umpqua River, and Siuslaw River. Florence on the Siuslaw River grew in the 1880s because of new salmon canneries that were built there. But the Rogue River was the most important location on the South Coast for this industry.

The spreading of farms up the Coos and Coquille Rivers and along the coastal terrace south to Port Orford began in the late 1850s. A group of settlers from Baltimore, Maryland came to the Coquille Valley in 1859. They provided the nucleus of early settlement in that fertile river valley. Early farmers on the Coos and Coquille Rivers experimented with many crops, including tobacco. But their major products were grains such as oats, wheat, barley, and corn; vegetables, especially potatoes and carrots; and hay for cattle. Some farmers turned marshland into cranberry bogs.

South of the Coquille River, cattle raising was a major activity, and for many years summer cattle drives came up the coast and then went inland up the Coquille Valley and over the Coos Bay Wagon Road to the railhead at Roseburg. South of the Chetco River, where a coastal terrace provided level land, farming also developed. In the 1890s, dairy farming became important all along the South Coast, and creameries were built to process milk into cheese for commercial export.

By the turn of the century, the South Coast had a well-established mixed economy of agriculture, logging, milling, shipbuilding, coal mining, and commercial fishing. On Coos Bay and the Coquille River, small towns had taken root. The largest, Marshfield (present day Coos Bay), had 1,391 people in 1900. At that time Coos County numbered 10,324 people and Curry County 1,868.

The South Coast Since 1900

In the years after 1900, the South Coast changed from a region dependent for its livelihood on a mixed economy of logging, lumber manufacturing, coal mining, shipbuilding, salmon canning, and agriculture to a predominantly forest industry-dependent economy. Coal mining peaked just after the turn of the century and then declined. By the early 1920s, the availability of fuel oil forced large coal mines in Coos County to close. Agriculture became more specialized with dairy farming becoming the principal form of production. During World War I, there was a temporary expansion of wooden shipbuilding, but after the war that chapter in the region's economic history closed. Steel replaced wood in the building of ships.

The single most important event signaling the new era of forest industrial development on the South Coast was the opening in 1908 of the C. A. Smith Lumber Company mill on Isthmus Slough next to Marshfield. By 1920, about half of the sawmill and woodworkers in Coos County were employed by this mill and the Smith-Powers Logging Company. The C. A. Smith Lumber Company bought extensive timberlands in Coos and Curry counties. Federal funding of harbor improvements beginning the 1890s, as well as the completion of a Southern Pacific Railroad line to Coos Bay in 1916, helped to support forest industrial growth.

The building of a railroad to Coos Bay led to the development of the town of Reedsport, at first as a camp for railroad construction workers and then as a permanent town. Its post office was established in 1912 when railroad construction was in its early stage. In Curry County, the town of Brookings got its name and start because the Brookings Lumber Company located there in 1913. The company manufactured lumber out of redwood trees logged just over the state border in California. On Coos Bay and the Coquille River, forest industrial expansion added to the size of pre-existing towns. By 1920, Marshfield had a population of 4,034; North Bend's population was 3,268. On the Coquille River, Bandon had a population of 1,440, Coquille 1,642, and Myrtle Point 934.

The major new development in forest industry in the 1920s was the growth of Port Orford cedar production, manufacture, and export. A Japanese market for Port Orford cedar boomed in the 1920s and 1930s. In addition, there was a national market for Port Orford cedar in the manufacture of battery separators and venetian blinds. In the 1920s, battery separator plants opened on Coos Bay and in the town of Coquille and became major employers of workers in the region.

Another obvious sign of progress in the region, and one that promoted closer ties among its people, was the construction of new roads and improvement of older ones. A reporter wrote in 1931 that Coos Bay now had roads leading into it from north, south and east—"roads not merely paths through the hills and forests. . . ." This change was demonstrated even more dramatically by the completion of the Oregon Coast Highway in 1932. With the completion of coastal bridge building in 1936, local and tourist traffic moved more quickly from one end of the South Coast to the other.

Developments in forest industry, transportation, and urban growth in the period between the two world wars continued in the post-World War II years. By 1946, as much lumber was being shipped from Coos Bay as from Portland. Weyerhaeuser Timber Company, Menasha Wooden Ware Company, and Georgia-Pacific Corporation set up new, forest industrial operations in Coos County in the late 1940s and early 1950s. The growth of the South Coast's larger towns and its overall population kept pace with expanding forest industry.

By World War II, most of the region's people lived in towns. Until the 1940s, small boats that operated on rivers, bays, and inlets were the main means of transportation. But after World War II, paved roads linked even remote communities to larger towns, so that people could travel by automobile and truck. As the larger towns grew, older buildings were torn down and replaced with new ones.

By 1949, lumber production in Coos County was double what it had been in 1929 before the Great Depression began. This was even before a new Weyerhaeuser mill opened at North Bend in 1951. But the peak year of employment in lumber and wood products in western Oregon came in 1960–1961. Even as early as 1956, forest researchers warned that the rise in log production was about to end.

In the early 1970s, studies of log production predicted a 20% decline in western Oregon by the year 2000. The decline hit much earlier and harder. By the end of 1981, 71 of 210 lumber mills in Oregon had closed down; 18,770 of 31,076 sawmill workers were out of work. In Coos County, on the South Coast, nearly 2,000 forest industry jobs disappeared in the three years 1981–1983. Beginning in 1979, one mill after another on Coos Bay shut down or laid off workers. In Gold Beach, the closure of a mill owned by Champion International Corporation terminated the jobs of 322 workers. Curry County unemployment escalated to 20%. All of Oregon suffered. In 1982, the annual timber harvest in Oregon was the lowest since 1939. That year, Weyerhaeuser Company still employed about 1,500 workers in Coos County; by early 1998, the company employed about 190 workers in Coos County.

The effects of the sudden crash of forest industry in Oregon, and particularly on the South Coast, caused great personal hardships for many families. It stimulated research on relationships between regional economies of the West and the nation as a whole. Oregon State University historian William G. Robbins wrote two books tracing the harsh impact of changes in corporate capital investments on small communities (*Hard Times in Paradise*, 1988; and *Colony and Empire*, 1994). But for many years, despite the dangers and uncertainties of forest industrial work, the timber economy provided workers with a good livelihood. Capitalism worked to the advantage of both corporations and workers, although not of the natural environment.

The effects of forest industrial decline in the 1980s–1990s scarcely were visible on the physical landscape of the South Coast in 1998, except for abandoned or converted mills. In most instances, mills were stripped of their machinery for resale as scrap and then dismantled, leaving little more than foundation traces. Forest industrial sites on Coos Bay that still existed were mostly log or woodchip storage facilities in the export trade. In 1998, only about ten forest-industry related manufacturing plants remained in all of Coos, Curry, and western Douglas counties. The growing national support for protection of fish and wildlife resources on coastal rivers promised further reductions in timber harvest and fewer logging and chip trucks on the highways for the foreseeable future.

In 1998, *Oregonian* correspondent John Griffith wrote: "If you build a treetop walkway in an old-growth forest, will people want to come? If they do, could a forest canopy anchor a local ecotourism industry and replace jobs lost to declines in timber and fishing?" Griffith's newspaper article highlighted the efforts of Curry County officials and residents to find economic alternatives, in the face of federal government decisions to put land "off-limits to logging, to protect habitat for endangered and threatened species, or in designated wilderness areas."

On Coos Bay, local officials and residents in early 1998 waited to see whether Nucor Corporation, a steel manufacturing company, would complete negotiations for purchase of land from Weyerhaeuser Company on which to build a steel recycling mill that would bring an estimated 250 new jobs to the area. Local economic trends showed a continuation of the decline in forest industry that began in 1979. As in other South Coast towns, Coos Bay's new economic growth came from retail business, serving a growing retirement population and tourists. Since the late 1960s, forest industry in the region had lost 4,000 jobs, and among those were 175 mill and 70 woods jobs lost when Weyerhaeuser Company at the start of 1998 closed an up-to-date North Bend sawmill in the export trade. The personal hardships related to these job losses were many, but they included an increase in divorces and out-migration of young workers.

The other side of the economic picture on Coos Bay in the late 1990s was, because of retirees and an aging population, an increase in health care employment, which almost doubled from the 1980s. The Bay Area Hospital was the Coos Bay area's largest employer in early 1998 with 556 employees. In that year, a new gaming casino, opened by the Coquille Indian Tribe on the site of Weyerhaeuser Company's former mill that closed in 1989, employed about 340 workers. But wages in newer retail, medical, and gaming jobs were less than what mill workers had once earned.

In 1998 the Coos County population stood at 61,400, less by 2,647 people than in 1980. Coos Bay's population grew from 14,424 in 1980 to 15,615 in 1998, an 8.3% increase; but North Bend's population barely budged, increasing only slightly (1.3%) from 9,779 to 9,910. By contrast, in the same period (1980-1998), Oregon's population increased by 24%. Curry County's population grew from 16,992 in 1980 to 22,000 in 1998, a 29% increase, largely due to inmigration of retired persons. Brookings, the largest town in Curry County, had a population of 5,510 in 1998. In western Douglas County, Florence was the largest town, with 6,715, while Reedsport had 4,860.

A Personal View of Recent Urban Changes

Despite many changes over the past 150 years, the South Coast in the late 1990s still reflected its geographically isolated, rural, small town, forest industrial, and maritime beginnings. It still reflected the nation's rural past more than its metropolitan present and future.

When I came to the town of Coos Bay with my family nearly thirty years ago to begin teaching history at Southwestern Oregon Community College, I liked the town's mix of history and new beginnings. At that time, a major downtown mall project was just being completed. Four blocks of Central Avenue had been turned into a pedestrian mall, the kind of urban renewal project many towns large (Eugene) and small (Coos Bay) were undertaking. It was called the "Coos Bay City Center Tomorrow" project. A later phase of the project envisioned a waterfront boardwalk with restaurants, shops, and views of the upper bay. At the time, I liked the idea of blending the old Coos Bay into a new urban design, and I still do.

In the mid-1990s, the three blocks of pedestrian mall was reopened to traffic. Covered walkways to protect pedestrians from rain were torn down to open streets and sidewalks to sunlight. The covered mall experiment turned out to be a failure. It didn't recapture business from newly built shopping malls, and the covered sidewalks kept out sunshine as well as rain. But while the early phases of urban renewal were reversed, the waterfront boardwalk (minus businesses) became a reality, offering tourists access to a walking view of the bay.

In other parts of the four-block-square "old" downtown area, many buildings were removed to make way for parking lots and a scattering of new professional office buildings. A new city hall was built to replace one built in the 1920s; in 1998, the old one housed a restaurant, dancing ballroom, and office spaces. An historic Elks Club Building was restored and remodeled into a bank headquarters. An old bank building was turned into a brewery. A 1930s post office building became an art museum.

Away from the old downtown center of Coos Bay (formerly Marshfield), four new shopping centers appeared in the 1970s to 1990s, anchored by Albertsons, Bi-Mart, K-Mart, Fred Meyer, Safeway, and Wal-Mart outlets. A publicly financed Bay Area Hospital, built in the 1970s, expanded. The Southwestern Oregon Community College campus, built in the early 1960s, added new classrooms, office spaces, playing fields, cafeteria, and dormitories in the 1980s and 1990s. The town of North Bend built a new public library, and Coos Bay was, in 1998, in the process of expanding its library facility.

All of these changes occurred as the old forest industrial base of the North Bend-Coos Bay community was disappearing. In 1998, all but one of the forest industry mills and manufacturing plants that operated on Coos Bay thirty years before were gone. In the early 1980s, it seemed as though the twin cities themselves would close down. But by the late 1990s, the number of "for sale" signs seemed to have decreased.

In these and many other ways, the Coos Bay-North Bend landscape had been transformed. The two towns, still administered separately, had grown together in the past thirty years. The old downtown areas of the "twin-cities" now were integrated into a larger pattern of multiple business centers linked by commercial streets and interspersed with old and new residential areas. The geographical center of the peninsula that pushes north into the Coos Bay estuary became one of these new commercial hubs, an area of the combined towns that consisted of wooded lots, wetlands, and a few small farms when I came to Coos Bay thirty years ago.

These are some of the elements of continuity and change that I see on the South Coast urban landscape where I live. It is a landscape that retains some of the features of an older, coastal-frontier West, but it also is one that has been continuously re-engineered to meet the changing needs of business, industry, government, and individuals. I think this makes the South Coast historically interesting—its blend of past and present, as well as its blend of regional and national identity.

Part Two
Historic Places, Sites, and Museums

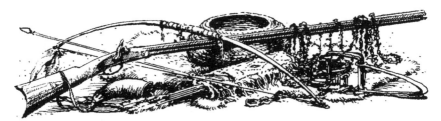

The Approach of the Jedediah Smith Expedition to Oregon in 1828

Jedediah Smith was one of this country's most important explorers of the American West. In recent years, scholars have come to appreciate his contributions to the mapping of the West. The journals kept by Jedediah Smith and Harrison Rogers provide the earliest observation of the South Coast by Euro-Americans after those of George Vancouver and Alexander McLeod.

There is no first-hand physical description of Jedediah Smith, but if, as biographer Dale L. Morgan suggests, he resembled his brothers, then he was probably just over six feet tall, slender, with brown hair and blue eyes. By the time he reached the South Coast, his face had been disfigured by a bear attack and subsequent field-stitching. Judging from the respect he earned from other mountain-men fur trappers and traders, he was serious, intelligent, self-assured, tough, and, surprisingly for a mountain man, religious.

The Jedediah Smith expedition approaching Cape Blanco in 1828.
Drawing by Kevin Kadar.

This guide to historic sites and museums on Oregon's South Coast has its beginning and end in the Jedediah Smith expedition's exploration of the South Coast in the summer of 1828. As we follow the expedition north from the Oregon-California border, we will take note of its campsites, describe its experience with the Indians of the South Coast, and view the South Coast landscape through the eyes of Jedediah Smith and Harrison Rogers, his second-in-command. We also will visit many earlier and later historic sites and related museum collections of importance to the history of the South Coast.

When Jedediah Smith reached Oregon's South Coast in 1828 at age twenty-nine, he already was a legendary figure. He was born on January 6, 1799 in the Susquehanna Valley of southern New York. In 1810, his family moved to Erie County, Pennsylvania, where a local doctor is said to have given him a copy of the 1814 Nicholas Biddle edition of the Lewis and Clark journals that encouraged a dream of becoming a western explorer. By 1817, the family had moved farther west into Ohio. In early 1821, after a river boat trip to New Orleans, Smith answered an advertisement for young men placed in a St. Louis newspaper by Missouri Fur Company owner William Henry Ashley.

Smith soon proved his mettle in skirmishes with Indians along the Missouri River. He became a leader among Ashley's men. By the summer of 1826, he had become a partner with David Jackson and William Sublette as part owner of the fur company Ashley had organized and made profitable. In the spring of 1824, Smith and his men rediscovered South Pass, a gap in the Rocky Mountains through which Smith's fur trading company brought pack mules and wagons to a summer rendezvous. Settlers eventually came through this pass by covered wagon on their way to Oregon and California.

In the next two years, Smith became the first American to reach California, the first to cross the Great Basin of Utah and Nevada, the first White person to cross the Sierra Nevada, and the first White person to lead an exploring expedition north from California into Oregon. In late summer 1826, he led an expedition of eighteen men from Cache Valley in the northeastern corner of Utah to the southwest. The expedition reached California with probably fifteen men and wintered there until the next spring, when Smith and two of his men crossed over the Sierra Nevada to return for supplies and reinforcements at the annual rendezvous. Smith headed back to California at the conclusion of the 1827 rendezvous with a new party of eighteen men. Mojave Indians attacked this second expedition; ten men and two Indian women traveling with the expedition were killed. Only nine survivors of the expedition reached the San Bernardino Valley.

After rejoining eleven of his men whom he had left behind in California, Smith laid plans to travel north into Oregon. By December 30, 1827, after troublesome negotiations with the Spanish, Smith headed northeast with nineteen men (and, in addition, possibly an Umpqua Indian boy named Marion) as well as about 300 horses. Initially, he followed a branch of the

San Joaquin River, eventually picked up the Sacramento River, and then in mid-April turned northwest down the Hay Fork of the Trinity River.

It took the expedition until June 8 to reach the Pacific Coast by following the Trinity River to its junction with the Klamath River and the Klamath River to its mouth. Some idea of the difficulty encountered in reaching the ocean may be gathered from Harrison Rogers' journal entry for June 3, 1828: "There was but little for our horses to eat; all hands working hard to get the horses on, as they have become so much worn out that it is almost impossible to drive through brush; we have two men every day that goes a head with axes to cut a road, and then it is with difficulty we can get along." The journals kept by Rogers and Smith also leave a record of day after day of fog and rain.

From Klamath, California, the party headed north along the coast. On June 20, it reached the river near the California-Oregon border that bears Jedediah Smith's name. The expedition made its last California camp at Castle Rock, then entered present day Oregon, just across the 42nd Parallel.

The Jedediah Smith Expedition on the South Coast left behind two legacies. One is a legacy of exploration and the opening up of new territory for westward expansion of Americans. The other is a legacy of insensitivity and violence in relations with the Indian people Smith's expedition met along the route of exploration. Beverly H. Ward's *White Moccasins* (1986), a book about the South Coast Indian experience based on stories told to her by her grandmother-in-law, Susan Ned, a Coquille Indian, expressed this second point of view. She wrote that the Indians feared the expedition, that the expedition tore down houses to make rafts, and that expedition members were killed by lower Umpqua Indians to protect their women from being raped. Hudson's Bay Company's Doctor John McLoughlin agreed with this Indian point of view, and many historians have supported it. Readers of this guide will have a chance to consider the evidence for themselves and to draw their own conclusions.

Chetco Valley to Rogue River

Travelers approaching Oregon from the south along US 101 pass over the Smith River just north of Crescent City. About fifteen miles east and south along Hwy 199, travelers from the east enter Jedediah Smith Redwoods. The name of Jedediah Smith has become affixed to this northwestern corner of California because of the exploring expedition he led up the coast from the mouth of the Klamath River into Oregon in 1828.

Jedediah Smith Campsites 1 and 2
Winchuck River to Chetco River

The expedition reached Oregon on June 23 and made its first camp in the state on the north bank of the Winchuck River. On this first day in Oregon, the expedition traveled along the shore or down on the beach. Smith noted that the nearby hills were "generally bare of timber." The expedition saw quite a few Indian villages that day. Smith commented that "many Indians visited camp in the evening bringing berries small fish and Roots for trade."

On June 24, the expedition advanced a few miles farther and camped on the south side of the Chetco River. The Chetco Indians have given their name to this river. They lived at its mouth and upriver along its banks for about fourteen miles.

Although its initial contact with Indians in Oregon had been friendly, the expedition received a different reception at the Chetco River. Jedediah Smith wrote: "Near my camp was a village of 10 or 12 Lodges but the indians had all ran off." Smith also made a few comments about Indian life: "Among the indians of this country I have seen a small kind of Tobacco which is pretty generally cultivated. These indians Catch Elk in Pits dug in places much frequented. They are 10 or 12 feet deep and much Larger at the bottom than top." Some men of the expedition stumbled into one of these traps with their horses and had trouble getting out.

Chetco Valley

Today, the Chetco Valley area is a beautiful, mile-wide strip of bench-land lying between the foothills of the Klamath Mountains and the Pacific Ocean. Fields of lilies merge to form a multi-colored floral tapestry in season. But it wasn't so cultivated or peaceful in earlier years.

The first White people came to this grassy valley in 1853. Twelve men divided the land and began to build cabins and establish farms. Trouble soon developed between these White men and Chetco Indians. Although condemned by other settlers, a man who ran a ferry and way station on the south bank of the Chetco River, together with some friends, attacked a Chetco village on the north bank of the river that winter. These and other Chetco

Indians on the river, perhaps numbering 350 persons, immediately became enemies of Whites and attacked and burned their homesteads. Although a temporary peace was arranged, it was broken again in 1855–1856 when the Chetco Indians joined the Rogue River Indians in a last stand against the White people. (See later section "War on the Rogue River" for more details.)

One of the early settlers in the area was Harrison G. Blake. His home, built about 1857, is now the Chetco Valley Museum. It is the oldest house to survive in the valley from pioneer days. Orvil Dodge in his pioneer history of Coos and Curry counties published in 1898 wrote about the Blake home: "Harry Blake's old home is one of the best in Oregon. It is situated about the center of the valley, and the buildings are surrounded with floral beauties and shade trees which have been brought from California and planted by Mr. Blake."

Although Blake gets the credit for building this beautiful pioneer home, it was his wife Mary who was the more important historical figure. She was one of the survivors of the John Geisel family that was attacked by Rogue River Indians in 1856. John Geisel and his three sons were killed. His wife, infant daughter, and older daughter Mary were taken captive, but they soon were ransomed for some blankets and an Indian woman who was being held by Whites. In later years, Mary was always remembered as a symbol of the tragic years of warfare with the Indians. (See later section "Geisel Monument Wayside" for more details.)

Chetco Valley Historical Museum

Location: 15461 Museum Rd., Brookings-Harbor; Milepost 360.7. Directions: Three miles south of Brookings on eastside of US 101; watch for road sign, "Oregon's Largest Monterey Cypress/Museum"; turn off on Museum Road parallel to US 101.

The Chetco Valley Historical Museum once was used as a stagecoach stop and trading post. It also was at one time the Chetco post office. Lewis A. McArthur, author of the book *Oregon Geographic Names*, noted that "old maps show this [post] office at various places on the coast between the mouth of Chetco River and the Oregon-California state line."

The museum stands back away from the highway on sloping ground. Its neatly trimmed yard, beautiful roses growing on an aging picket fence, and nearby record-size Monterey cypress, which stands ninety-seven feet tall and measures twenty-seven feet nine inches in circumference, makes it an inviting way station to start on the South Coast historic trail.

The rooms of the old Blake House now consist of a living room, bedroom, and kitchen furnished with late nineteenth-century artifacts. Two other rooms contain a variety of artifacts and photographs related to early Chetco Valley history. The photograph collection shows the development of Brookings and the surrounding area; pioneers and family members also are

Chetco Valley Museum. Author photo.

highlighted. A number of patchwork quilts are on display throughout the house, one said to date from 1844. The kitchen is well stocked with items of kitchenware, a wood stove, and a Hoosier kitchen cabinet. In the two rooms used for general displays, there is a collection of local Indian arrowheads and basketry items. An adjoining annex has other Indian artifacts, carpentry tools, an exhibit on Scouting, and an old post office window.

Chetco Valley History: 1860s–Present

Settlement of the Chetco Valley by White people took place slowly. There were only 215 people living in the Chetco Valley in 1860. A. G. Walling, in his description of southern Oregon in the early 1880s, noted that for about twelve miles along the Chetco River, settlers had cleared homesteads. South of the river, he said, "are some very fine farms, mainly devoted to wheat raising, but possessing orchards and other improvement." Wool, hides, fish, dairy products, wheat, and oats left the Chetco bar on the *Mary D. Hume* and other coastal schooners. A few early dairy farmers had upwards of 80 to 100 cows. Manufacturing, however, was absent. Walling remarked that although "the Chetco country has often been called Egypt since at one time it supplied nearly all of Del Norte county with wheat," it had to send wheat to Smith River to be milled. Lumber mills and fish canneries also were located over the California line.

Between 1863 and 1910, the Chetco post office was located at different locations in the valley, but there was no town. In 1891, a group of local town developers announced plans for a new town site called "Harbor." The Chetco post office was relocated there in 1894, but it later was moved when a feud broke out between two local families, the Coolidges and Van Pelts.

Ambitions to create a town were realized in 1913, when the owners of the Brookings Timber and Lumber Company built a mill and laid out a company town on the north side of the Chetco River. The company already

View of Brookings, Oregon, 1914.
Courtesy of Coos Historical & Maritime Museum.

owned mills in California. Between 1906 and 1912, company owners John and Robert Brookings bought nearly 27,000 acres of timberland between the Pistol and Chetco rivers. In 1912, they located a new sawmill operated by electricity on the Chetco River site. Famous California architect Bernard Maybeck designed the new town.

One distinctive feature of Maybeck's design was the laying out of streets so that they followed the contours of the land. In May 1914, about 350 persons lived in the new town. In 1926, an observer described the town in this way: "The town is not like the usual type of industrial village. The cottages are all different and very attractive. . . each was placed on a large lot, affording space for garden and flowers."

The Brookings Timber and Lumber Company merged with the California and Oregon (C. & O.) Lumber Company within a few years of the town's beginning, but the town kept its name and continued to grow. By 1920, Brookings had about 421 residents, and Chetco (Harbor) 451. In 1922, the C. & O. Lumber Company sold the houses and business property in the town to its residents.

The Chetco Valley still was isolated from the outside world in the 1920s. A section of the Coast or Roosevelt Highway was completed in 1924 between the California border and Brookings. But the road north was primitive. The residents of Coos, Curry, and Del Norte (California) counties lobbied for further improvements. By 1932, the Roosevelt Highway extended from Brookings to Gold Beach and a bridge had been constructed over the Rogue River. Before the highway's extension, it took about four hours by Model-T to reach Gold Beach in the wintertime.

Transportation improvements were essential to the Chetco Valley's survival. This was especially true after 1925 when the C. & O. Lumber Company shut down its mill in Brookings. Within a year, most of Brookings' residents left. The company's mill, railroad tracks, and wharf disappeared, as the company sold it for salvage. But farming in the Chetco Valley continued.

The lily bulb industry in the Chetco Valley grew out of three men's contributions. Louis Houghton, who worked in the Bandon area for the U.S. Department of Agriculture during World War I, became interested in the potential for lily bulb-raising on the South Coast. His enthusiasm led Sidney Croft of Bandon to raise lily bulbs. When he moved to Harbor after the Bandon fire of 1936, he grew lily bulbs and persuaded W. L. Crissey to do the same. Crissey, like Croft, wrote William Lundquist, "played a 'Johnny Appleseed' role with his bulbs, encouraging area farmers to grow them."

When World War II cut off Japanese bulb growers from the American market, South Coast lily bulb production boomed. The wartime expansion in lily bulb production led to a market collapse after the war. From a thousand growers at the end of the war, the industry in Curry County shook out all but ten farms by the 1990s in the Smith River to Harbor area. These farms produced 95% of the Easter lily bulb world market.

During World War II, on Wheeler Ridge five miles east of Brookings, a Japanese pilot, Nobuo Fujita, dropped two incendiary bombs. They were the first to be dropped on the United States mainland. The Japanese hoped to create forest fires that would distract Americans from their military mobilization. The wet forest conditions that existed on the day of the bombing, September 9, 1942, made the resulting fires easy to control. Three more bombs dropped near Port Orford malfunctioned.

In 1944, Jerry Phillips was working on the Chetco Peak Lookout. After Pearl Harbor and the 1942 incendiary bombings, lookouts were built to watch for Japanese planes. Phillips in *Caulked Boots and Cheese Sandwiches* (1996) recalled the "set of cards, showing the silhouettes of all Japanese aircraft, in our lookout towers."

A two-mile long "Bomb Site Trail" is located east of Brookings near the Wheeler Creek Natural Area off the South Bank Chetco River Road. It is located at mile 18.5 (10 miles on gravel roads) off a South Bank Chetco River Road to Forest Service Road 1205 ("Mt. Emily Road") tour route. Nobuo Fujita, the Japanese pilot who dropped the bombs on Wheeler Ridge, returned in 1962 as an act of post-war reconciliation and presented a 400-year-old family samurai sword to the Brookings-Harbor community. It is displayed in the Chetco Community Library. He returned again in 1992, on the fiftieth anniversary of the bombing, and planted a redwood seedling at the bombsite. (See later section "Cape Blanco: Lighthouse, Shipwrecks, and Japanese Fire Bombs" for more information on the Japanese bombings.)

Kalmiopsis Wilderness

Location: East of Brookings up the Chetco River. Directions: Obtain maps from the Chetco Ranger District office in Brookings; several trailheads can be reached from county road #784 (North Bank Road) and connecting forest service roads.

The Kalmiopsis Wilderness, located at the northern end of what has come to be called the Klamath-Siskiyou Ecoregion, is 180,000 acres in size, stretching from Chrome Creek at the south end to Bald Mountain at the north end. It takes in the headwaters of the Chetco and Illinois rivers, and borders on the Rogue River. It is named for its rarest plant, *Kalmiopsis leachiana,* a miniature, prehistoric rhododendron. Elevation in the wilderness ranges from 400 to 5,100 feet. The wilderness has a total of thirteen trailheads and 160 miles of hiking trails.

The U.S. Forest Service managed the Kalmiopsis as a wilderness for many years, although mining and logging activity occurred within the area. But when Congress established the landmark National Wilderness Preservation System in 1964, the Kalmiopsis was included. Then, in 1978, Congress enlarged the area from the original 76,000 acres to 180,000 under The Endangered American Wilderness Act. Its creation reflected the growing environmental consciousness of the 1960s–1970s that led to much ground-breaking legislation. The Kalmiopsis was only a small parcel in the initial nine million-acre, national wilderness system created in 1964. In addition to the Kalmiopsis expansion in 1978, another 36,000 acres on the Rogue River was established as The Wild Rogue Wilderness, which ranges from Mt. Bolivar at the northeast end to a point southwest of Illahe at the south end.

The Wilderness Act of 1964 was historically important because of the wild areas it preserved and because of the commitment it represented to the idea of preserving the few remaining wild natural areas in the country from business, tourist, and road development. The prohibition against development sets wilderness areas apart from national and state parks and recreation areas.

In recent years, as people have learned more about the Kalmiopsis Wilderness, its special geological and biological features make it seem even more important than it did in 1964. No one did more to bring to public attention the Klamath-Siskiyou Ecoregion and the Kalmiopsis's place in it than David Rains Wallace. His book, *The Klamath Knot* (1983), made people outside of the region aware of what had been a largely unknown place.

Gold mining spilled over into the Kalmiopsis in the 1850s, and the mining of chromite went on there as recently as the 1950s. So the Kalmiopsis had not existed in pristine isolation prior to wilderness designation. David Rains Wallace's explorations of the Kalmiopsis brought him into contact with many old mining sites: "Some of these old mining sites are eerie, like Taggart's Bar in the Kalmiopsis. Taggart's Bar is on the Chetco River, which runs between steep cliffs of volcanic stone and is only accessible from above in a few places. I camped several days on the cliffs and have rarely felt such wildness and loneliness in a place."

Wallace, however, was interested primarily in the plant, animal, and insect life of the Kalmiopsis:

> *The Chetko in the Kalmiopsis is another place where a river approaches the wonder of dreams, not only in its waters but in its setting. As I waded along the bank, I passed under umbrella plants with leaves a yard across and found dozens of big orange and purple stream orchids in the thick sedges. The cliffs above were a rock garden of azaleas, rhododendrons, lilies, maiden hair ferns, and ankle-high patches of Kalmiopsis leachiana, the rare little plant for which the wilderness is named. With half-inch leaves and dime-size red flowers, Kalmiopsis is the oldest living relative of azalea and rhododendron, an almost extinct species that grows only on the Chetko, Illinois, and Umpqua drainages, and that wasn't discovered until 1930.*

In the Klamath-Siskiyou Ecoregion as a whole, Wallace confronted some historic implications of the theory of evolution. He saw a "mosaic forest—"—a mix of many different conifers, but also oaks, maples, dogwoods, yews, shrubs, and smaller plants. It suggested to him that evolution might be as much about cooperation as competition.

By Wallace's estimate, about half of the Kalmiopsis consists of red-rock mountains of peridotite and serpentine rock. Dwarfed incense-cedar and Jeffrey pine predominate. Therefore, the Kalmiopsis is different from the rest of the Klamath Mountains ecoregion with its more abundant conifers. The soil lacks calcium, making it inhospitable ground for many plants. But it also favors certain plants, not only the Jeffrey pine, but also bunch grasses, which have been squeezed out elsewhere by non-native grasses. The Kalmiopsis also harbors the unusual, insect-eating pitcher plant that "has a bright green hood from which a forked, tonguelike appendage protrudes." Insects that land on its tongue eventually are trapped and fall down into the plant's inner pool of water, where they dissolve and are absorbed.

The cobra plant, which grows in wet ground in the red-rock forest of the Kalmiopsis, has its origins in earlier Oligocene period Klamath Mountain swamps. Wallace characterized the mini-swamps, where it grows today, as "the last vestiges of a landscape that otherwise vanished millions of years ago."

The larger Klamath-Siskiyou ecoregion to which the Kalmiopsis Wilderness belongs has gained world attention in the 1990s. It has been proposed as a World Heritage Site and UNESCO Biosphere Reserve, and the World Conservation Union has listed it as an Area of Global Botanical Significance. In 1997, the World Wildlife Fund rated it a "globally outstanding ecoregion" that is considered to be one of the world's five most endangered regions. The Fund's selection was based on a conservation assessment compiled over a two-year period by more than seventy scientists. This recognition is part of an effort at local, national, and international levels to restrain commercial exploitation and development of the world's last natural areas. Locally, it means trying to expand the protected status enjoyed by the Kalmiopsis Wilderness to more of the larger ecoregion to which it belongs.

Within South Coast boundaries of the Klamath-Siskiyou ecoregion, attention recently has focused on the headwaters of the Elk and Sixes rivers. Between these two rivers lies a third wilderness area on the South Coast, the Grassy Knob Wilderness. It is a small, 17,200-acre wilderness, only about nine miles northeast of Port Orford. Just to the east of Grassy Knob lies an area of 10,900 acres at the meeting point of Middle Fork Sixes, North Fork Elk, and Johnson and Salmon Creeks of the South Fork Coquille rivers. It has been proposed as a Copper Salmon Wilderness. This area has one of the last surviving stands of Port-Orford-Cedar on the South Coast. It also provides the cold, fresh water that makes the Elk and Sixes rivers two of the most important coho and chinook salmon and steelhead trout spawning areas on the Northwest Coast.

In a recent report on the ecological benefits of a proposed Copper Salmon Wilderness, fisheries biologist Christopher A. Frissell pointed out that the Kalmiopsis, Wild Rogue, and Grassy Knob wildernesses could be linked together more closely by establishment of a Copper Salmon Wilderness. Together they form "an archipelago of old growth habitat areas."

The Kalmiopsis, as the oldest South Coast nature preserve, symbolizes the values of preserving wild nature. An historic struggle continues on the South Coast and elsewhere in the Klamath-Siskiyou ecoregion between the demand for timber harvesting and jobs and the preservation values for which such well-known nineteenth-century conservationists as Henry David Thoreau and John Muir fought. To those nineteenth-century preservationist values that link wilderness to the nation's cultural history, today's conservationists have added the future-oriented ecological value of protecting biological diversity.

**Jedediah Smith
Campsite 3**
Thomas Creek

After leaving the Chetco River, Jedediah Smith and his expedition followed as close to shore as possible. But Smith soon found that the hills pushed down to the ocean, so for much of June 25 the expedition was forced to travel along the upland.

The expedition must have turned inland near Cape Ferrelo. It is named for Bartolome Ferrelo, pilot for Juan Rodriguez Cabrillo who sailed along the Pacific Coast in 1542. But it is not known for sure that Ferrelo ever came within sight of the cape.

The day's travel also took the expedition across Whalehead Creek. Offshore lies Whalehead Island. It has been eroded in such a way as to form a hole through which incoming waves rush and "spout" like a whale.

Although there were numerous ravines to cross, the expedition made twelve miles on June 25. Smith wrote that it "was much the best march I had made for a long time." He also noted: "Deer plenty and some Elk." The expedition camped that night on the north bank of Thomas Creek, within what is today Samuel H. Boardman State Park.

Samuel H. Boardman State Park

Oregonians may take them for granted (until they go out-of-state), but Oregon's state parks and roadside rest areas are among its most important and historic environmental achievements. Because it bears the name of the person most responsible for building the state park system, Samuel H. Boardman State Park is a good place to reflect on the history behind the park system.

Location: Mileposts 343–353; the park begins about three miles north of Brookings on US 101; it continues for about eight miles with numerous viewpoints and trails.

Two of the earliest state parks were created on the South Coast: Cape Sebastian (1925) and Humbug Mountain (1926). Governor Oswald West (1911–1915) led the way in promoting the idea of setting aside land for public use when he declared Oregon's beaches to be a public highway. Governor Ben Olcott (1919–1923) proposed the first acquisition of land for "parks, parking places, camp sites, public squares, and recreational grounds." The state legislature acted on Olcott's proposal in 1925. Support for a "scenic preservation and park program" waned in the late 1920s, until 1929, when Samuel H. Boardman was appointed by the Highway Commission to be the first state parks engineer.

Since the first two South Coast parks were established, another twenty-seven overnight and day-use-only parks have been added. Altogether, there are 75 state parks along the Oregon Coast and nearly 100 more in other parts of the state. As early as 1938, coastal parks received 942,345 (or 67%) of the 1,407,429 visitors to state parks.

By the 1920s, Americans increasingly took their new Model-T Fords out on roads for day trips and vacations. Samuel H. Boardman had the imagination to realize that Oregon had the scenic beauty to make its developing highway system a national model. By the time of his retirement in 1950 at age 75, Boardman had expanded the park system from forty-six small parks totaling 6,444 acres to a system of 181 parks encompassing 57,195 acres.

Boardman had long been a tree-planting advocate. He had a romantic's love of trees, which he believed inspired a serenity that could calm the "troubled minds" of contemporary Americans. Before going to work for the Oregon Highway Division, he homesteaded in eastern Oregon (the town of Boardman is named after him), where he launched a tree-planting project along the Columbia River Highway.

Coastal visitors in the early 1950s on the Coast Highway south of Cape Sebastian, just north of Samuel H. Boardman State Park. Courtesy of Oregon State Archives.

Although he was a romantic visionary who wanted to put Oregonians in touch with nature, he also was a practical man, a civil engineer by training. He early saw the link between highways and tourism. He didn't have adequate financing to make large acquisitions, but he was very successful in persuading private citizens and companies to donate land to the state for park use. During the depression years of the 1930s, he made use of Civilian Conservation Corps (CCC) workers, young men in need of work, to do the hard labor of constructing park facilities. (See "Jessie M. Honeyman Memorial State Park" for more information.)

Samuel H. Boardman State Park itself was established late and named in Boardman's honor. The first land was acquired in 1949. The Borax Consolidated, Ltd., of London, England donated 304 acres of land in 1950 and an additional 63 acres of right-of-way. U.S. Bureau of Land Management acreage was added in 1957. Altogether it includes 1,471 acres of land that Boardman originally hoped would be the centerpiece of a National Recreation Area along the Curry County coastline stretching from Pistol River to Brookings. As proposed, it would have totaled 30,000 acres. The National Park Service prepared a study, but the idea met local opposition, especially from stock grazers, and a bill to create a National Recreation Area in Curry County died in Congress in 1940 for lack of funding.

Samuel H. Boardman State Park, like some of the other parks, started with small initial land parcels and then expanded with later private donations or purchases. Humbug Mountain State Park began with a thirty-one-acre tract near the mouth of Brush Creek that was purchased in 1926. Between 1930 and 1975, sixteen additional pieces of land brought the whole area adjacent to and including Humbug Mountain into the park.

The protection of coastal headlands through private and public funding continues. In 1998, The Nature Conservancy of Oregon made a $1.9 million purchase of 134 acres with 6,200 feet of shoreline adjacent to the south boundary of Pistol River State Park. In May 2000, the U.S. Fish and Wildlife Service purchased the property from TNC. It is being managed as part of the Oregon Islands National Wildlife Refuge. Its tidal areas play host to harbor seals, sea lions, and several hundred thousand seabirds, including Leach's Storm Petrels. Crook Point headland is also home to many special plant species.

Boardman State Park is a day-use-only state park. Boardman himself thought state parks should be primarily for day use and that private campgrounds should provide for overnight visitors. However, a demand for overnight facilities at state parks led to the building of the first campgrounds in 1952 at Honeyman, Umpqua Lighthouse, Humbug Mountain, and Harris Beach state parks.

On June 26, the expedition left Thomas Creek and pushed on to the south bank of Pistol River, which takes its name from James Mace's pistol, lost to the river in 1853. Indians lived at the mouth of Pistol River, and during the day the expedition followed an Indian trail over the coastal ridge that lies between Thomas Creek and Pistol River.

**Jedediah Smith
Campsites 4 and 5**
Pistol River to Rogue River

The next day, June 27, the expedition passed over Cape Sebastian. This cape is a prominent headland that bears the name of Sebastián Vizcaíno. He may have sighted this landmark while exploring north from Mexico in 1603. It is impossible to tell whether this was actually the cape he sighted and named Cape Sebastian at what he thought to be 42 degrees north latitude. However, the United States Coast and Geodetic Survey adopted the name Sebastian in 1869.

Another ship of this expedition captained by Martín de Aguilar is supposed to have reached a "Cape Blanco" at 43 degrees north latitude. But McArthur in *Oregon Geographic Names* concluded that "the recorded latitudes of this expedition are too great and there is nothing to show that the members ever reached the coast of Oregon or saw what is now Cape Blanco." McArthur's conclusion also would apply to Cape Sebastian.

Once over Cape Sebastian, the expedition found easy traveling along the beach the rest of the way to the Rogue River. Jedediah Smith wrote on reaching campsite five on the south side of the Rogue River: "I encamped on the south side of a bay and close to its entrance which was 150 yards wide."

A morning fog sometimes envelops the mouth of the Rogue River. It confines a view of the river to the straight, narrow, pedestrian channel that leads between two jetties into the ocean. But when the fog begins to lift and one looks upstream, a wide valley opens up, islands appear in the river delta, and the coastal mountains loom in the distance. This, one realizes, is no ordinary coastal river, but a great water artery of the mountainous country from which it flows. It is known far and wide for its legendary salmon runs, thanks to the romanticizing of its wildness and Shangri-La seclusion by Zane Grey, the writer of western fantasies, in the late 1920s and since then by many other sports writers.

Like any special river, the Rogue River has a history as varied and extensive as its own course from the winter snow pack of the Cascade Range near Crater Lake to the Pacific Ocean. The upper, middle, and lower Rogue River sections each have their own unique history centering around the Indian tribes and White settlers who lived there, commercial and sport salmon fisheries, and more recent conflicts over how the river should be used and protected.

The origin of the name Rogue River still is something of a mystery. It has been suggested that it derived from the French word "rouge" meaning red. McArthur in *Oregon Geographic Names*, argued that this interpretation was mistaken. Several references to the river in early journals indicated that it was called "La Riviere aux Coquins," or River of the Rogues, by French fur traders. The "rogues," of course, were the Indians of the region, who early acquired a reputation for being unfriendly toward Whites. A map of the Oregon territory published in 1838 identified the river as "Rouge, Clamet or Tut-to-nez or McLeod's River."

Alexander McLeod was a Hudson's Bay Company explorer who visited the Rogue River in 1827. In his journal on January 11, 1827, he wrote: "This stream is called in the native dialect Toototenez, it falls short of the description report has given it, in size and depth for it does not exceed a quarter of a mile in breadth, where we fell upon it about four miles from the sea at a village containing about a dozen Indians. . . ." In contradiction to McLeod, however, McArthur stated that the Indians called the Rogue river "Trashit."

On reaching the Rogue River in 1828, Jedediah Smith took note of beaver signs, and he no doubt thought it might be a place with good fur trapping possibilities. He also observed the freshness of the water at low tide and "infered that it received a considerable river." However, the human inhabitants of the lower Rogue River, the so-called "rogues," kept their distance. Smith noted in his diary for June 27 that "on each side of the Bay were several indian villages but the indians had all run off." They couldn't have been pleased to see the expedition tear down one of their houses to make rafts for crossing the river.

The Rogue River proved to be a difficult crossing. On June 28, Smith and his men began driving their horses across the river. Some twelve of fifteen horses drowned under the flailing hooves of the massed herd straining to reach the river's north bank.

Rogue River Indian Villages

If Jedediah Smith had explored upriver, he would have discovered many Indian villages located from the mouth of the river to the Big Bend of the river at Illahee just above the fork of the Illinois and Rogue rivers. The narrow canyons, bench-lands, and meadows of the rugged Rogue River country provided Indian inhabitants with a livelihood and secluded home for many thousands of years, as recent archaeological excavations have revealed.

In late July 1850, the Klameth Exploring Expedition, a group of adventurers from San Francisco looking for potential town sites, entered the Rogue River. One of their members, Captain Albert Lyman of the schooner *Samuel Roberts*, described in his journal the Rogue River Indians he met. He noted that the Indians near the mouth of the river were numerous, friendly, unused to seeing White men, and lacking in trade items. He described them as "mostly naked or wrapped in a deer skin. Some had a closely woven conical cap made basket fashion and the chiefs had a deer skin cap with feathers on top. They paint their faces with black and red and wear pearl ornaments in their nose & ears. Some have feathers stuck through the perferature in their nose. Their Bows and arrows are of very nice workmanship." Lyman saw only "two old muskets among them." Some of their arrows had iron points, others flint. Their knives were made of copper or iron. "Their canoes," Captain Lyman wrote, "are rather rude being square at each end."

Anthropologists identify the Indians of the lower Rogue River as belonging to the Athapaskan linguistic group. The largest and most influential village on the lower Rogue River was that of the Tututni, located about five miles upstream from the ocean. White settlers called other Indians of the area by that name, but in fact the people of each village had their own name.

A census of the Indians of the lower Rogue River was made in 1854. It identified the Yah-shute or Joshua Indian band at the mouth of the river, the To-to-tin (Tututunne or Tututni) a short distance upstream, the Mack-a-no-tin (Mikonotunne) from Lobster Creek to the Illinois River, and the Shis-ta-koos-tee (Shasta Costa) from the fork of the Illinois and Rogue rivers to Big Bend. In all, the census reported 517 Indians living on the lower Rogue River. However, smallpox and measles had reduced the population over the previous thirty years or so.

The terms "Rogue River Indians" or "Rogues" are misleading. The Indians living on the Rogue River differed in language and customs. Anthropologist Dennis J. Gray in a University of Oregon Anthropological Paper, *The Takelma and Their Athapascan Neighbors* (1987), has discussed the three major language families (Athapascan, Takelma, and Shasta) on the upper and lower Rogue River. He explained that each language group had its own villages and even dialectical differences, indicating a long period of habitation and language development. Lower Rogue River Indians belonged to the Athapascan language family, but upper Rogue River Indians belonged to all three of these language families. Among the Takelma Indians, some were more dependent on riverine resources than others. Lowland Takelmas, for example, traded salmon for deer hides and meat with the Upland Takelmas. Lowlanders also used canoes instead of log rafts for river transportation. The semi-subterranean, gabled structures of the Upland Takelma were more likely to be covered with bark slabs and earth than planks. The geographical dividing line between these two Takelman groups was somewhere between Evans Creek and Gold Hill.

The Galice Creek, Illinois, and Applegate River Indians were "islands" of Athapascan-speaking Indians extending into Takelma territory. Lowland Takelmas probably stuck to the north side of the Rogue River and Athapascans to the south side. It seems uncertain how much use was made of the stretch of Rogue River from Grave Creek to the Illinois River. At the time Whites arrived, Shasta Costa Indians (Athapascan-speaking, as were other lower Rogue River Indians) had their main village site on the north bank of the Rogue opposite the Illinois River. But they probably went upstream on the Rogue to fish and hunt. An archaeological site at Marial, upstream from Illahe, is believed to have been a place of temporary use for thousands of years. (See later section, "Rogue River Ranch: Mule Creek").

War on the Rogue River

In the years 1855 and 1856, the river became a broken line of skirmishes and battles between Whites and Indians. The Rogue River War of 1855–1856 was one of the hardest-fought conflicts on the western frontier, and it occurred many years before the better-known Modoc, Nez Perce, and Plains Indian conflicts.

The rush to the beaches of the South Coast by gold miners in the early 1850s brought immediate danger to the Indians of the region. In early 1854, miners at Randolph (Whiskey Run) north of the Coquille River attacked and massacred at least sixteen inhabitants of an Indian village near the mouth of the Coquille. On the Chetco River, two villages were attacked and twelve men of the village were killed. There were numerous incidents in other places involving attacks on Indians by rough, quick-tempered, Indian-hating White men of the mining camps.

In early October 1855, a vigilante company of White "exterminators" from Jacksonville attacked a Shasta Indian village on Little Butte Creek on the upper Rogue River. Twenty-three Indians were killed, mostly old men, women, and children. This act mobilized Indians who had been opposed

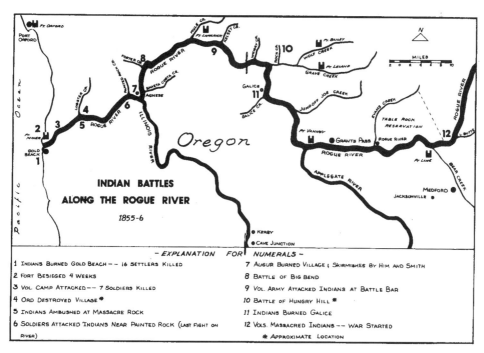

Indian battles along the Rogue River. Map by Kathy Hartman originally published in *Indian Battles Along the Rogue River 1855–1856* (1972), courtesy of Frank K. Walsh.

to going onto the Table Rock Reservation near Fort Lane that had been established under the Table Rock Treaty of 1853.

An Indian force made up of Applegate, Cow Creek, Galice Creek, and Shasta Indians retaliated against Whites along the middle Rogue River between Evans Creek and Grave Creek. The approximately 300 Takelma Indians on the reservation remained at peace.

By the end of October and early November, several hundred White volunteers and 104 U.S. Army regulars under the command of Captain Andrew J. Smith from Fort Lane mounted an attack on hostile Indian bands in the Grave Creek Hills. This became known as the Battle of Hungry Hill (October 31–November 1); it took place on the divide between Grave Creek and Cow Creek. About 100 Indian warriors repulsed the much-larger White force. Whites suffered an estimated twelve killed and twenty-six wounded; the Indians suffered seven to twenty deaths and unknown wounded.

Meanwhile, Oregon Territorial Governor George Curry called up a volunteer militia force—the Oregon Mounted Volunteers. Later in November, 386 volunteers and 50 U.S. Army regulars attacked an encampment of about 200 Indians, probably half of them women, children, and old men, located at Battle Bar on the south side of the Rogue River below Grave Creek.

News of events taking place upriver carried quickly to lower river Indian villages. Fearful of White reprisals on the coast and of plans for their removal to a reservation on the north Oregon coast on the Siletz River, lower Rogue

River Indians attacked White miners and settlers near Gold Beach in late February 1856. The sub-Indian agent for the area, Benjamin Wright, and twenty-two other Whites were killed; sixty cabins or houses were burned down. A surviving group of about 130 Whites took refuge in a temporary fortification called Fort Miner on the north bank of the Rogue River near its mouth, where they stayed for twenty-seven days and came under repeated Indian attacks.

Although he was strongly opposed to the war and mobilization of White volunteers, Major-General John E. Wool, commander of the Army of the Pacific, planned a three-pronged attack on hostile Rogue River Indians. He ordered approximately 100 soldiers from Fort Lane in the Rogue River Valley, another 100 from Crescent City, and 70 from Fort Orford to converge on the meeting point of the Rogue and Illinois rivers (at present-day Agness). The soldiers from Fort Lane arrived at the rendezvous point too late in March to link up with the soldiers from Fort Orford. But in the meantime, Colonel Buchanan, the field commander in charge, arrived at the mouth of the Rogue River from Crescent City, and relieved the siege of Fort Miner.

By mid-April, the Oregon Mounted Volunteers began preparations for a spring offensive. The volunteer forces skirmished with Indians in late April between Little Meadows and Big Meadows, but bad weather consisting of both snow and rain delayed arrival of the regular forces. Finally, in early May, a force of 343 U.S. Army regulars moved up the Rogue River. This army force consisted of the soldiers under Captain Smith from Fort Lane, as well as the contingents from Fort Orford and Crescent City. The volunteers renewed their pressure from the east. Through intermediaries, Colonel Buchanan urged the Indian bands at war to surrender, and on May 19–22 he held a peace council with Indian chiefs and their people at Oak Flat on the Illinois River.

But Chief John of the Applegate River, the main leader of the hostile Indian forces, and Enos, a man of mixed White and Indian background who led the attacks on Fort Miner, still refused to make peace. On May 26, Captain Smith arrived at Big Bend (near Illahee) to meet surrendering Indians, but Chief John attacked Smith's company with about 150 warriors. By May 28, Captain Augur's company had rescued Smith's men from defeat. Augur and Smith's companies suffered the worst casualties of the war, twelve dead and seventeen wounded. Despite their heroic last battle, the Indian force was reduced to about thirty-five men, who retreated into the surrounding hills with their women and children.

After the Battle of Big Bend, the Rogue River Indian war-coalition collapsed. In the days that followed, in late May to early June, Indians were rounded up by army regulars or straggled into the army encampments. For the most part, the regulars were successful in keeping those who surrendered out of the hands of the extermination-prone volunteers.

Captain Edward O. C. Ord described the suffering of the Indian women and children in his diary. "At 2 PM lot of Indians 4 men 9 squaws & some children came limping and crying (the squaws) into camp—a girl 12 years was drowned coming down the river—poor devils—the decrepid and half blind old woman are a melancholy sight—to think of collecting such people for a long journey through an unknown land—no wonder the men fight so desparately to remain."

The steamer *Columbia* arrived at Port Orford on June 19 to take on board 729 Indians bound for the coastal Siletz Reservation (which they would finally reach via the Columbia and Willamette rivers to the Yamhill River, and then by foot over the Coast Range). 592 Indians left later on July 8, bringing the total Indian removal to about 1,300 persons.

Chief John and the remaining Applegate Indians surrendered on June 29. His band consisted of approximately thirty-five men, ninety women, and an equal number of children. Captain Ord described their surrender: "There comes [down the hill] a long file of fierce looking fellows—in paint & feathers each with a fine rifle & at their head steps sternly & erect a hard faced grisly thin old man [about fifty-five years old]—in shirt sleeves & a small rimmed old Hat on top of his Head—its Old John I know at sight."

Chief John's band had to walk all the way up the coast to the Siletz Reservation.

From summer 1856 to winter 1857, William Tichenor, founder of Port Orford, tracked down an additional 152 Indian "holdouts" (19 were ambushed and killed on their way to Fort Orford).

Gold Mining on the South Coast

The name of the town of Gold Beach is a reminder that the South Coast once was a place where people came in search of gold. Unfortunately, there is no accessible place to go to see evidence of early gold mining activity on the South Coast, even though one may come across remains of early mining activity and even claims being worked today in the coastal mountains. But however fugitive the remains, gold mining, especially the gold rush of the 1850s, played a major role in bringing White people to the South Coast.

In February 1852, gold was discovered in the Rogue River Valley of southern Oregon. The town of Jacksonville sprang up overnight in close proximity to the diggings. The gold rush spread west to the Applegate and Illinois rivers, and down the Rogue River to the coast. Mining camps were scattered throughout the Klamath Mountains, which extend inland from the coast to the Cascade Range and north from the California border to the Coquille River. Thousands of men with gold pans, picks, shovels, and other equipment swarmed over the region in search of gold.

The heaviest concentrations of gold in the Klamath Mountains were found along the Rogue River, Applegate River, and upper Illinois River. But extensive mining took place along South Coast beaches at Ophir, Pistol River, Gold Beach, Port Orford, Cape Blanco, and just north of the Coquille River in Coos County. Mining also occurred on the Chetco, lower Illinois, and Sixes rivers, and on the upper reaches of the Coquille River's south fork as well as the Elk and Sixes rivers. These major locations of gold mining activity can be separated into four groups: beach placers, Salmon Mountain-Sixes area, Mule Creek-Bolivar area, and Illinois-Chetco area.

By 1852, miners had discovered gold on South Coast beaches as far north as Whiskey Run, just north of the Coquille River. In 1853, the gold mining camp of Randolph, which had upwards of a thousand men, had been established there. The beach placers stretched from Pistol River to Whiskey Run.

The most successful beach mining occurred where ocean waves had concentrated deposits of black sand containing gold, platinum, and chromite. According to an Oregon Department of Geology and Mineral Industries report (1977): "The better concentrates occur near sea cliffs on beaches where wave action during high tides and storms washes away the lighter minerals and leaves a residual rough concentrate of heavy minerals, pebbles, and driftwood." These beach concentrates were mined with various placer mining sluices and rocker boxes.

Recent mapping of offshore mineral deposits indicates the continued presence of black sand concentrations. The geologist John Eliot Allen has written that "one patch of black sand 5 miles long and 2 miles wide, only a mile or so northwest of Cape Blanco, contains the richest concentration of heavy minerals, more than 30 percent. These sands may also contain gold in amounts of about .005 parts per million. Smaller, gold-laden, black sand areas are located offshore from Gold Beach and Euchre Creek.

Late in the nineteenth century, the search for gold in black sand extended inland from the beach onto the beach terraces. The Pioneer Mine on Cut Creek (between the Coquille River and Whiskey Run) eventually had three tunnels, one of which reached 1,340 feet. The operators of this mine followed

Coastal beach placer mining.
Reprinted from *Harper's New Monthly Magazine* (Oct. 1856).

a pay streak of black sand about three feet thick that contained traces of gold that were recovered by sluicing. Terrace placer mines like the Pioneer and nearby Eagle Mine continued to be worked in the twentieth century. Salvaging of black sand concentrates at the old Pioneer Mine site was going on as late as 1964.

Extensive placer mining also took place in the Salmon Mountain-Sixes area east of Cape Blanco. J. S. Diller wrote in 1903 that "nearly all of the gold which has thus far been obtained in the Port Orford quadrangle has come from placer mines, some of which are along beaches in marine deposits and the rest in river gravels, especially along the South Fork of the Sixes and at the heads of Salmon and Johnson Creeks. . . ." Diller estimated the value of gold production from this area to be about $1,000,000. The only lode mine of importance in this area was the Salmon Mountain Mine, whose value of production up to 1936 was between $75,000 and $100,000.

The Mule Creek-Bolivar area lies to the northeast of the Blossom Bar-Marial section of the lower Rogue River. This was an area of lode deposits, the mountains consisting of broken sections of high-grade quartz veins containing gold. The first lode mining in this area began in the 1890s as a result of placer mining on the Rogue River itself below the mouth of Mule Creek on Red River bar. By 1914, four lode mines were operating in the area: Paradise, Lucky Boy, Red River, and Mule Mountain mines. As part of the Lucky Boy and Mule Mountain operation a two-stamp mill and cyanide plant were set up. The lode mines, however, were not very productive. In addition to early placer mining in the 1850s on Rogue River near Mule Creek, the Red River Gold Mining Company operated a hydraulic mining operation at the mouth of Mule Creek around the turn of the century.

The Illinois-Chetco mining area lies between Brookings-Harbor and Cave Junction. Gold miners moved west from the Kerby-Cave Junction area down the upper forks of the Illinois River. Josephine Creek was a major area of placer mining. Miners also crossed over to the upper reaches of the Chetco River. Several lode-mining claims still exist in the Kalmiopsis Wilderness area.

In addition to placer and lode mining for gold in the Klamath Mountains, some copper and chromite has been mined there. Wartime stockpiling of chromite in World War I and II and in early 1950s has resulted in the mining of a total of about 2,500 tons from about twenty mines and test sites in the Chrome Ridge area. The Kalmiopsis Wilderness also contains about eight chromite-mining sites near Chetco Peak.

Although the black sand gold deposits on South Coast beaches have washed away, the ocean might again at some future time open up its treasure chest. Along coastal rivers and at places like Whiskey Run, it is still possible to come across recreational miners. For some the search for gold on the South Coast continues.

Curry Historical Society Museum: Gold Beach

Location: Alice Wakeman Building, 29419 Ellensburg, Gold Beach, across the street from the Curry County Fairgrounds on US 101.

Although the first White settlement in Curry County was at Port Orford and today's largest community is Brookings-Harbor at the county's south end, the focus of the county's history has been the Rogue River. It is here in Gold Beach, originally called Ellensburg, near the mouth of the Rogue River, that the Curry Historical Society Museum is located.

The museum with its many photographs of early life in the region surrounding Gold Beach offers a good starting point for finding out about Curry County's history. Logging, gold mining, and salmon fishing and canning were mainstays of the local economy in the late 19th and early 20th centuries. The museum's many historic photographs of these industries illustrate a way of life that has long since disappeared. Mining and logging industries employed many young, single men who lived in camps and boarding houses. A boarding house exhibit complete with a table set for dinner helps to bring that experience back to life.

As described in the next section, Robert D. Hume played a major role in the life of people living on the lower Rogue River between 1876 and his death in 1911. Hume turned the lower Rogue River into a major commercial salmon fishing and canning center. The museum displays Hume's writing desk, letters of correspondence, photographs, and business ledgers.

The museum also has several excellent examples of Indian basket making. An exhibit of a basket made by Adeline Billings in 1917 also displays such material for making baskets as willow sticks, maidenhair fern, bear grass, and spruce roots.

A petroglyph exhibit that used to be located at the museum can now be viewed at the Agness-Illahe Museum in Agness. Removed in 1977 from the Twomile Creek petroglyph site about six miles up the Rogue River from Agness, the petroglyphs have been returned closer to their original home. According to local Indian tradition, the Twomile Creek Petroglyphs were associated with the encouragement of a good salmon and eel harvest. The cupules characteristic of these petroglyphs have also been associated in northern California Indian cultures with rain making and fertility. The Twomile Creek Petroglyphs have been estimated to date from about 1,500 years ago, based on comparisons of their patina with petroglyphs in Nevada and California. They are another reminder of ancient Native American life in the region.

The Curry Historical Society Museum contains many valuable photographs, historical documents, and artifacts. The museum encourages use of these materials for genealogical and historical research.]

Robert D. Hume, Salmon King: Wedderburn

Wedderburn gets its name from the ancestral home of Robert D. Hume, who once owned the land on both sides of the river for miles upstream. He was a tough, hard-working, and shrewd businessman. The history of the lower Rogue River is largely a history of his enterprises from the time of his arrival in 1876 until his death in 1908. In 1895, he replaced a fish cannery that burned down with a new one on the site of today's Rogue River Mail Boat Trips dock and office.

Location: Wedderburn is located on the north bank of the Rogue River, just across the Rogue River Bridge at the north end of Gold Beach.

In the early days of pioneer settlement, the coastal rivers ran thick with salmon during the annual runs. Old-timers talked in only slightly exaggerated terms of being able to walk across the rivers on the finny backs of salmon. In 1857, the first fish plant was opened on the Rogue River for salting down salmon in barrels to be shipped to San Francisco.

Hume got his start a decade earlier working for his brothers, who had started the first salmon canning plant on the Pacific Coast on the Sacramento River in 1864. His brothers moved their operation to the Columbia River in 1866, producing a pack of 4,000 cases (forty-eight cans each) in 1867. Hume soon built a cannery of his own at Astoria, later opened a business office in San Francisco, and then in 1876 acquired property and built a salmon cannery on the south bank of the Rogue River at Ellensburg (officially named Gold Beach in 1890).

Hume called himself a "pygmy monopolist," and rightly so, because within a few years he owned about 15,000 acres of river frontage and controlled most of the lower Rogue River. When his cannery burned down in 1893, he built a new plant on the north bank of the river and named the site Wedderburn. It was named after his family's place of origin in Scotland. Wedder is a variant of "wether," which in Middle English means male sheep, while "burn" means a stream or creek.

The packing of salmon at Hume's canneries on the Rogue River reached about three-quarters of a million cans annually between 1880 and 1900. Seine fishing and salmon canning was the mainstay of the economy on the lower Rogue River. During the canning season upwards of a hundred Chinese were brought down from Astoria to work in Hume's plant. His business enterprises on the river extended to cattle and sheep ranching, and dairy farming. He also owned a general store and a local newspaper.

Orvil Dodge captured the spirit of R. D. Hume when he wrote that "Mr. Hume, who does nothing by halves nor is the least appalled by big ventures, actually floated all of the chief buildings of Ellensburg across the broad river on scows, including a big two-story hotel."

Hume's holdings on the lower Rogue River made him a controversial figure. He was accused of hiring men to run off fishermen on the river who didn't work for him. One irate Port Orford fisherman at the turn of the

Delivering salmon at Rogue River cannery. Reprinted from R. D. Hume, *Salmon of the Pacific Coast* (1893), courtesy of Curry County Historical Society.

century asked: "Since when did our government grant a franchise to any man to own a navigable river?"

In 1911, soon after Hume died, the lower Rogue River was temporarily closed to commercial fishing by action of the Oregon legislature. The Macleay Estate Company in Portland purchased Hume's interests on the river in 1913, and it got the lower twelve miles of the river reopened to commercial fishing. The town of Wedderburn, which by 1913 had dwindled to about five people, revived. But conflict of interest between sport and commercial fishermen raged on for the next two decades. Zane Grey wrote a fictional treatment of this struggle in his novel *Rogue River Feud* (1945).

Like Hume in his day, the Macleay Estate continued to dominate the lower river with its holdings on both banks that extended upstream for about thirteen miles. By controlling land adjoining the river, the company effectively limited access to the river and restricted seine net fishing to its own fishermen. By 1925, however, the courts began to insist that rival fishermen be permitted to enter Macleay Estate lands. Ten years later, sport fishermen won the battle against commercial fishing interests, corporate and small fry alike. The river was closed for the final time to commercial fishing.

Wedderburn today is the starting point for mail boat trips that take passengers on runs up the Rogue River as far as Blossom Bar Rapids, a 104-mile roundtrip. Mail boat service began in 1895, when the first mail was brought downstream from Illahe to Gold Beach. This began a regular weekly service of delivering mail and merchandise from the Wedderburn post office and Hume's general store to people living upstream on the river. The story of the mail boat service is interestingly told in Gary and Gloria Meier's book *Whitewater Mailmen: The Story of the Rogue River Mail Boats* (1995).

The first mail boats were rowed (and poled to get over gravel bars). Gasoline-powered boats began working the river in 1900, but even then it took the use of a pole to get over some of the riffles. The boats had to be pulled around difficult rapids. There were a number of different mail boat operators in the early years. Passengers could ride the boats, and help with getting over riffles and rapids, for a dollar per roundtrip. From 1913 to 1921, the postal authorities experimented with mule pack train delivery into the "Rogue River Canyon" area. But in 1921, they gave up their experiment and ordered that from then on, all mail service on the river would go by mail boat.

In the 1930s, many movie celebrities discovered the Rogue River, and they liked to take the mail boat. One of these was Clark Cable, famous star

U.S. Mail Boat *Chinook*, a double-ender, propeller-driven boat built by Lex Fromm in 1948 and piloted by him in 1949. Courtesy of Oregon State Archives.

of "Gone With the Wind," who had spent two years in Oregon in the early 1920s before going to Hollywood. He worked in the woods, in a sawmill, on a coast survey crew, and at various other jobs to make money while acting off and on with a Portland theatre group. In 1930, he made his first fishing trip to the Rogue River and kept coming back. The Meiers have written that "Clark Gable loved taking the Mail Boat trip, and Abe Fry recalls piloting the star up to Agness with the mail on a number of occasions." Sometimes Gable would get off the mail boat to go fishing, and then hop on again on its return downstream.

Zane Grey and Sport Fishing on the Rogue

On Winkle Bar, upstream from Marial and accessible only by trail or river boat, is a privately owned cabin. It was built by Zane Grey, the famous writer of popular westerns, and stands as a reminder of the major influence he had on changing the Rogue River from an unknown coastal stream to a major sport fishing and tourist destination.

Zane Grey was born in Zanesville, Ohio, in 1872. He received a degree in dentistry from the University of Pennsylvania in 1896 and began his dental practice in New York City in hopes of achieving financial independence early in life so that he could pursue his passion for fishing. Grey showed some interest in writing as a young boy, but he didn't begin writing seriously until 1902, just after he met his wife Lina Roth, whom he called Dolly.

Dust jacket of Zane Grey's novel, *Rogue River Feud* (1948), about conflict among commercial fishermen on the lower and middle Rogue River.

Grey's first novel, *Betty Zane*, published in 1903, was a historical novel based on stories he had heard from his great-grandfather about the American Revolution. This was the first of three books he wrote about settlement of the Ohio River Valley. In 1907, he traveled to Arizona with an old buffalo hunter. This trip provided the material for his first western, *The Last of the Plainsmen*, published in 1908. In the period 1914–1928, Grey became one of America's most popular writers, publishing one western after another.

Grey's love of fishing led to many fishing expeditions, especially in the 1920s and 1930s, and to the writing of many fishing stories for sports journals. The first collection of these fishing stories to appear in book form came out in 1919. This was three years after Grey made his first fishing trip to the Rogue River. He was unsuccessful in catching steelhead on this first trip, but he came back in 1920. Again, either the fishing was poor, or Grey couldn't get the knack of steelhead fishing. But he came back in 1922 and caught his first steelhead. Grey made his first trip down the lower Rogue from Grants Pass in September 1925. Writer Mary Korbulic has quoted Grey's son Loren as saying that his father quit fishing the Rogue River when the Savage Rapids Dam was built a few years later.

Grey's stories about fishing on the Rogue were collected in his book, *Tales of Fresh Water Fishing*, published in 1928. In addition, the stories he heard from his river guides provided the material for a serialized novel about conflict among commercial fishermen on the lower and middle Rogue River. This novel first appeared in 1929 in the magazine *Country Gentleman* as "Rustlers of Silver River," and was published after Grey's death as *Rogue River Feud* in 1948. Even though his own interest turned away from the Rogue River to the North Umpqua River in the early 1930s, Zane Grey's stories about the Rogue River helped to make known its sport fishing attractions, especially on the middle and lower sections of the river.

It was river guides like Glen Wooldridge and Claud Bardon who made boat trips down the lower Rogue River possible for Zane Grey and other "dudes." Florence Arman tells Glen Wooldridge's story in her book, *The Rogue: A River to Run* (1982). After a couple of years gillnetting salmon on the Rogue west of Grants Pass, the nineteen-year-old Wooldridge and his friend Cal Allen decided to try running the river to Gold Beach. They launched a homemade boat and set out on September 5, 1915. This was the first of many trips Wooldridge made downriver over the next half century.

Grey's 1925 fishing expedition marked the beginning of the river's popularity with celebrities—writers, fighters, movie stars, and even a United States President. Glen Wooldridge recalled that Jack London, the writer, and Jim Jeffries, the fighter, fished the Rogue. Wooldridge also guided Herbert Hoover on the river when he was President. In the 1930s and 1940s Hollywood discovered the river.

As a result of Wooldridge's years of guiding on the river, he came to know its rapids better than any other person. He built boats designed to run the river's dangerous, rocky course. He also took it upon himself to alter some of the more impassable rapids. "The blasting along the river was done over a wide number of years," he recalled. "Blossom Bar was the big job, of course. We sure burned a lot of powder there before we learned how to shoot the rocks out. But we blasted many other places to clear a safer channel all the way down to Agness." Wooldridge's engineering, as well as his guide work, has made the Rogue River what it is today, still wild and scenic, but a lot less difficult for boats to run than it used to be.

In recent years, the Rogue River has become one of the most popular rivers in the West for river-running vacationers. Travel writer Julie Sterling captured the excitement, river-lodge-luxury, and attraction to this new kind of wilderness experience in describing breakfast before a day of white-water adventure.

Huevos rancheros, muffins, bacon and fried potatoes creak around the Lazy Susans that serve our breakfast at several round tables in the dining room [of Marial Lodge]—just as they did our Swiss steak dinner last night. We eat as though it is our last meal. Conversation focuses on Coffee Pot, the first nasty hazard in the Mule Creek descent, the entrance to the canyon is marked by "Guardian Rocks," which the guides lovingly call "jaws" . . .

The Rogue River received special recognition under the Wild and Scenic Rivers Act passed by Congress in 1968. An eighty-four-mile segment of the river extending from the mouth of the Applegate River near Grants Pass to the mouth of Lobster Creek near Gold Beach is protected by the Act. The Rogue River as a whole (215 miles in length) is one of the longest rivers inside of Oregon; only the John Day (the longest interior river at 284 miles) and the Deschutes (252 miles) are longer.

In recent years, there has been much concern about wild salmon runs on the Rogue River and other South Coast streams. In the summer of 1998, Oregon's coastal coho salmon were added to the national listing of threatened and endangered species because of a 9th U.S. Circuit Court of Appeals ruling that scientific concerns about the survival of coho salmon required their being listed. Oregon previously had launched its own Governor's Coastal Salmon Restoration Initiative in 1996 and had implemented a Wildlife Diversity Program, but state budgets for fish and wildlife biologists who work on these programs had been significantly reduced. The question remained whether federal regulation alone could restore coho salmon runs. Geoff Pampush, executive director of Oregon Trout, argued that "the key to salmon restoration lies in protecting and restoring key habitats and their functions in every watershed." That would require the cooperation of private landowners.

The listing of coho salmon as a threatened and endangered species will affect future logging in coastal forests. It has been estimated that logging revenues to South Coast counties may be reduced substantially as a result of efforts to save the coho salmon. But coho salmon represented a significant part of Oregon and the South Coast's natural heritage. The task of saving coho salmon represented, in Pampush's words, the "largest watershed restoration effort in Oregon's history."

Rogue River Ranch: Mule Creek

The most well-preserved historic landmark on the wild stretch of the Rogue River is the Rogue River Ranch located on Mule Creek a short distance upstream from Marial. This is the former George Billings ranch built around the turn of the century. The Rogue River Ranch, which is managed by the Bureau of Land Management as a historic site, is a striking reminder of the way of life on the river enjoyed by a small number of pioneer families.

George Billings was the son of a White man, John Billings, and a Karok Indian

Location: North bank of the Rogue River at mile twenty-three from Grave Creek, eighteen miles upstream from Illahe on the Rogue River Trail; the Marial Road provides vehicle access to the middle portion of the Rogue River Trail at Mule Creek. Contact Bureau of Land Management, Medford District, or Siskiyou National Forest, Gold Beach Ranger District, offices for directions.

woman, Adeline, from the Klamath River, who gave birth to ten children. The families of John Billings and two brothers, James and Abraham Fry, who also were married to Karok women, left the Klamath River for the Rogue River in about 1868. There already were miners living and working along the Rogue, including some Chinese. The Billings and Fry families made a living by mining and farming. In 1878, John Billings moved his family upriver to

Rogue River Ranch at Mule Creek.
Courtesy of Bureau of Land Management, Medford District Office.

Foster Creek. In the early 1880s, he built a flourmill. The family lived off the land, raising its own food, grazing cattle, and hunting and fishing.

George Billings was born in 1865. By the time he came to Mule Creek as a young man in 1890, it had long been a center of gold mining activity. George married mining camp cook Sarah Ann Huntley in 1894. They settled down to live and raise a family in the Mule Creek area. At first they lived in an old miner's cabin. George operated a store out of the cabin, and he packed in goods from the community of West Fork on Cow Creek to the east, where the railroad passed through. Over the years, he built a house and outbuildings, which now make up the Rogue River Ranch. The downstairs of the new house was operated as a store and boarding house for travelers.

Kay Atwood, whose fine book *Illahee* (1978) tells the stories of early families on the river, has commented that "George Billings' home served for years as a gathering place on the Rogue River. Miners, packers, and river families stayed there, voted on election-day at the trading company, danced above the barn, were born and died in the main house." Sometimes fifteen to twenty people would stay for the night at the Billings ranch. In addition to running the store, George, Sarah Ann, and their children developed an extensive farm-ranch on the river. They planted oats and vetch for their cattle, tended an orchard, and grazed cattle up Mule Creek canyon.

Gold mining in the Mule Creek area continued up to about 1912 or 1913. In the 1890s, a large flume was built on Mule Creek to bring water for placer mining operations near the river. George Billings built an eighty-three-foot-high trestle bridge across Mule Creek to carry the flume. In 1906, the Red River Gold Mining and Milling Company bought claims in the Mule Creek area and worked the area for six years without much success. The company built a sawmill to construct a three-and-one-half-mile-long flume from the east fork of Mule Creek. At one point, the flume was suspended 310 feet in the air on a trestle above the creek. There were also several lode mines in the Mule Creek Area. George Billings worked one of them, the "Tina H," where, according to Ivin Billings, there was a two-stamp mill, crushing machine.

Rogue River Ranch is still a stop for travelers along the river. The activity of the Billings family and the coming and going of miners, packers, and river families ceased years ago. But one still can experience through its buildings, its farm tools and implements, and the land of the old ranch itself, the unique wilderness isolation enjoyed by the river's early pioneers.

On the west side of Mule Creek at the Rogue River is a recent archaeological site that has yielded material radiocarbon dated to 8,560 years ago. It is known as the Marial Site. Material from this site is the oldest that has been dated on the South Coast. However, there may be even older materials at greater depths at the site. The stone tool technology that was found in the oldest levels of this site shows stability until about 2,800 years ago. Archaeologists call this the Glade Tradition. It is an early indigenous culture pattern that has been described by Thomas J. Connolly in a recent report on the Standley Site in Camas Valley. He wrote that it is "characterized by foliate and shouldered, contracting stem projectile points, broad-necked stemmed points, edge faceted cobbles, stone bowl mortars, hammer and anvil stones, and a linear flake technology that most consistently appears on distinctive steep endscrapers."

The Marial Site is located within the territory of the Shasta Costa Indians. Takelma Indians from upriver also may have made use of the resources of the surrounding area, but the western limit of their territory probably was closer to Grave Creek. Dennis J. Gray, in *The Takelma and Their Athapascan Neighbors* (1987), has noted that the farthest point downstream mentioned by Indian informants questioned by early twentieth-century anthropologists was Rainie Falls. But both Shasta Costa and Takelma Indians entered the region long after the people who originally made use of the Marial site.

The material excavated at the Mule Creek or Marial site consists of stone tools, which include projectile points, scrapers, and drills. Scrapers were found in greatest abundance. Archaeologists interpret these tools to mean that the site was used for hunting, fishing, plant gathering, and preparation of animal hides. It may have been a seasonal rather than permanent site.

Many prehistoric sites have been identified between Galice Creek and Gold Beach on the lower Rogue River but few have been scientifically investigated. Unfortunately, there has been much illegal artifact hunting along the river, to the detriment of future scientific investigations. It is against the law to excavate or remove archaeological objects without proper authorization.

The Rogue River Ranch site, with its evidence of prehistoric Indian habitation and later White mining and ranching activity, symbolizes the fateful collision of White and Indian cultures. And in the story of the Billings family itself is interwoven the history and traditions of those two cultures.

Rogue River or Isaac Lee Patterson Bridge

On leaving Gold Beach, northbound travelers cross over what commonly is called the Rogue River Bridge. Although they may take it for granted, this bridge, like the others that leap rivers and canyons the length of the Oregon Coast, belongs to a unique collection of engineering artifacts. One historian of bridge building has called it "the most interesting concentration of concrete bridges in America." In 1982, the Rogue River Bridge was designated as a National Historic Civil Engineering landmark by the American Society of Civil Engineers. It is named for then-Governor Patterson.

The Rogue River Bridge, built in 1931 and officially opened in May 1932, now is almost seventy years old. It was built in a "golden age" of bridge building in Oregon under the engineering direction of Conde B. McCullough, Bridge Engineer for the Oregon State Highway Department (1919–1932). McCullough has come to be recognized as a major figure in the history of American bridge building. (See "McCullough Bridge: Coos Bay" for more

The Rogue River Bridge between Wedderburn and Gold Beach, c. late 1930s.
Courtesy of Oregon State Archives.

information on McCullough.) The Rogue River Bridge is one of fourteen surviving bridges built under McCullough's direction. Four of these are on the South Coast: Rogue River Bridge, 1932; Coos Bay or McCullough Bridge, 1936; Umpqua River Bridge, 1936; and Siuslaw River Bridge, 1936.

The Rogue River Bridge illustrates the key features of McCullough's bridge-building style. It is characterized by its graceful wide arches providing support for the overlying roadway; high, narrow, Gothic-style arches on approaches to the bridge's main section; and decorative ornamentation on the main level of the bridge, including Art-Deco obelisks or gateway markers at the south and north bridge entrances.

The obelisk, a four-sided stone pillar that comes to a pyramidal point, is an Egyptian architectural feature that symbolized the sun's life-giving rays. A revival of interest in Egyptian architectural design in the 1920s led to incorporation of Egyptian motifs in buildings and bridges built in the 1920s and 1930s.

But what makes the Rogue River Bridge and others designed by McCullough so visually interesting and beautiful is his sensitive application

Detail of the north end of the Rogue River bridge.
Photo by author.

of an ancient architectural and engineering form—the arch. Despite the flatness of the deck or roadway itself, McCullough's varied and contrapuntal use of arches makes the bridge seem to float in the air above the river and to blend into the contours of the surrounding hills.

At the time of its completion, the Rogue River Bridge, with its seven 230-foot-long ("open-spandrel rib type reinforced concrete deck arch") spans and 1,898-foot length, was the largest bridge that the State Highway Department had engineered. Viewed from a distance, the bridge's arches harmonize with the curving lines of the coastal landscape—the arcs and curls of ocean waves, the rounded contours of sandspits and dunes, the sinuous patterns of coastal rivers, and the arching movement of coastal hills. Even without being engineers, we can appreciate the Rogue River Bridge as a unique example of engineering with nature rather than against it.

Rogue River to Bandon

Geisel Monument Wayside

Directions: At mile post 322.4 on US 101, 4.6 miles north of the Rogue River Bridge; watch for Geisel Monument $^1/_4$ Mile sign, then turn at the State Park sign. The narrow, poorly marked entrance is on the ocean or west side of the highway.

A good place to make a final reflection on the Rogue River War of 1855–1856 is the Geisel Monument. About five miles north of Gold Beach off Highway 101 there is a day-use-area wayside and monument to one of the White families that was attacked by the Tututni in late February 1856. Here one can see the tombstones of John Geisel and his three sons who were killed by Indians. His wife Christina and two daughters were taken captive by the attackers, but later were returned alive through the exchange of ransom. Although Christina lived until September 20, 1899, when she was murdered for her pension check, and although she remarried and became a widow several times, she too is buried in the Geisel memorial plot.

The Geisels were among those who were attracted to the area near the mouth of the Rogue River in 1853 by the gold to be found on nearby beaches. They built a cabin at the gold-rush town of Elizabethtown, located where the park is today. The sufferings of this family symbolized the horror felt by White pioneers at the terrible loss of life experienced in the early days of the war on the lower Rogue River. Their memory is enshrined in pioneer narratives and memories of those days.

A pioneer of Ellensburg, F. A. Stewart, has left an account of the aftermath of the "Geisel Massacre." Indians who remained after the main body left Port Orford by ship in June 1856 were tracked down by bounty hunters. One group of Indians, after being marched through Ellensburg, was taken

Gravesite of Geisel family at Geisel Monument Wayside. Author photo.

across the Rogue River and up the coast toward Port Orford. Within about a quarter mile of where the men of the Geisel family were killed, the Indians came under attack. "A number of citizens rose up from the low brush, and poured a preconcerted and well directed volley upon the doomed Indians, all of whom, nineteen in number, were slain, and thus was the Geisel massacre avenged, as far as was in the power of man to do," Stewart wrote.

There is no monument on the lower Rogue River to commemorate the Indians who lost their lives and homes in this tragic episode of Indian-White conflict on the northwest frontier.

It took the Jedediah Smith expedition from June 28 to June 30, 1828, to travel from the Rogue River to Brush Creek at the base of Humbug Mountain. This rugged coastal country placed a strain on horses and mules. Smith lost twelve to fifteen just crossing Euchre Creek.

Jedediah Smith Campsites 6 to 8
Rogue River to Humbug Mountain

The expedition alternated between the beach and higher ground. The incoming tide at times forced the expedition off the beach. Smith's entry for June 29 on Mussell Creek reads in part: "The traveling for the last two days much alike alternately on the beach and over the hills which generally closed in to the shore near which the country was generally prairae with some thickets. Farther back from the coast the hills were high rough and covered with thickets & timber."

In sunshine, Brush Creek today makes a beautiful, rippling accompaniment to the drive around the backside of Humbug Mountain. US 101 must follow fairly closely an old Indian trail that avoided the precipitous ocean-side slopes of Humbug Mountain. But in all likelihood, it wasn't such an easy

Otter hunting by early white hunters. Reprinted from *Harper's New Monthly Magazine* (Oct. 1856).

and scenic trail to follow with a large herd of horses. The party must have crossed and recrossed Brush Creek many times.

In the 1850s, a miner named Herman Francis Reinhart and his partner moved north from gold diggings at the mouth of the Rogue River and built a cabin along the trail at Mussell Creek. For a number of years, Reinhart ran a small way station selling liquor, tobacco, food, and overnight lodging to travelers. The Indian village on Mussell Creek was small and the Indians (the Co-sutt-hen-ten) were friendly. Reinhart recalled: "We had all the fresh fish we wanted; eggs from ducks (wild) or gulls, large and nice, and mussels, and with good ham, elk, deer, and bear meat, we could get up a good meal for anybody for one dollar."

Reinhart's life as a wilderness hotel manager also allowed him plenty of time for observing ocean animals. He noted that "all along the coast sea otter were very plenty and some old hunters made it a business to kill them and send their furs to San Francisco. . . . I could see plenty of whales (the small humpback whale) in whole schools of them, blowing and spouting a few miles out from shore and lots of porpoises or sea-hogs tumbling over and over like an endless chain."

Humbug Mountain

Location: Humbug Mountain State Park is at milepost 305.5 on US 101.

Nothing seems to be recorded to show the significance of this mountain for local Indians. However, its Indian name is believed to be "Me-tus," and it did serve as a dividing line between the Qua-to-mas of the Port Orford area and the Cosutt-hentens, Eu-qua-chees, and Yahshutes south to the Rogue River. Landmarks of this kind were extremely important because the coastal Indians took their territorial rights seriously.

Although this enormous headland projecting into the Pacific Ocean received several names in the early days, only one of them stuck. Captain William Tichenor, founder of Port Orford, sent a party to find a good route to the interior. He told the men to head south to Sugar Loaf Peak. Instead the party got lost, wandered as far north as the Coquille River, and when it returned took out its frustration by changing the name Sugar Loaf Peak to "Tichenor's Humbug." Thus it remains to this day in shortened form.

American and British Discovery of Port Orford

The town of Port Orford got its name from the English explorer George Vancouver who named Cape Blanco after the Earl of Orford in 1792. The small cove to the south of Cape Blanco beneath the present-day town is the only large offshore natural harbor on the South Coast. It attracted explorers in the late eighteenth century, when competition between European powers for the Pacific Northwest motivated them to investigate the shoreline more closely.

Robert Gray in the *Lady Washington* anchored in this bay in 1788. The second mate of the ship, Robert Haswell, wrote in his journal: "We now ran for a place that looked like an inlett this place was in a large deep bay to the southward and Eastward of Cape Mendocino [Cape Blanco] having ran in within about a mile of a small Island we hove the Jolley boat out and sent her to sound the Channel. . . ." Haswell noted that "birds were so numerous they were of maney speces but most of them Pelicons" on a small offshore island. He doesn't mention contact with Indians.

In 1792, George Vancouver reported contact with local Indians and described their physical features in great detail. "Their countenances indicated nothing ferocious," he wrote, "their features partook rather of the general European character; their color a light olive; and besides being punctuated in the fashion of the south-sea islanders, their skin had many other marks, apparently from injuries in their excursions through the forests."

Vancouver's description of the local Indians also is noteworthy for its recognition of their honesty. "They brought but a few trifling articles to barter," he wrote, "and they were scrupulously honest, particularly in fixing their bargain with the first bidder. . . . They did not entertain the least idea of accepting presents; for on my giving them some beads, medals, iron, etc., they instantly offered their garments in return, and seemed much astonished, and I believe not less pleased, that I chose to decline them."

The Indians of the Port Orford-Cape Blanco area were the Qua-to-mas. They lived from the Port Orford area north to present day Langlois. There was a large village at Port Orford, as well as villages at the mouth of the Sixes River and Floras Creek.

Battle Rock

Probably the most well-known historic site on the South Coast is Battle Rock. Motorists approaching Port Orford from the south come upon this small but close offshore island as they enter town. Those going south can't fail to see it on their right before leaving town, because

Location: At milepost 301, opposite the Battle Rock Historic Wayside at the south entrance to Port Orford, on the ocean side of US 101.

it lies in plain view at the foreground of one of the most beautiful ocean vistas on the South Coast. The Battle Rock Historic Wayside visitor center overlooks the site.

It is one of the ironies of history that small matters with little major influence on the subsequent course of history often loom larger than life. The battle fought at Battle Rock is one of these. I have just described Vancouver's peaceful encounter with the Indians of the area in 1792. Yet Battle Rock is famous as a site of Indian-White combat. Could this be the same place?

Battle Rock at Port Orford. Lithograph reprinted from A. G. Walling, *History of Southern Oregon* (1884).

The place is the same. But one wonders what bad experiences with Whites the Qua-to-mas had between 1792 and 1851 when Captain William Tichenor sailed his small schooner *Sea Gull* into the harbor in order to land nine men he had persuaded to help him build a town on this isolated part of the coast. The men of the party landed on June 9 and began immediately to build a breastwork of logs on Battle Rock to protect themselves. Tichenor left for San Francisco in the *Sea Gull* for more men and supplies, but not before the men pleaded with him to leave behind an old cannon. The Indians who met them on the beach looked hostile and the men prepared for an attack with only a few weapons at hand.

The next day, June 10, a large war party of perhaps a hundred Indians gathered and attacked. With the air full of arrows, the men used pine boards as shields to protect themselves as best they could. Two men were wounded in an early volley and another took cover in fright. As the Indians charged up the ridge of Battle Rock, the men readied the cannon. When fired, it killed about seventeen attackers. After some hard hand-to-hand skirmishing, the rest of the Indians were cleared from the rock.

At the conclusion of this first day of fighting, the Indians carried away their dead. No further fighting occurred for another fourteen days. Then a second and larger force of Indians, perhaps numbering several hundred, attacked the White men on the rock. But the defenders' deadly fire kept the Indians away. That afternoon, following the Indians' retreat to campfires down the beach, the White men decided that, with their ammunition running out, they had better try to escape. So, led by one of their number, John M. Kirkpatrick, they left their crude fortification and struck out for White settlements they knew lay to the north.

At the Coquille River, the escaping party came upon a large Indian village, which they quickly left because the Indians there also seemed hostile. Continuing north, they were helped by Indians on Coos Bay and finally reached the White settlement of Umpqua City at the mouth of the

Fighting off Indians at Battle Rock in 1851.
Reprinted from *Harper's New Monthly Magazine* (Oct. 1856).

Umpqua River on July 2, 1851, a little over three weeks after their landing at Battle Rock.

When Kirkpatrick, the group's leader, stopped on his way to Portland at Jesse Applegate's home in Yoncalla, Applegate told him: "Why those Indians down the coast, combined with their brothers, the Rogue River Indians, are the worst Indians on the American continent, and the bravest. Every old settler in Oregon knows that. The man or company that persuaded [you] to go down with a view of making a settlement at Port Orford was guilty of a great wrong."

If Kirkpatrick agreed with Applegate's opinion, he also took pride in getting himself and his eight partners out of Indian hands alive. He looked back on his experience as a great victory against the Indians. Whether the nine men actually stood off three hundred Indians, as Kirkpatrick said, there is no way to know. Unfortunately, Indian versions of this story have not survived.

Port Orford and Port Orford Lifeboat Station

Captain William Tichenor, after leaving his party of men at Battle Rock, returned to San Francisco. He didn't come back to Port Orford until late June or early July. Finding only scattered evidence of the fighting that had taken place on Battle Rock, he again left for

Location: On US 101 at milepost 301.

San Francisco and arrived there on July 10. But by July 14, he had returned again to Port Orford with some sixty-seven men and enough provisions for four months. Tichenor and the men proceeded to establish the town of Port Orford, the oldest platted townsite on the Oregon Coast.

Two blockhouses were erected to defend the new settlement, and its development began. As Captain Tichenor sailed the *Sea Gull* between San Francisco and Portland, he left lumber at Port Orford with which to build a home for his wife and three children.

Trouble with Indians on the Coquille River in September 1851, where five men of an ill-fated expedition exploring for a route to the interior were killed, prompted the dispatch of two companies of U.S. Army dragoons to Port Orford. By November, there were 205 soldiers stationed there. Fort Orford was laid out within the town Captain Tichenor had established. By 1854, the Fort Orford detachment had constructed quarters for officers and soldiers, a hospital, store houses, ordinance store house, guard house, and officers' mess hall—fourteen buildings altogether. The fort was built just west of Battle Rock on the hillside above the bay and wharf. In 1854 and 1855, the number of soldiers at the fort never exceeded fifty-one. Nothing of the fort remains.

When the Rogue River War reached the South Coast in the spring of 1856, the personnel at the fort increased to 244. About 1,100 Indians were held captive in the vicinity of the fort before being removed by steamer to the Siletz and Yamhill reservations. By September 1856, however, the war having ended, only four soldiers remained.

Tichenor fought the United States government for another twenty-five years to regain control of what had been part of his original donation land claim. The fort itself, however, served no further military purpose.

In the early 1850s, Port Orford was a thriving small town. Herman Francis Reinhart recalled that it was "a lively town of about a thousand inhabitants." It had "a garrison and fort and some troops stationed there, and many stores and hotels and saloons, and there was lots of business done by miners from Cape Blanco and the mouth of Sixes River and Floras Creek had some very rich gold claims all along the beach for ten or twelve miles."

But the early boom days didn't last. When the mining died out and the Indian fighting was over, the town shrank. In 1868, a terrific forest fire swept the plateau land and hills above the harbor. Only two homes and a barn were left standing, one of them belonging to the Tichenors. The town had to be rebuilt all over again. Louis Knapp rebuilt his hotel and others built new homes and businesses until, by the 1890s, the town numbered nearly seventy-five buildings.

Sawmills, sheep ranches and farms, and fishing kept the town alive through the years. It's as though local people wanted to prove late nineteenth-century historian Hubert Howe Bancroft wrong when he wrote uncharitably: "Port Orford is a little hamlet on the wrong side of the mountain with no reason on earth for being there."

A few of the "new" Port Orford buildings constructed at the end of the nineteenth century still stand today. A map showing the location of

Early town of Port Orford.
Reprinted from *Harper's New Monthly Magazine* (Oct. 1856).

these buildings is available at the Battle Rock Historic Wayside. They are the Nygren Hotel 1888, constructed as a stage stop; Long House 1891, constructed by Pehr Johan Lindberg, a Swedish carpenter, in a simple Victorian Gothic style; Lindberg House 1892, constructed by Lindberg in a elaborate Victorian Gothic style with Queen Anne tower; and Masterson House 1898, also constructed by Lindberg in Victorian Gothic style.

The Port Orford Lifeboat Station located on Coast guard Road in Port Orford Heads State Park (turn left/ west at 9th St., off US 101) has been restored as a museum. Built in 1934 and decommissioned in 1970, it houses exhibits related to Coast Guard life, shipwrecks, and Japanese World War II incendiary bomb attacks on Curry County. Walking trails open onto spectacular coastal views.

Cape Blanco:
Lighthouse, Shipwrecks, and Japanese Fire Bombs

The Cape Blanco road heads west across a broad benchland, through sheep and cattle country, to the tip of Cape Blanco. In the summer, stiff winds blow out of the northwest across this exposed headland that extends farther out into the Pacific Ocean than any other point on the South Coast. On a clear day, the view from Cape Blanco is breathtaking; on a foggy day, the lighthouse is barely visible from the end of the road. In winter, Cape Blanco receives gale-

Directions: At milepost 296.6 turn off US 101; watch for the Cape Blanco Junction $^1/_2$ Mile sign, 4.4 miles north of Port Orford. It is 5.5 miles from US 101 to the Cape Blanco Lighthouse.

force winds. This is a good place to observe the force of nature, and perhaps that is why local Indian people consider it to be sacred ground.

This is the cape that Spanish sea captain Martín de Aguilar may or may not have reached in 1603. Although it was identified by Aguilar as "Cape Blanco," it also appeared on a Spanish map in 1775 as "Cabo Diligensias." If you arrive at Cape Blanco on a day when fog shrouds the cape and the wind blows cold, you can imagine how shadowy this coastline must have seemed to the early Spanish and English sea captains who explored these waters. Many ships lie buried in a watery grave off the reefs at the foot of this rugged headland.

George Vancouver in 1792 described Cape Blanco's shape as "the northernmost extremity of the main land, which is formed by low land projecting from the high rocky coast a considerable way into the sea, and terminating in a wedge-like low perpendicular cliff." He named it "in honor of my much respected friend the noble Earl [George] of that title [Orford]." Vancouver's name for this cape, however, failed to displace that of Cape Blanco, officially adopted by the United States Coast and Geodetic Survey.

Construction of a lighthouse on the cape was completed in 1870. The bricks to build the lighthouse were made locally from local clay. The tapered lighthouse tower consists of a double wall of bricks with a hollow space inside that allows for air circulation to the top of the tower. Recent restoration work on the lighthouse has removed interior layers of plaster that prevented the brick walls from breathing properly—as essential to the life of a lighthouse as to a human being.

Cape Blanco Lighthouse is the oldest continuously operating light on the Oregon Coast. It also is the most westerly lighthouse in Oregon, and only the Cape Flattery Lighthouse in Washington State extends farther into the Pacific Ocean. The ground on which it stands is 245 feet above the ocean, and the cone-shaped tower of the lighthouse is 59 feet tall.

At the visitor center where the flow of summer tourists to see the lighthouse begins and ends, there are many early photographs of the lighthouse and lightkeepers. Lightkeepers and their families lived in housing on the site. One of the early lightkeepers was James Langlois, who became an assistant lighthouse keeper in 1875 and head keeper in 1883. He served at the lighthouse for forty-two years, living there with his wife and five children. His son Oscar eventually became head lightkeeper on the Coquille River until that lighthouse ceased operation in 1939.

It was the job of the lightkeepers to keep oil lamps light lit and lenses polished and in good working order. The original lens was a non-rotating or fixed Fresnel lens designed by Augustin Jean Fresnel and used for the first time at the mouth of the Gironde River in France in 1822. It was replaced in 1936 by a rotating Henry-LePaute Company-made Fresnel lens.

The light has an eight-sided cylindrical shape consisting of a brass frame that holds rows of small prism lenses. These focus the light source through

Cape Blanco light and lighthouse keeper's house.
Lithograph reprinted from A. G. Walling, *History of Southern Oregon* (1884).

glass rings that have a bullseye center. The light is like a huge jewel that at close range seems to reflect light in all directions, but that from the sea appears as a single beam of light that flashes every twenty seconds and can be seen from twenty-four miles away. The Cape Blanco Lighthouse lens is four feet eight inches in diameter and six feet eight inches tall. This makes it intermediate between a first-order and second-order lens. Eventually, electrification increased the Cape Blanco light's candle-power approximately seven times. The lights of other South Coast lighthouses were also of French manufacture, except for the British-made light installed at the Heceta Head Lighthouse.

The Cape Blanco Lighthouse became a popular stop for turn-of-the-century visitors. James A. Gibbs in his book *Oregon's Seacoast Lighthouses* (1994) commented that "the Langlois' were known for their friendly acceptance of visitors who ventured over the rough wagon road and its washboard contour in order to gain their destination. From 1896 until 1916, the lighthouse recorded 4,050 visitors." It has received upwards of 175 visitors daily during summer days in the late 1990s.

Oregon lighthouses are aesthetically as well as historically appealing. They symbolize the ties between sea and land in the lives of early coastal residents. They also remind us of the dangers of ocean travel and marine industries. They are monuments to the courage of those who lost their lives at sea, and of the loved ones who survived after them. Befitting its significance, the Cape Blanco Lighthouse was placed on the National Register of Historic Places in 1993.

Several major shipwrecks have occurred in the waters and on the reefs off Cape Blanco. One of the worst involved the *Alaskan* that was lost off Cape Blanco on May 13, 1889. The *Alaskan* was a side-wheel steamer built at Chester, Pennsylvania in 1888. The steamer was 275 feet long and had a 40-foot beam and 13-foot depth. Although she was built for inland water use, the *Alaskan* was considered a good ocean-going vessel.

The ship left Astoria on May 1 and headed south for San Francisco to be overhauled. As a result of heavy weather, the ship sprang leaks and began to break up. It made it as far south as Cape Blanco, when the order was given to abandon ship. As many crewmen as could be accommodated put to sea in four lifeboats. The rest of the ship's crew had to take their chances with makeshift rafts. Only sixteen of the forty-seven men on board survived. The tug *Vigilant* picked up three men as well as the ship's captain, R. E. Howes, who had been afloat on wreckage for thirty-three hours. Another crewman drifted off the coast for about a week before being washed ashore. Still another crewman ended up in Hong Kong, after everyone thought he had lost his life at sea. He was rescued from drifting wreckage by a British ship bound for the Far East.

An even greater disaster occurred to the tanker *J. A. Chansler* in 1919. The *J. A. Chansler* was 378 feet long with a 52-foot breadth and a 29-foot depth. It, too, was heading south from Portland to San Francisco. Heavy fog and rough weather forced the ship off course and an inshore current drew the tanker onto a reef. The collision broke the ship into two parts and the stern sank with twenty-eight men in it. Thirteen men on the forward section of the ship took to a lifeboat. They drifted all night and through the next day, during which time two men died of exposure. The remaining crewmen tried to bring the lifeboat through the surf at Whiskey Run north of the Coquille River for a landing, but the boat capsized, drowning seven more. Only three men survived the ordeal. The foresection of the ship finally was pushed to shore by the force of the sea near the Sixes River. The ship's captain, A. A. Sawyer, had his license suspended for two years because of improper navigation.

During World War II, Cape Blanco Light played a brief but historically interesting role in one of several scattered incidents of strategic Japanese attacks on the West Coast of the United States. Cape Blanco Light was used as a navigational orientation point for two of these attacks. The attacks are described in detail in Bert Webber's book, *Silent Siege: Japanese Attacks Against North America in World War II* (1984). In retaliation for American bombing raids over Tokyo and several other cities, the Japanese high command decided to start forest fires along the South Coast of Oregon by dropping incendiary bombs.

On September 9, 1942, the Japanese submarine I-25 surfaced off the Oregon-California border. A small Zerotype reconnaissance plane was assembled on the deck of the submarine and lifted into the water for take-off. Within a few minutes, the plane had taken flight for Cape Blanco Light, its navigational orienting point. As pilot Nobuo Fujita explained in a letter to Bert Webber in 1983, Japanese military leaders believed that if big forest fires could be started "it would cause panic if the people knew Japan could bomb their country, their factories, and their homes." From Cape Blanco, Fujita flew southeast, dropping two 170-pound incendiary bombs on Wheeler Ridge in the mountains east of the town of Brookings between the Chetco and Winchuck rivers. (A two-mile long "Bomb Site Trail" is located east of Brookings near the Wheeler Creek Natural Area off the South Bank Chetco River Road.)

On September 29, the submarine again launched its small bomber about fifty miles west of Cape Blanco. This time, pilot Fujita dropped two incendiary bombs on the Grassy Knob area east of Port Orford. The first bombing touched off small forest fires. Webber described the Wheeler Ridge burn as an area about fifty to seventy-five feet across. A firefighting patrol found no evidence of fire after the second bombing.

After the two bombing runs, the submarine sought safety in South Coast ocean depths and lay in wait for merchant vessels. On October 4, 1942, it spotted the oil tanker *S. S. Camden* about fifty miles west of Winchester Bay, on its way from San Pedro to Puget Sound. Two torpedoes set the ship ablaze. The fire was temporarily brought under control, and the ship was towed north; but it burst into flames and sank off Gray's Harbor, Washington.

On October 5, submarine I-25 attacked another oil tanker, the *Larry Doheny*, which it torpedoed between Cape Sebastian and Cape Blanco. The *Larry Doheny* sank almost immediately off Port Orford. Forty of the forty-six men on board were rescued. Webber noted that the sinking of the *Larry Doheny* was the "final loss, and final attack, on an American ship along the west coast of the mainland of the United States in the Pacific War."

Jedediah Smith made no special mention of Cape Blanco. He referred to a "bluff from 30 to 100 feet in height," in the vicinity of an outlet from a small lake, that was probably Garrison Lake. After crossing "prairae" land on the bench of the cape, the party reached the Sixes River, which forms a fairly wide river valley with open grazing land on either side of the river.

Jedediah Smith
Campsite 9
Sixes River

In his journal on July 1, 1828, Smith wrote: "Encamped on a river 60 yards wide on which was some beaver sign. I found the tide too high to cross. For the three past days but one deer had been killed but as we had dried meat we did not suffer from hunger. We saw appearances of Elk have been abundant in the vicinity when the grass was tender. For many days we had hardly got sight of an indian and but one had visited camp since my horses were killed. In the course of the days travel one of my horses was crowded off from a cliff and killed."

Harrison Rogers, Smith's second-in-command, observed the possibilities for farming and ranching in the surrounding countryside: "The country for several days past well calculated for raising stock, both cattle and hogs, as it abounds in good grass and small lakes a little off from the beach where there is good roots grows for hogs."

There is some disagreement about how the Sixes River got its name. In Chinook jargon, the word "Sikhs" means friend. It is spelled differently but pronounced the same as "Sixes." However, the local Indian word for the river was "Sa-qua-mi." One variant of the name of a local Indian tribe was "Sik-ses-tene." Lewis A. McArthur in *Oregon Geographic Names* argued that the Sixes River got its name from this shortening of the local tribal name.

The Hughes House on Cape Blanco

Location: 3.8 miles off US 101 on the Cape Blanco Highway; it stands on the north side of the road above the Sixes River.

The Hughes House is the most well-preserved Victorian house in Curry County. Local builder Pehr Johan Lindberg, who built many buildings in Port Orford, built the Hughes House in 1898.

Patrick and Jane Hughes, who emigrated from Ireland in the 1850s, settled on the south side of the Sixes River in 1860. They built up a successful dairy farm. In addition, Patrick had a black sand mining operation south of Cape Blanco that yielded about $1,100 a year. The couple raised a family of five sons and two daughters. Their beautiful Victorian home, built to demonstrate the success of the family's nearly forty years of pioneering, commanded a view of 2,000 acres of land that the family acquired over those years. The family's first home lay about a half mile to the northwest, closer to the sea, where the family lived for their first thirty-eight years.

The Hughes family was Catholic and to have a place to worship, they built a church on the cape above the farm in 1893. It was called "Mary, Star of the Sea." For about two decades it was used whenever a priest was available to hold services. All that remains of the church grounds today is a small cemetery plot along the lighthouse road. One of the Hughes sons became a Catholic priest. Patrick Hughes died in 1901, only a few years after the new house was built, and his wife Jane died in 1923.

The Hughes House is owned and has been restored by the state of Oregon. It is part of Cape Blanco State Park that includes the 1,800 acres of the old Hughes ranch. It is a large, two-story structure built in a Folk Victorian style common in the period 1870–1910. It has a gable front and wing design with decorative gingerbread ornamentation in the manner of the English furniture designer Charles Eastlake. The house's decoratively shingled

The Hughes House overlooking the Sixes River. Courtesy of Pat Masterson.

exterior is painted in subdued red and golden colors. Sawn woodwork features include circle and triangle-shaped shingle siding, gable trim, and front porch braces and capitals.

Inside, the house has been restored by the nonprofit Friends of Cape Blanco. It is furnished with many handsome period pieces, although they were not part of the original house. A small room upstairs served as a chapel and attests to the family's religious devotion. The ceiling of this room, and the downstairs bathroom, is hand-painted. Small tufts of clouds trail across the ceiling of the chapel, while the downstairs bathroom ceiling has a delicately colored floral border pattern. In the center of the kitchen is a wonderfully large, brick-walled oven and range (French Range No. 2, Geo. H. Tay & Co., San Francisco). The dining room is large enough to hold a table that would serve up to twenty guests. In nearly all the rooms of the house on sunny summer days, light streams through tall, narrow, double-sash windows, giving the house a delightful, airy feeling.

The house's builder, Pehr Johan Lindberg, was born in Sweden in 1851. He went to sea at age fourteen and eventually settled at Port Orford in 1882. He built barns as well as houses, and he also served as local coffin maker and undertaker. He was a successful businessman who served terms as school board member, constable, and county commissioner.

The Hughes House would have looked handsome in any American town around the turn of the century. But located in this isolated coastal setting, it stood erect on its hillside site with an especially self-important bearing, a testimony to the hard work and achievement of the pioneer Hughes family.

Langlois

Location: At milepost 287.8 on US 101, about eighteen miles south of Bandon.

The small town of Langlois has several historic buildings, now housing art galleries and antique stores. One of the buildings, at the corner of First St. and US 101, was the Hotel Langlois that used to provide room and board for loggers who worked for Danish-born Asmus Adolphsen. By about 1910, Adolphsen had moved his logging operations and sawmill from the small community of Denmark (about three miles south) to Langlois.

Alexander H. Thrift and Frank M. Langlois were the original settlers of the Langlois area. Thrift platted a town called Dairyville because of the dairy farms nearby. Orvil Dodge called it "a pretty town of cheese, milk and butter." In the 1890s, it had two hotels, one store, wagon shop, blacksmith shop, harness shop, feed stable, two cooper shops, school, and creamery. Thrift owned one of the largest dairy farms in the area, with a herd of about 100 cows. Thrift had been a member of the Coos Bay Commercial Company, a group of men who came to Coos Bay from Jacksonville in 1853.

At the time pioneer historian Orvil Dodge wrote, the town was still called Dairyville by local people, although the post office had been named Langlois, after the family of that name, since 1881. The government rejected the name Dairyville and named the post office after Langlois, who was postmaster.

Main street of early Langlois, looking north.
Courtesy of Coos Historical & Marittime Museum.

Otto Heckel, Coast Hi-Way Auto Service, north side of Langlois, c. 1920s.
Courtesy of Curry County Historical Museum.

The country lying between the Sixes River and Coquille River provided easy traveling for Jedediah Smith and his party. Their route followed the shoreline most of the way. Smith mentioned "passing a small lake" that is now known as Floras Lake. According to Lewis A. McArthur, Floras Lake was named for a miner, Fred Flora, who mined the

**Jedediah Smith
Campsite 10**
South of the Coquille River

nearby beach in the early 1850s. His name may have been spelled Florey, but McArthur rejected the possibility that Floras Lake was named for Martín de Aguilar's pilot, whose name was Flores. As mentioned earlier, it is unlikely his expedition made it this far north.

Both Smith and Harrison Rogers responded to the changing landscape. Smith described the land between the beach and foothills as covered with "grassy prairae brush, sand hills & low Pines." Rogers was fascinated by the broken nature of the country they passed through over the previous three days (from Mussell Creek south of Humbug Mountain to the Coquille River). He wrote that it "appears to leave the effects of earth quakes at some period past." He also was impressed by the "good grass and clover." On the night of July 2, the expedition camped about two miles south of the Coquille River.

Historian Alice B. Maloney referred in her article about the expedition to an old Indian trail that ran south from the Coquille River in pioneer days. With the help of an older resident of the area, Maloney was able to find traces of it as late as 1934. In his book, *Pioneer Trails of the Oregon Coast*

(1971), Samuel N. Dicken showed on maps where this and other coastal Indian trails may have been located.

After camping just south of Bandon on the night of July 2, the expedition reached the Coquille River the next morning. Smith noted that as soon as he came to the river, he saw Indians in a canoe. They moved upriver as fast as possible, but Smith on horseback cut them off, forcing them to shore, where the Indians began to demolish their canoe. Smith yelled and succeeded in scaring them away. The expedition used the canoe to ferry supplies and beaver pelts across the river. What is curiously lacking in Smith's and Roger's journal entries, as well as those of Alexander McLeod the previous year, is any mention of Indian village sites near the mouth of the Coquille River. They were well established there in the early 1850s when the first White settlers arrived.

Bandon

Location: On US 101 at milepost 270; turn north off US 101 at the Welcome to Old Town Bandon sign.

Today Bandon is a tourist town known for its cranberries; its cheese factory; its restaurants, art galleries, and craft shops; and its scenic beaches and offshore island rookeries. What it is best known for historically can't be seen—that is the Bandon fire of 1936.

By the end of the nineteenth century, Bandon had become important as a port for goods entering and leaving the Coquille River, and for serving communities farther upstream. George Bennett gets credit for founding Bandon in 1874, when he requested that a separate precinct of Randolph be established and named for his hometown of Bandon in County Cork, Ireland. Bennett, who was descended from Irish nobility, was an energetic man who contributed importantly to Bandon's development.

Bandon grew as local sawmills, salmon canneries, shipbuilding yards, and even a woolen mill provided jobs for newcomers, and as the farming population of the Coquille Valley also grew. Downstream to Bandon came the milk, potatoes, coal, lumber, and other products grown, mined, or manufactured along the river. Retail goods and food from San Francisco went upstream to Prosper, Randolph, Beaver Hill, Riverton, Coquille, and Myrtle Point. Harbor improvements, including the building of jetties that were completed in 1912, helped Bandon grow. Its population in the first half of the twentieth century peaked in 1910 at 1,803 people.

When the road system in the county developed to the point in the 1920s that automobiles could reach the coast from the Willamette Valley, Bandon became a popular resort town—known as Bandon-By-The-Sea. But its prosperous downtown then looked nothing like it does today.

Although Bandon suffered a fire in 1914 along the waterfront, it was a far more disastrous fire twenty years later that transformed the appearance and future of Bandon forever. In the summer of 1936, in the midst of the Great

Bandon business district in the 1920s with First National Bank of Bandon right-center. Oregon Historical Society, #OrHi 59335.

Depression and after several years of dry summer weather, hot winds started fires throughout Coos County. A small fire on the outskirts of Bandon spread and turned the town into an inferno. The highly flammable gorse or Irish furze that Bennett had introduced from Ireland helped spread the fire, like an endless chain of explosives. Once started, the fire swept through Bandon, destroying everything in its path except for a few buildings.

One of the buildings that survived is the Masonic Temple building at 2d Street SE and Alabama, one block from the waterfront. This building was built by a newly organized First National Bank of Bandon in 1913. It has a fine neo-classical facade, which looks surprisingly like the facade of the United States Bank of Boston built in 1798 by Charles Bullfinch. The pilasters are in the Ionic rather than Corinthian style; the building is reduced in scale; it lacks arched entrances on the lower level; and other decorative features are different, but otherwise it shows a striking similarity to the Boston bank.

Ironically, although the First National Bank of Bandon had to close in 1925 because of financial difficulties, it provided a convenient headquarters for the Bank of Bandon after the 1936 fire. The brick building was one of the few that could be reused. The Bank of Bandon, which had been established in 1904 even before the First National Bank, had a fine building of its own prior to the fire. But after the fire, what remained of it was unusable. In 1954, the Bank of Bandon moved to a new building in Bandon, and in 1960 its name was changed to Western Bank, which then began expanding its branches to other towns on the South Coast and elsewhere in Oregon.

At 460 First Street SW on the way to the south jetty is another older building (next to the last along the waterfront) that survived the fire—the Breuer Building, named for Michael Breuer, who had a shoe business. He

Bandon business district after the 1936 fire,
First National Bank of Bandon building in background.
Wesley Andrews photo, Oregon Historical Society, #OrHi 14010, 80-A.

had learned the shoemaking trade in his home country of Austria, and came to Bandon in 1894. He continued to work in a cobbler shop attached to the building until 1952 when he was 93 years old. The Breuer Building is on the National Register of Historic Places.

The building next door to the Breuer Building on the eastside used to be the Coquille River Coast Guard Station. It is owned now by the Port of Bandon. This colonial style building was built in 1939 to replace the one built in 1891 that was destroyed by the 1936 fire. A boat ramp leads directly down from the rear of the building to the river. Coast Guard personnel had their quarters on the second floor. The building has a whitewashed exterior and interior, a double bank of shuttered windows, a hip roof with projecting dormers, and a quaint second-level balustrade outside what once was an officers' suite. These features combine to make this building the most interesting in Bandon after the Masonic Temple and next-door Breuer Building.

The building, when it was a working Coast Guard station, normally had a complement of about seventeen men. But during World War II, 118 Coast Guard servicemen were stationed at Bandon. Some lived in the attic of the building, others in temporary quarters. In addition to the normal routine of maintenance work, boat drills, and assistance to commercial and recreational boats in distress, the Coast Guard patrolled the beaches north and south of the Coquille River to protect against possible Japanese or German landings. By 1944, they were patrolling on horseback.

Bert Webber in his book *Silent Siege*, which describes Japanese attacks on the West Coast during World War II, wrote that: "By April 29, 1942, there were about 13 life boat stations and 26 coastal lookout stations keeping watch over

Coast Guard Station, Bandon, c. 1939. Oregon Historical Society, #OrHi 14095.

the coastline." In addition to lookout and patrol surveillance, the Coast Guard checked all ships entering and leaving local harbors. Although Webber stated that the beach patrols "never had to report an enemy landing," the danger was real, as shown by Japanese incendiary bombings in the mountains of Curry County and submarine attacks on merchant ships. (For information on these attacks, see the "Cape Blanco" section.)

Highway 101 now brings millions of motorists through Bandon each year, but for more than a half century after the first settlers came to the South Coast, the region was very isolated from the rest of Oregon. How, then, could people get to Bandon, even as late as 1915? This was the local *Western World* newspaper's advice:

> *Take the steamer Elizabeth from San Francisco for $10; take either the Alliance or Breakwater from Portland to Marshfield, then take a train to Coquille at 9 o'clock connecting with the Coquille River boat, landing you at noon the same day in Bandon, combined fare, not counting lodgings is approx. $12; over stage from Roseburg, Oregon to Myrtle Point, from which place you take the river boat to Bandon as before, fare being $5 for stage and $1 boat. We recommend boat clear through in the wintertime at least. It is quicker and pleasanter for those not afflicted with seasickness.*

Each year, Bandon has a cranberry festival. The cranberry has come to replace lumber, cheese, woolens, ships, coal, potatoes, and other products as Bandon's major export. The wild bog cranberry (*Vaccinium oxycoccos*) is native to Oregon. In 1885, Charles McFarlin introduced to the South Coast a wild variety from Massachusetts that now bears his name. McFarlin established a bog at Hauser north of Coos Bay. In 1895, experiments with raising cranberries in the Bandon area began. McFarlin had five acres under cultivation in 1898; by 1924 the number of acres planted in cranberry bogs on the South Coast had increased to about 120; and by 1995 there were about 2,000 acres. Cranberry bogs can be easily seen from Highway 101 south and north of Bandon.

Bandon's Indian Village

Location: South side of First Street between Bandon Avenue and Cleveland Avenue at the foot of the bluff.

Beginning in 1978, evidence of the existence of an ancient Indian village site on First Street in Bandon began to be dug out of the ground. Oregon State University graduate students in archaeology, Isaac Barner and John Draper, under Professor Richard Ross' supervision, undertook a test excavation of what was believed to be an "open shell midden." Several other possible sites were being investigated that summer, elsewhere in Coos County.

This test excavation was part of a process of inventorying archaeological sites on the Oregon Coast that began as early as 1951. By 1995, archaeologists had identified fifteen known sites near the mouth of the Coquille River and about 100 sites in all of Coos County.

Roberta L. Hall, a professor of anthropology at Oregon State University, had been doing research on the Coquille Indians since 1976. In a collection of articles entitled *People of the Coquille Estuary: Native Uses of Resources on the Oregon Coast* (1995), she told the story of the search for the prehistory of these people.

In 1978, Barner and Draper found shell and faunal remains (of seal, sea lion, whale, clams, etc.), as well as stone artifacts (waste flakes, utilized flakes, cores, projectile points, etc.). In 1986, the Coquille Tribe and the city of Bandon requested that Professor Hall excavate several human burials uncovered by the digging of trenches for power lines. In this emergency salvage project, faunal remains and an engraved sea mammal tooth were found.

Two years later, in 1988, further excavation uncovered more human remains and artifacts, including a small antler-spoon and bone whistles. Radiocarbon dates for site 35CS43, its official designation, ranged as far back in time as 140–420 AD for some charcoal material. In 1993, a core sampling and sediment study revealed an even older layer of shell-midden material. Professor Hall concluded: "We have taken the site back several millenia—at least 2,300 years, and if results from Core 5 are corroborated, more than 3,500 years."

In Professor Hall's opinion, there was no doubt that the site first excavated by Barner and Draper was a village site: "After the 1990 excavation, which recorded a deep burial, numerous and varied stone and bone tools, a very extensive midden of shell and bone, and two clay cooking vessels, I can no longer conceive of CS43 as anything but a permanent settlement—a 'village'—at least for a significant part of its history."

Bandon Historical Society Museum

The centerpiece of the Bandon Historical Society Museum is its collection of photographs on early maritime history of the Coquille River. The photographs of the many schooners that crossed the Coquille bar, the tugs that pulled them through treacherous water, and the courageous work of the life-saving and Coast Guard crews that manned stations on the river bring to life an exciting era in Coquille Valley history.

Location: In Bandon on US 101 at Fillmore Street .

The museum also has exhibits of Indian artifacts from the Coquille Valley. These exhibits are a reminder of the Indians who lived for thousands of years along the Coquille River before the arrival of White people. The exhibits illustrate the ways the Coquille Indians used the natural resources of the area, the kind of living shelters they built, and other aspects of their life.

In addition to its maritime and early Indian history exhibits, the museum also features the Bandon Fire of 1936, with many photographs and newspaper clippings. Other exhibits illustrate with photographs the full range of economic activity associated with historic Bandon, including sawmilling and logging, cranberry raising, dairy farming, mining, fishing, and town business.

The museum is housed in the spacious quarters of the old Bandon City Hall, one of the first buildings to be built after the 1936 Bandon fire. Only two blocks north of the museum, one can walk along the Bandon waterfront with its marina, shops, and fishing dock and pier. From almost any vantage point, the river itself becomes an artifact. With a little imagination, one can see sailing schooners, shipwrecks, Indian villages, busy wharves, and riverboats waiting to take passengers upstream to Riverton, Coquille, and Myrtle Point.

Coquille Valley Eastward

Farms and Early Towns along the Coquille River

Directions: Continue on US 101 beyond the Coquille River Museum to the first stop light; turn onto Hwy 42S; Coquille is seventeen miles east along the Coquille River.

A side trip off the Jedediah Smith Trail along the Coquille River to Powers offers a variety of coastal valley scenery and historical sites. Early settlers in the Coquille Valley made their way upriver by boat or Indian canoe to new homesteads. The history of the valley can be read in the pattern of its farms, occasional old farm houses, pilings along the river banks that mark old riverboat landings, dikes and canals built to control flooding, and in the slow, muddy tidal current of the river itself.

The earliest historian of southern Oregon, A. G. Walling, has left this description of the Coquille River in the early 1880s:

> *The Coquille, from Norway to the sea, is a sluggish, deep and comparatively narrow stream, well adapted for navigation. . . . Sea-going vessels, mostly schooners, come in from the Pacific and load with lumber at Parkersburg or Coquille City, or with salmon at the cannery [near Parkersburg], and by the aid of a tug pass down stream and put to sea. Local traffic on the river is already very considerable, for about 2,000 people derive their necessary supplies of merchandise through this one artery of commerce. Two steamers ply the river, the propeller Ceres and the stern-wheeler Little Annie. They make alternate trips between Bandon and Norway, or Myrtle Point, touching at all the landings upon the river, which are many. The length of their trip is forty miles, and they occupy a day in making it, and return the next day.*

The establishment of farms in the Coquille Valley dates back to the late 1850s when the valley first began to be settled. Farm production on small family farms became an important part of the local economy. Early farmers in the valley raised a variety of crops ranging from wheat, oats, and barley to potatoes, carrots, and beets. There was even experimentation with the raising of tobacco. Hay was a major crop; cattle and hogs also were raised. But by the 1890s, dairying had become next in importance to crop production. By the mid-twentieth century, the value of dairy farming and beef and sheep production far exceeded the value of other activities. Dairy farms still are a prominent feature of this rural landscape.

It is an historic landscape. Although most land has changed hands many times, there still are farms owned by the descendants of families who homesteaded the Coquille Valley in the late nineteenth century. In size, relation to the river and surrounding hills, ties to local communities, layout of fences and dikes, and even use of the land for dairy farming, Coquille Valley farms have changed little in the past half-century or more. In their

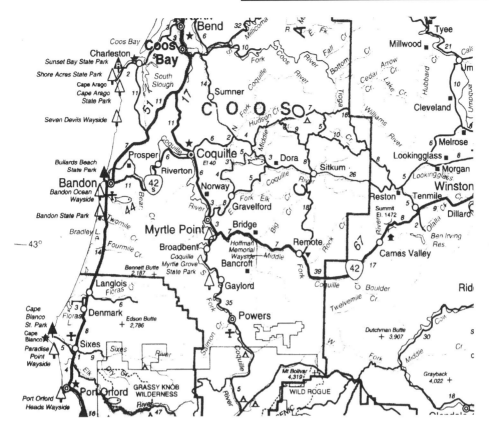

technology and management, however, dairy farms today have to be up-to-date to survive.

Three sites of historic river towns lie along the south shore of the Coquille River between Bandon and Coquille. They were Prosper, Parkersburg, and Riverton. The site of one historic river town—Randolph—lies on the north shore. At the end of the twentieth century, these places consisted of little more than a few houses clustered together along the road. But they could once boast of having sawmills, wooden shipbuilding yards, and coal mines.

Prosper was the first of these towns along the river. Shortly after the turn of the century, it was the site of a shipyard owned by Emil Heuckendorff, who had come to Oregon in 1880 from Denmark. Another enterprise that once could be seen here was the Prosper Canning Company's salmon cannery. It operated from 1904 to 1925, closing when seine nets were outlawed on Oregon coastal rivers.

A few miles upstream from Prosper on the north side of the river was the town of Randolph, the fourth place in the vicinity to take that name. This description of the town by A. G. Walling in his *History of Southern Oregon* (1884) provides an excellent impression of the hustle and bustle of community life along the river:

> *The present village of Randolph stands at the foot of a rather steep bluff a few hundred yards north of the Coquille and two or three miles from the mouth of that stream. The little river steamers come to the wharves of this*

small city, making their way up a small but deep slough which furnishes sufficient water for that species of navigation. Randolph has a post office, a store or two, a brewery of very fair beer, and a small number of cosy residences, and contains perhaps 100 inhabitants, whose chief occupation is lumbering and salmon catching. Near town is a lumber chute leading from the brow of the bluff spoken of and ending at the slough, where the logs, launched from the steep height, come down like a flash of light, and plunge into the waters.

Parkersburg was the next town upriver. It was established by Captain Judah Parker, who had experiences as whaler, gold miner, ship's carpenter, and explorer for sunken treasure ships before he came to Coos County and established Parkersburg in about 1876 at age forty-seven. He built a sawmill and shipyard on the site. There were fish canneries nearby.

Many of the early pioneers of the South Coast led adventurous lives before settling down. Judah Parker is a good example. He was born in New Jersey in 1829. He left his parents at age twenty-one to work aboard a whaling ship for eighteen months. After sailing the Arctic Ocean, the whaler came to port in the Hawaiian Islands, where Parker signed on with another ship to return to the Atlantic Coast. Parker soon returned to the Pacific Coast, arriving in San Francisco in 1854. For the next four years, he was a gold miner in the Sierra Nevada foothills. After leaving the gold fields, he spent several years as a ship's carpenter. Then, together with a venture capitalist, he embarked upon a search for the sunken treasure ship *Golden Gate* off the Mexican Coast. Parker made three attempts to find the *Golden Gate* and then tried his hand at recovering treasure off the coast of South America. When this effort failed, he returned to San Francisco, and then he headed north for Coos County in 1875. The next year, he founded Parkersburg on a beautiful bend of the Coquille River.

Highway 42S bypasses Prosper and Parkersburg, but it goes through the former coal-mining town of Riverton. Nathaniel Thrush homesteaded there in 1870. But the coal resources of the area were not exploited until J. H. Timon in 1894 or 1895 opened the first successful mine. Pioneer historian Orvil Dodge remarked that Timon made Riverton coal famous in San Francisco. Without capital, but full of "pluck, perserverance and frugality," he "pierced those rocky hills with subterraneous passages and brought forth the hidden treasure."

Within a short time, other mines opened. The Liberty Mine started in 1897. It reached a depth of 1,300 feet. A number of smaller mines were started before and after. They operated for short spans of time. Two of the more successful in this century were the Gage Mine (1912–1915) and the Alpine Mine (1930–1941).

In 1896, Riverton had a population of about 300 people. In addition to its coal mines, it had a sawmill, a general merchandise store, a hotel, and several saloons. Some of the first African-Americans to move to the South

Riverton, c. 1920. Courtesy of Coos Historical & Maritime Museum.

Coast came as coal miners and worked mines in Riverton and elsewhere in Coos County.

At the peak of its coal production in the late 1890s, Riverton must have been a busy place. Its hills were honeycombed with mine shafts; schooners waited to be loaded with coal; and the sound of mill steam whistles, whining saws, and clanging machinery could be heard up and down the river.

For many years, the main means of transportation up and down the Coquille River was by riverboat and steamer. Riverboats made frequent stops at the small river towns, dairy farms, and creameries along the river.

Travel on the river was a time to meet and talk to friends and neighbors. But sometimes competition between rival boats heated up. Ernest L. Osborne wrote in *Wooden Ships and Master Craftsmen* (1978) of a rivalry between the *Telegraph* and the *Charm*. The *Charm* was a seventy-five-foot, gas-propelled boat built in 1913. The *Telegraph* was a 103-foot steam stern-wheeler built the year after. "Once, as the *Charm* was going into Jarman's landing to pick up a passenger," Osborne wrote, "the *Telegraph* put her bow against the stern of the *Charm*, pushed her out of the landing and picked up the passenger. . . Obscene language turned the air blue; oil cans were thrown; tie-up lines were cut, and as a final result, the U.S. Steamboat Inspectors were called [to investigate]."

Coquille

Before turning off Hwy 42S onto Hwy 42 to enter Coquille, stop at Sturdivant Park to view a marker. It calls attention to the work of the "Spruce Soldiers" during World War I. The United States entered the war in 1917, and steps immediately were taken to boost lumber production. Twenty-seven thousand six hundred sixty-one enlisted men and 1,222 officers of the U.S. Army performed their national service by working together with civilians in logging camps and sawmills throughout the county. Sturdivant Park was the site of one such sawmill. Spruce was used to make wing-beams, ribs, and struts for World War I airplanes. One such airplane was the Curtiss JN-4 "Jenny" (U.S.).

A little upstream from the bridge that crosses the Coquille River at Sturdivant Park, there used to be a riverboat landing that was the gateway to the town of Coquille. Small riverboats, sternwheelers, and even schooners used to crowd the narrow channel of the river at the Coquille wharves. Now there are two boat landings for fishers, but the town itself has turned away from the river.

Orvil Dodge, who came to the Coquille Valley in 1866 and made it his home, described the daily arrival of steamers at Coquille. "The river steamers from the upper and lower river met at about midday . . . When the whistle of the approaching boats were heard everyone who was not busy immediately started for the landing, little boys, girls, men and women rushed down to meet friends, or for idle curiosity." There was even a town

Coquille waterfront (c. 1920) with stern-wheeler *Relief* (left) built in 1916 and gas-propelled *Charm* (center) built in 1913. Courtesy of Coos Historical & Maritime Museum.

dog called "Coquille" who used to run down every day when the steamer whistles blew. The wharves along the river stretched for about a half-mile, with lumber from the Lyons sawmill taking up much of the space.

Development in the Coquille Valley was slower than on Coos Bay and Coos River in the 1860s. Orvil Dodge remembered the trip from Coquille to Empire City on Coos Bay to get the mail. "We used to go by dugout to Beaver Slough a few miles below Coquille City," he wrote. Then, after poling up Beaver Slough as far as possible, he would walk over a divide and down to Isthmus Slough and then catch a boat to Empire City. Coquille got its own post office in 1870.

The old brick buildings that still give the downtown of Coquille a turn-of-the-century look came after a growth spurt in the 1890s. By 1898, with a population of about 728 people, Coquille had general merchandise, hardware, drug, clothing, and grocery stores, as well as two weekly newspapers, five churches, a sawmill, broom handle and shingle mill, and a new courthouse under construction. It also was the largest town on the river.

There is some confusion about the origin of the name "Coquille." Although the spelling is French, meaning "shell," the origin probably is Indian. Local Indians are believed to have called the river Nes-sa-til-cut, but "scoquel' is said to have been the local Indian word for eel that were caught in the river. Another source indicates that the Indians farther south on the coast called the Indians of this area "Ku-kwil-tunne," or a variation thereof. Thus, from a fairly lengthy discussion of the question in McArthur's book *Oregon Geographic Names*, one might conclude that there were several words in the local Indian language that sounded similar to the present name of Coquille.

It's the spelling that gives a French identity to what probably was a local Indian word or words. Anthropologist Robert L. Hall has argued that "the more common spelling was 'Coquelle,' and pronunciation was Coe-KWELL with the accent on the second syllable. Some Coquilles believe that this word was used by the Upper River peoples to refer to 'river' and possibly to their own river." George B. Wasson, Jr. has added to this discussion the fact that Coquel Thompson, an upriver Coquille Indian, in a 1942 interview with ethnologist John P. Harrington, said: "This name [Coquille] is of Whiteman origin and has nothing to do with the South Slough word for bow." Wasson also noted that the change in pronunciation from Coquel to Coquille probably occurred at the initiative of local businessmen in the early 1900s, when an annual event called "The Kokeel Korn Karnival" got started.

The town of Coquille is a place to walk in order to view historic buildings. If you enter Coquille from the west, turn left at the first stop light onto N. Central Blvd. Begin your own walking tour at the Coquille Valley Sentinel newspaper office. This historic small town newspaper office has old newspapers and typecases on display. Pioneer historian Orvil Dodge started the newspaper in 1905. From the Sentinel office, walk around a two-block area of business buildings out of the 1920s to 1940s era. Coquille City Hall

Andrew J. Sherwood House built in 1901 illustrates Queen Anne style architecture. A large myrtlewood tree stands in left foreground. Author photo.

on the corner of N. Adams Street and 2d St. is on the National Register of Historic Places. It was built in 1912–1913 in the American Renaissance style using bricks from the nearby community of Arago. The Sawdust Theatre at the intersection of E. First St. and N. Adams St. is a new building, but it presents late nineteenth-century melodrama during the summer.

Coquille also has a number of well-preserved older homes that can be located by using a Chamber of Commerce descriptive guide. One of these homes, the Andrew Jackson Sherwood House (257 E. Main St.), a private residence built in about 1901, is one of the outstanding examples of Queen Anne-style architecture in Oregon. Set in a grove of myrtlewood trees, this house with its decorative chimneys, tower, array of projecting gables and windows, and ornately sawn and turned Eastlake spool-and-spindle porch is a unique example of architectural exuberance and virtuosity. The John Paulson House (86 N. Dean St.), built in 1906, is another fine Queen Anne-style home. Other interesting examples of turn-of-the-century homes can be found on nearby blocks off E. First Street.

Coos Bay Wagon Road

Directions: To get to the Coos Bay Wagon Road from Coquille, take Central Blvd. to the Fairview-McKinley-Laverne Park sign, just below Coquille High School. Turn north toward Fairview, nine miles northeast.

In 1872, when the first wagons came over the Coos Bay Wagon Road from Roseburg, it was the only way to get to Coos Bay entirely by land from the Umpqua Valley. Until then, people coming to Coos Bay from the Willamette Valley had to change modes of travel. First they went by horse or stage to Scottsburg on the Umpqua River, then by steamer to Winchester Bay at the river's entrance, then by stage down the beach to the north spit of Coos Bay, and finally by riverboat across the bay to Empire City, North Bend, or Marshfield. From Portland or San Francisco, people came by coastal schooners or coastal steamers.

The Coos Bay Wagon Road is nearly fifty miles in length. Today's road follows almost exactly the original course between Coos Bay and the Umpqua Valley. It originally was called the Coos Bay Military Road, but later became known as the Coos Bay and Roseburg Wagon Road, or simply, the Coos Bay Wagon Road. The Coos County section of the old road is shown on some maps as the Sumner-Fairview Rd., Fairview-McKinley Rd., and Myrtle Point-Sitkum Rd., with only the stretch from Sitkum to Lookingglass called the Coos Bay Wagon Rd.

The builders of the Coos Bay Wagon Road hoped it would become the major land route to Coos Bay. But it proved to be an endurance test for horses, stage drivers, and passengers. Like a roller coaster, the road goes up and down, around and through range after range of coastal mountains, following for about a third of its length the beautiful East Fork of the Coquille River. The difficulties of the Coos Bay Wagon Road prompted Orvil Dodge to write in the 1890s that it "had proved a miserable failure." He added that construction of a new road from Myrtle Point to Camas Valley along the Middle Fork of the Coquille River "caused a great rejoicing."

The Coos Bay Wagon Road cuts through the heart of the Coast Range. In 1870, four men paddled canoes up the East Fork of the Coquille River as far

Fairview stage station on the Coos Bay Wagon Road, c. 1890.
Courtesy of Douglas County Museum.

as Dora. They continued on upstream until they came to a small mountain valley. It was named after Horace Brewster who was a member of this exploring party. Alva Harry, who came to the valley in 1870 with Brewster, settled there. Orvil Dodge wrote that Brewster Valley "in its wild state resembled a beautiful picnic ground, the elegant tall myrtles and maples forming shady dells where twilight seemed to linger through midday."

Alva Harry built about five miles of a steep grade on the Coos Bay Wagon Road that leads eastward out of Brewster Valley toward Roseburg. He died in 1874, leaving a wife, children, and a reputation, according to Dodge, as "one of nature's noblemen." His wife remarried to James Laird, and they and their family ran the stage stop in Brewster Valley for almost half a century. This last stop on the coastal side going east is no longer there, but Brewster Valley still resembles the Shangri-la Dodge described.

On the coastal side of the Coast Range, the Coos Bay Wagon Road begins at Sumner on Catching Inlet. The link to Coos Bay was by riverboat or stage along Catching Inlet or Isthmus Slough. East of Sumner, the road went up Blue Ridge Mountain, twisting and turning steeply. It required a major effort for horses and drivers to get wagons and stages up this grade and the others that follow. Way stations were located about every eighteen to twenty miles—Sumner, Fairview, and Sitkum on the Coos Bay side, and Reston on the Roseburg side.

Because the road from Sumner to Fairview is graveled and not very scenic, travelers on the Coos Bay Wagon Road should join it at Fairview (see "Directions" above). It will take about two hours of driving time to reach Hwy 42 Tenmile on the Douglas County side of the Coast Range. The stretch of the Coos Bay Wagon Road from Sitkum to the Douglas County line is narrow and graveled. On this stretch of the road, expect to meet cars and logging trucks on sharp curves with little road margin. The road is signed as hazardous, therefore motorhomes and vehicles pulling trailers should not attempt this route.

The large mountain valley of scattered farms where Fairview is located used to be called Burton Prairie after an early pioneer, Eliza Burton, who settled there in 1853. Fairview is a small community of houses, a church, a school (built in 1927), and a grocery store. From here it is eight miles to Dora and seven miles from Dora to Sitkum; it is about twenty miles from Sitkum to Reston.

Fairview to Sitkum

The wagon road climbs out of Burton Prairie from Fairview and goes over another mountain and down to McKinley. At McKinley, the Cherry Creek County Park offers a look at some fine examples of myrtle trees. The next stop along the wagon road is Dora. Near Dora is Frona Park, one of five parks that one-time county judge Reuben Mast helped create. The Coos Bay Wagon Road originally was financed through government land grants. In

1916, much of this land was taken back for failure of the land grant holders to fulfill their legal obligations. The five parks were created out of the reclaimed government land.

Between Dora and Sitkum, the East Fork of the Coquille River winds through the coastal mountains, splashing down over boulders and around huge granite blocks. The wagon road has been carved out of the mountainside above it. The road narrows in places to one lane, falling off steeply to the river. It was up this river that the exploring party consisting of Horace Brewster, Alva Harry, and two other men came in 1870.

Sitkum in Brewster Valley

The community of Sitkum, located in Brewster Valley, is encircled by cone-shaped mountains with granite columns protruding in places like flying buttresses on a medieval church. Although the valley is fenced off into farms, and cows graze in its green pastures, it still impresses one with its primitive isolation.

Brewster Valley's history is inseparable from that of the Laird family. James Laird was a stage driver and carried the mail for many years. He and his wife ran an inn called "Half Way House" for almost a quarter-century where travelers on the wagon road stopped. Up until about 1887, tolls were collected from travelers on the Coos Bay Wagon Road at the Lairds' "Half

Half Way House in Brewster Valley operated by the Laird family on the Coos Bay Wagon Road, c. 1900. Courtesy of Coos Historical & Maritime Museum.

Automobile stage on the Coos Bay Wagon
Road, c. 1915.
Courtesy of Douglas County Museum.

Way House." It cost $2.00 for a horse-drawn wagon, and fifty cents for a
horse and rider. The Lairds charged travelers who stopped over "two bits
(25 cents)" for a bed and meals.

The first "Half Way House" was a log cabin. It evolved into a ten-bedroom
combination of home and inn that burned down in 1903. It was replaced
by still another, smaller inn that operated until about the end of the First
World War. James Laird's son Jimmy, his wife Nancy Belle, and later, their
daughter Eva, carried on the "Half Way House" tradition. They also operated
a telegraph station out of their house until 1917, a year after the Southern
Pacific Railroad reached Coos Bay.

In winter, the mountain between Brewster Valley and the Roseburg side
often was deep in snow. Then the only way across was on horseback, and
freight went on pack animals. Winter rains and melting snow often caused
mudslides that damaged the trail. In the winter of 1880–1881, melting snow
caused such a gigantic landslide that it closed the trail for two years, and
nearly destroyed "Half Way House."

Summers brought cattle and sheep on drives from Curry County to the
railhead in Roseburg over the Coos Bay Wagon Road. Hundreds of cattle
and sheep would stay overnight in Brewster Valley before going over the
final coastal mountain barrier to the inland valley. Dairy cattle came in the
1920s, after road development and the introduction of trucks to haul milk.

The first automobile to come over the wagon road arrived in Brewster
Valley in 1908. Mr. and Mrs. Henry Harth of Roseburg, Al Dailey, and Ed
Abernethy, acting as the expedition's photographer, took a week to travel

the wagon road to Marshfield on Coos Bay. One of the Harry children, a boy of fourteen at the time, later recalled their appearance:

I was helping a brickmason build a chimney. I heard this terrific clatter coming up the road, so I waited there to see what this awful noise was. Pretty soon these two men came walking along, one with a shovel, one with a pick axe, just ahead of this car. There had never been a car over the road and the ruts were real deep, made by the wagons. When they found a place too high centered and they couldn't straddle it, they would take the pick and take rocks out of the road to fill in the deep ruts so they wouldn't hang up.

The Lairds bought their first automobile in 1913 or 1914. For a few years, they ran an auto stage line between Coos Bay and Roseburg. Every day, the stage left Coos Bay in the morning and reached Roseburg in time to meet the train. That run was shortlived because of the coming of the railroad from Eugene to Coos Bay in 1916.

Sitkum to Reston (or Lookingglass)

From Brewster Valley, the road follows along the East Fork of the Coquille River up a steep mountain canyon. It is a gravel road that narrows dangerously in places. But in counterpoint to the road, the East Fork twists and turns down the canyon in beautiful riffles, pools, and falls. Historic landmarks appear unexpectedly: a bridge of logs planked over; a tree stump with notches cut in it for springboards that once held up men chopping and sawing away at old-growth Douglas-fir and cedar. But the road itself, in Brewster Canyon, is the real historic artifact, with its little more than one lane cutting in and out around the mountainside. In places it is breathtakingly high above the river below.

The descent of the eastside of the mountain is a more relaxing drive over a wider road, although its steep grade made it a dangerous and difficult descent for horse-drawn vehicles. In places through tall stands of Douglas-fir, one can see the foothills on the eastside of the Coast Range and the small valleys where early travelers found a place to stop and eat before continuing on to Lookingglass and Roseburg. (After the descent, turn onto the Reston Road to reach Hwy 42, at Tenmile.)

The Coos Bay Wagon Road was the earliest-constructed transportation route into the Coos Bay region. It helped to open up the region to newcomers from the inland valleys of Oregon. But it wasn't greeted with open arms by early pioneers. Most of them were skeptical that a wagon road would succeed. Orvil Dodge commented that "when they talked wagon road to the old pioneers they would only be laughed to scorn and say we could not keep them open if we had them." When the wagon road was finally built, they believed it was "the greatest curse that ever happened" because they feared that "the people of the valley will now ship their products here, and will completely ruin our butter and egg market."

The road proved to be less of a threat to the region's economy than a failure. It was easier to reach the region through Camas Valley and down the Middle Fork of the Coquille River, the route taken by Hwy 42. But the wagon road survived, still used by farmers who lived along it and by logging companies. It survives today for the same reasons, as well as to serve fishermen, hunters, and history-minded travelers, and as the route of a new natural gas pipeline.

Myrtlewood in the Coquille Valley

The drive from Coquille to Myrtle Point on Hwy 42 provides a beautiful view of the Coquille River Valley as it narrows toward the Coast Range. The name Myrtle Point is a reminder of the tree of the same name, and this particular part of the valley offers many opportunities for travelers to see this species.

Although we marvel at the beautiful grain of this hardwood when it is worked into furniture, bowls, lamps, or other items, it was a nuisance to the early settlers in the valley. Myrtle and maple trees grew thickly along river bottomland, so pioneers cut and burned it. Orvil Dodge deplored the waste. "The myrtle is the loveliest tree of Coos County, and perhaps of all the temperate zone . . . When growing closely together these trees make up a grove of unequalled beauty," he wrote. The trees reminded Dodge of "grand and antique arches and colonades," and on some stretches of the Coquille River, maple and myrtle trees grew together overhead and "interlaced."

The Oregon-myrtle is actually a California-laurel (*Umbellularia californica*) and has other common names such as spice tree and mountain laurel. It is not true, as some people believe, that the tree exists only on the South Coast and in the Holy Land. In fact, the Holy Land "myrtle" is a different, if related tree.

The range of the California-laurel extends from Coos County south to Baja, California, and from the coast to the Sierra Nevada in California. Myrtle trees can grow to be over 100 feet in height. The myrtle tree also may live to be several hundred years old. Donald Culross Peattie in his book *A Natural History of Western Trees* (1952) noted that "like the classic Laurel or Bay (*Laurus nobilis*) with which ancient victors and poets were crowned, it has a spicily aromatic and evergreen leaf."

In 1826, David Douglas, the British botanist for whom the Douglas-fir is named, discovered and described the myrtle tree as he found it near the Umpqua River: "This elegant evergreen tree . . . forms the connecting link between the gloomy pine forests of northwest America and the tropical-like verdure of California. The foliage when bruised, gives out a most powerful camphor-like scent, and even during severe hurricanes I have been obliged to remove from under its shade, the odor being so strong as to occasion violent sneezing."

People have found many uses for the myrtlewood. Douglas wrote that fur trappers with whom he traveled "often make use of a dedoction of the leaves, which they take without any bad effect; indeed, it stimulates the system, and produces a glow of warmth. . . ." Patent medicine manufacturers in the nineteenth century mixed oil made from myrtle with nutmeg and cardamom and sold it as a cure for everything from a nervous headache to meningitis. Myrtlewood proved useful to shipbuilders both for interior paneling on ship cabins and for such external fixtures as bits and cleats that had to hold up under hard wear. Today, because of its rarity, we appreciate it primarily for its use in making household furnishings and decorative pieces.

Myrtle Point

Myrtle Point acquired its name because of the abundant myrtle groves that grew on this point of land overlooking the Coquille River. It originally was called Meyersville, then Ott, and finally, in 1876, Myrtle Point.

Myrtle Point has always been a small town. But because it has changed little from year to year, it is the best-preserved town on the South Coast. Many business buildings and residences in the town haven't changed in nearly a hundred years.

On Spruce Street, which is the main street of town, there are six buildings constructed between 1889 and 1895. The best preserved of these is a building at 333 Spruce Street that was built in 1895 and originally housed the Bank of Myrtle Point. In recent years, it has been occupied by a department store. It is a stolid-looking old brick building that wraps around the corner of a block. Its upper-level arched windows and roofline cornice details declare

Presbyterian Church in Myrtle Point, built in 1890. Author photo.

its classical origins. There is nothing fancy about this building, but it has a quiet dignity and sense of proportion.

Myrtle Point is located on a promontory overlooking the upper end of the Coquille Valley. By river it is thirty-eight miles from Bandon on the ocean, although only sixteen miles as the crow flies. It once was the site of or was near an upper Coquille Valley Indian village or villages; the exact locations of upper Coquille River Indian villages in the period before Whites arrived cannot be located precisely from historic documents.

Pioneer historian Orvil Dodge wrote that "the location where Myrtle Point stands was selected by the natives as a central place, and here they congregated and established their villages, as they retired from the seashore and engaged in the chase for the elk which roamed the hillside and wallowed in the cool ponds along the spacious and shady valleys." Although suggestive, Dodge's comment also is vague and romanticized. Hudson's Bay Company explorer Alexander McLeod reported a village at the forks of the Coquille River near Myrtle Point, but he didn't describe its exact location. Pioneer Daniel Giles, in his reminiscence of early days, recalled an Indian village about a mile below the juncture of middle and south forks of the Coquille River, which is about where Myrtle Point developed as a town.

Ephraim C. Catching established a donation claim to the land in the 1850s. He also married a local Indian woman. According to Orvil Dodge, he went back on a promise to his mother not to have anything to do with Indian women, and "the wedding was consummated and royal wedding feasts according to customs of the natives were enjoyed by the tribe . . . ." The story of Catching's marriage also suggests the existence of a nearby Indian village or villages.

Henry Meyers purchased the site and in 1861 had it platted as a town, the first town site platted in the Coquille Valley. Chris Lehnherr bought it in 1866 and farmed the land. But ten years later, he had it resurveyed as a town site. Binger Hermann built a two-story store on the site, and together with Lehnherr's gristmill, the town got its start. Other businesses joined these two in the late 1870s and 1880s. The town was incorporated in 1887. Dodge wrote that "in 1888, the town began to assume a more important air, built up rapidly, and in 1890–[9]1 a new and vigorous impetus took hold and two hotels were doing a good business."

It was this business boom that led to the construction in 1890 of several brick buildings on Spruce Street. A three-story Hermann Building went up in 1892. The first story housed a mercantile store, the second an "opera hall," and the third a Masonic Temple, which gives some idea of the town's cultural as well as business interests.

The business boom owed its existence to a few years of optimism fostered by railroad construction from Marshfield to Myrtle Point in the early 1890s. The line was completed as far as Myrtle Point, and the first train arrived on September 15, 1893. One can imagine the excitement the train's arrival caused. Visitors came from Coos Bay, bands played, speeches were given, and pioneers were photographed. The celebrants feasted on barbecued venison. The Ladies Military Band from Roseburg gave a concert. The celebration climaxed in a grand ball at the opera house.

In the days, months, and year that followed, a number of Myrtle Point businessmen lost their shirts, when the railroad line to Roseburg failed to materialize. At least one of the investors in the Hermann Building went broke. A national economic depression also reached the South Coast at about the same time.

But the short boom, however disappointing at the time, left a modest architectural legacy. Although business and industry make a town, the residences of a town reflect its relative degree of prosperity and their owners' appreciation of architectural craftsmanship. Myrtle Point's architectural heritage offers a look at a fairly wide range of late nineteenth-century homes.

Architectural styles vary from plain one-story bungalows, to two-story salt-box type houses with transverse gables, to larger Victorian style houses. There are no ornate Queen Anne-style houses in Myrtle Point. But as you walk or drive along the residential streets of town, you will find houses with decorated wood trim on the gables, projecting porches with tapered posts and lathe-turned balusters, and clapboard siding alternating with decorative bands of fish-scale shingling.

Myrtle Point residents also realize that they have a legacy of trees. They have designed a walking route through the old part of town that is called the "Myrtle Point Tree Trail." The trees on the route include such native trees as the Oregon-myrtle, Port-Orford-cedar, and Pacific madrone, among others.

Coos County Logging Museum

A visit to Myrtle Point would be incomplete without a stop at the Coos County Logging Museum. It is housed in a strange-looking, onion-shaped building. It was built in 1910

Location: Corner of 7th St. and Maple St. in Myrtle Point.

for the local congregation of the Reorganized Church of Latter-Day Saints. Samuel Giles, son of a local pioneer, designed the building after the Salt Lake tabernacle. It is small in scale, only forty-five feet in diameter and twenty-four feet high. But the circular building interior that once served as a church, later as an American Legion meeting hall, now contains a very special set of exhibits on logging history.

According to Myrtle Point historian and museum founder Curt Beckham, some local people used to poke fun at the building by saying that it was "built round so that the devil could not corner" church members. Whatever the truth of the story, it does underscore the fact that the building is an interesting example of religiously inspired folk architecture. It takes its shape from studs that run like curved ribs of a wooden ship's hull from floor to cupola.

This museum contains a collection of historic logging tools and equipment, photographs of logging camps and mills, and other memorabilia of early logging days. There are spike hammers for driving railroad spikes, pike pole ends used to handle logs in the water, branding hammers and axes to mark logs and lumber, broad axes and adzes, bull team yokes, mauls, chain binders—the equipment on view runs the gamut of logging tools. The historic photographs on exhibit nicely illustrate the uses made of this equipment and larger logging trains, yarders, and the like. These photographs also convey a lively sense of what turn-of-the-century logging camps looked like, as well as showing us the faces of the men who worked in them.

The highlight of the museum's exhibits is nine carved myrtlewood panels depicting early logging scenes. These are the work of the late Alexander Benjamin Warnock (1922–1991), a Portland diesel mechanic by trade and self-taught wood carver of many years. Warnock completed the works between 1986 and 1990 in a burst of creative activity near the end of his life.

These are masterfully done panels that can be enjoyed as fine works of craftsmanship, as well as for the way they bring the artifacts of the museum to life. The panels were presented to the museum in 1998 by the Roundhouse Trust. The panels complement nearby photographs of similar subjects by

Early loggers working on a Douglas-fir tree with crosscut saw while standing on springboards.

giving three-dimensional sculptural representation to these archetypal images of early logging days.

The Coos County Logging Museum is a window that opens onto a larger world of the timber industry. It is ironic that for all the importance of the timber industry to South Coast history, there no longer are any accessible working lumber mills. That day is past; the surviving mills are small, tucked away, specializing in shakes or small-dimension lumber.

Men still work in the woods. Logging trucks still bull their way down backroads and highways. Sometimes logging operations can be seen near a roadside, with men in cut-off pants and suspenders, tin hats, and proudly grubby. But this is a rare sight.

What, then, is the significance of the artifacts in the Coos County Logging Museum to the larger historical picture of the timber industry? There are at least three major stories they tell about the industry. One is the story of early logging and milling with oxen, steam donkeys, and waterside steam-powered mills. This was the late nineteenth-century timber industry. The second is a story of twentieth-century technological innovation and large-scale corporate investment and control. From sawing lumber, the timber industry moved on to making battery separators, plywood, paper pulp, and wood fiber products. In Coos County, the C. A. Smith Mill began this era; Weyerhaeuser, Menasha, and Georgia Pacific corporations continued and pursued this profitable path to its end. The third story is one of small, independent "gyppo" loggers. And running through all three stories is a fourth one, the story of the sometimes courageous, sometimes foolhardy, always hard-working men and women in the woods and forest products manufacturing plants.

The Coos County Logging Museum has a plaque dedicated to those who lost their lives working in the timber industry. Like traditional fishing communities, death was an ever-present fact of life in timber communities.

What many contemporary historians miss in their story of capitalistic industrialization of the American West is the pride that timber industry workers felt in their work. The timber industry, for all its dangers and uncertainties, also gave workers a chance to realize their dreams of opportunity and independence. The Coos County Logging Museum helps us to better understand all of these stories.

South Fork of the Coquille River to Powers

Deep in the Coast Range is the once-thriving logging community of Powers. The turn-off to Powers just outside of Myrtle Point leads onto a narrow, winding, but paved road along the South Fork of the Coquille River.

Directions: Three miles east of Myrtle Point take the turn-off to Powers; distance to Powers is eighteen miles.

On the eastside of one of the first bends in the river, one passes the small community of Broadbent. It was to this upper end of the Coquille Valley that some of the earliest settlers came in 1859. Along a road west of Broadbent, Dr. Henry Hermann, a physician and leader of a group of German immigrant families from Baltimore, Maryland, built a wooden frame house in 1861–1862. He wrote to a friend in Baltimore: "Our buildings we put up ourselves and cut, split, prepare and plane all timber and boards with not a plank from a sawmill."

The road to Powers offers fine views of the South Fork of the Coquille River, sometimes from high above its swift-flowing course. Particularly spectacular whitewater spills out of the river's canyon in the vicinity of Powers. Myrtlewood trees abound along the South Fork. As one approaches Powers, the coastal mountains rise ever more steeply on either side, forming a canyon through which one enters the remote mountain valley where the town of Powers was established in 1914–1915.

Indians inhabited the South Fork long before Whites came. The Hudson's Bay Company fur-trapper and explorer Alexander McLeod traveled along the South Fork in 1826. He passed several small Indian villages from the forks of the Coquille River south to Powers. In his journal entry of December 11, 1826, he wrote: "As soon as day light enable us to see our way we moved forward, after passing a short belt of wood we opened into a fine plain at the extremity of which, we came to a village of five dwellings rather unexpectedly. Our sudden appearance amazed the inhabitants who had not observed us, till we reached their door their fear was soon dissipated, we obtained some dried salmon, indifferently cured for which in return they got a few trinkets." Near Powers, the expedition encountered "another village greater and more populous than the last." McLeod commented on the South Fork: "it becomes rocky, with many cataracts, some perpindicular falls, that afford the means of spearing the salmon trout. . . ."

American White people first visited the South Fork Valley in the early 1850s. A party of men set out from Port Orford under W. G. T'Vault in September 1851 for the purpose of cutting a trail to the inland valleys. The party became lost in the coastal mountains and finally wandered out by way of the South Fork. In 1853–1854, a man named "Coarse Gold" Johnson found nuggets on a tributary creek of the South Fork. A nearby mountain is named for him.

Pioneer (Wagner) House and Railroad Museum: Powers

Location: On the right as you enter Powers after crossing the bridge. Closed to entry, but tours may be arranged. Local telephone numbers are posted.

The first major group of settlers arrived in the Powers valley in the early 1870s. Just as the lower South Fork had its Baltimore Colony, the upper South Fork became home for a colony of families from North Carolina. David Wagner and his wife led the way in 1871. His son John, with his new wife Mary, together with about seventy-five to eighty other people, left North Carolina in April 1872. They reached the upper South Fork area in August of that year.

Pioneer (Wagner) House in Powers built in 1872. Author photo.

The town of Powers is located on the David Wagner Donation Land Claim. In 1872, David and his son John built the Pioneer House that now stands beside the road leading into town. It shares with the Tower House in Empire on Coos Bay the distinction of being the oldest building in Coos County. It was restored in the early 1970s, thanks to the generosity of Mrs. Albert H. Powers and the work of local residents.

The Pioneer House is a one-and-a-half-story, hand-hewn log house. It is divided into two rooms downstairs and two upstairs. The downstairs consists of a combined kitchen, living room, and dining room, and a master bedroom. It has sash windows on either side of the front door and at both ends of the house. The south end also has a stone fireplace. The downstairs ceilings are approximately eight feet high.

Furnishings in the Pioneer House recreate a feeling of the period. The bedroom has a bed, nightstand, and closet with clothes in it. A spinning wheel stands near a front window. In the living-dining room, a table is set with plates and eating utensils. The furniture is handmade. An interior stairway leads to the upstairs rooms, which contain assorted historical artifacts. The downstairs living-dining room, too, contains memorabilia of the Wagner family and pioneer days. In various places throughout the Pioneer House are photographs of later Powers and its logging era.

In the early days, the Wagners and other families on the South Fork were linked to the Coquille Valley by only a narrow Indian trail. It took approximately two days for them to reach the town of Coquille. By the time they settled on the South Fork, only a few Indians still were living there. Chinese miners, however, were working gold diggings along creeks in the nearby mountains. They were run off in the mid-1880s.

When David Wagner died, his son John took over Pioneer House. He and his wife Mary raised ten children in the house; nine children were born to them there. For many years, the house was a stopping place for travelers. John was known for his smoked hams and bacon, and the women of the house spun, wove, and made their own clothing. They raised, grew, or hunted for most of their food. A post office named Rural was established at the Wagner home in 1890.

Early Powers

The South Fork valley community of Rural might have remained the hub of scattered farms and ranches if the valley hadn't been located in the center of one of the Pacific Northwest's richest stands of old-growth Port-Orford-cedar and Douglas-fir. The forest industry in Coos County doubled its productive capacity with the arrival of the C. A. Smith Lumber Company in 1907–1908. The Smith-Powers Logging Company, owned by C. A. Smith and Albert H. Powers, provided the lumber mill with cut timber, and Al Powers ran the logging operations. Up to 1912, the company logged on the sloughs of Coos Bay. That year, the company bought the Wagner claim and began preparations to build a railroad extension from Myrtle Point to the South Fork valley where the Wagners and other families from North Carolina had settled fifty years earlier.

In the spring of 1913, railroad construction began. As the tracks were laid along the South Fork, camps sprang up and logs began to be hauled to the Marshfield mill. Victor Stevens in his book *The Powers Story* (1979) commented that "completing the [rail]road to Powers was not the end but the beginning of the operation." Rail lines were built beyond Powers up Mill Creek, Salmon Creek, and Yellow Creek.

While the tracks were being laid, workers and family members lived in tents and railroad shacks. But afterwards, families moved into the new town of Powers. The company had laid out lots, sewer, and water lines. Rather than run a company town, lots were sold to workers and businesses. The town planning commission insisted that houses in the town had to have double walls and a toilet. Building by workers, businesses, and the company continued through 1914 and 1915, the year that the post office's name officially was changed from Rural to Powers.

The town's businesses consisted of J. T. Ross's grocery store, the town's first business; the office of Claud C. Moon, optometrist; the Busy Corner Drugstore; W. K. Wiseman's furniture store; a rooming house; Gagnon's Restaurant; a general store; several pool halls and barbershops; a clothing store; a tavern; the Pioneer Theater; and, by December 1, 1915, the Powers Bank. The town was divided into a North Town and a South Town. The latter was where, as Stevens puts it, the "brass" lived and "some who thought they were 'brass'"; it also was the location of the company warehouse, office, and store. Most of the loggers, of course, lived in camps up nearby creeks at logging operations sites.

By the early 1920s, four trains a day ran from Powers to the mill in Marshfield, which by this time had changed names, becoming the Coos Bay Lumber Company mill. By the mid 1920s, Al Powers had retired to

California, ending about a thirty-year career in the logging business that began in Hibbing, Minnesota and ended on the South Fork of the Coquille River.

There still is evidence of Powers' logging past scattered about—an old steam donkey at the Powers County Park, the old mill pond behind the Pioneer House, and the old-fashioned panoramic photographs of logging camps, trains, and men hanging on the walls of the Pioneer House itself. The sound of chainsaws still can be heard in this coastal mountain valley, and the historical traveler has to be prepared to share the mountain roads with logging trucks.

Local historian Victor Stevens remarked that Al Powers wanted to name the new town he laid out on the South Fork after the Wagner family. But the Southern Pacific Railroad already had a town by that name, "so by popular demand of all of the people, the name Powers was chosen; which is as it should be."

Port Orford Cedar

Old-growth Port Orford cedar and Douglas-fir trees are unmistakable by their girth, sparlike straightness, and height. At a distance, the Port Orford cedar is distinguishable from the Douglas-fir by the vertical lines of its outer bark and by its slightly drooping, fernlike branches.

Next to the Oregon-myrtle, the Port Orford cedar has been the region's most special tree. Port Orford cedar (*Chamaecyparis lawsoniana*) has a small range stretching from the Coos Bay region to Eureka, California in a coastal zone of up to forty miles inland. For many years, it was the most highly valued species of timber in the region. Stands of timber were cut for this species alone, leaving Douglas-fir and other species behind. Now there are few of these trees left, and a root disease fungus threatens those remaining. The fungus spreads from water runoff, streamflow, cattle, and vehicles that carry it to previously uninfested areas.

The name "Port Orford" cedar is due to its abundance in the Port Orford area in pioneer days. It is also called Port Orford white cedar, Oregon cedar, Lawson false cypress, and Lawson cypress. The first recorded use of Port-Orford-cedar by White settlers was in the building of a fort at Port Orford in 1851. In the 1890s, Orvil Dodge wrote: "Port Orford cedar sells in San Francisco for several times the price of fir. It is used principally for finishing and is by far the most valuable timber in Oregon, and there are still large quantities yet remaining in the forests."

Directions: Drive south from Powers on County road #219 to Forest Service Road #33 and just past Daphne Grove National Forest Campground to Road #3348. Drive one mile up Road #3348 to the Coquille River Falls trailhead. The adjacent Coquille River Falls Research Natural Area contains old-growth stands of Douglas-fir, hemlock, and Port Orford cedar. Trees can be seen from the road or trail.

The Port Orford cedar is a noble tree that is almost extinct. "Shining and gracious in youth, gigantic and glorious in age, possessed of a fragrant wood of great beauty and scores of the most valuable uses" is the way Donald Peattie in his book, *A Natural History of Western Trees* (1952), described it. It grows to immense heights, upwards of 200 feet, and reaches a diameter of 4 to 6 feet. But its foliage is delicate and fine, with what one writer describes as "feathery or fernlike sprays." In advanced age, Donald Peattie wrote, "the forest monarch which may have lived 600 years, will have an awesomely long straight trunk covered with a soft, fibrous, fluted bark, and a very narrow crown of branches which droop with a grand but sorrowful gesture."

It is a wood that can be used for the heaviest industrial purposes and for finely finished wood pieces. Because of its resistance to decay, it was used to build ships, shore up mines, and support railroad tracks. During World War I, it was discovered that the tree's resistance to acid made it a perfect material for making separators in automobile batteries. During the 1920s and 1930s on Coos Bay and at Coquille, battery separator plants were built that employed upwards of 1,000 people. The Coos Bay region was one of the largest producers of battery separators in the country.

It was the Japanese and Chinese who recognized the values of this wood for finer purposes. Donald Peattie noted that in Japan and China it was used to make caskets. The reason was "its lightness, satiny texture when finished, its pungent odor compared by some to ginger, by some to roses, and the fact that it ranks, in contact with the soil, with the most durable of all woods." The Japanese still use it as a substitute for native cedar in making woodenware and in the construction of shrines and temples. The export of Port Orford cedar to Asia began at the end of World War I and has continued ever since.

Bandon to Coos Bay

Bullards State Park: Prehistory

Bullards State Park is an important historical site for several reasons. The north and south banks of the lower Coquille River once were the sites of Indian villages. The mining of gold on the nearby beaches north of the Coquille River made the state park area a logical place for early homesteading. Because the Coquille

Location: Eleven miles north of Bandon at milepost 259.2, just across the Coquille River bridge on US 101; watch for the Bullards Beach State Park/Coquille Lighthouse road sign.

River narrows where the bridge now spans the river, it also was a good place to locate a ferry. Bandon's development as a coastal port led to the construction of a lighthouse on the river's north spit. A cemetery plot near the camping area of the park is a reminder of early settlement.

Several important archaeological excavations have taken place in the park. The existence of at least three village sites near the Coquille River mouth when the first White people came made the park a likely area for investigation. Alex Krieger and Kenneth Leatherman from the University of Oregon first excavated on the lower Coquille River in the 1930s. They uncovered three house pits and associated artifacts at Bullards Beach. The site level probably dated from the early 1800s. Krieger and Leatherman excavated another side about five miles upriver called the Schwenn site, which is believed to date from an earlier time.

In 1952, Luther Cressman, also from the University of Oregon, excavated a site near the Bandon lighthouse. He also discovered several house pits. The remains showed that the people living there depended for their livelihood on fish, shellfish, and sea mammals, but also, to a considerable degree, on elk. Further investigation in 1974 of the Krieger and Leatherman site at Bullards uncovered several burials and many glass trade beads, broadening the possible time range of Indian occupation in Bullards State Park to an estimated period of from 500 to 1856 A.D.

A nearby archaeological site just east of Bullards Bridge on the north bank has been radiocarbon dated. Known as the Philpott Site, it is now part of the Bandon Marsh National Wildlife Refuge. Excavation at the site in 1978 by Oregon State University archaeologists uncovered fish weirs, as well as stone tools and mammal bones. The site was placed on the National Register of Historic Places in January 1980, the first prehistoric Oregon Coast site to be so designated.

Over hundreds of years, the level of the Coquille estuary has changed. At one time, the lower Coquille River tidal area near Bullards was much larger. It gradually shrank in size, creating tidal channels where local Indians placed fish weirs. But it is believed that about 300 years ago, an earthquake caused the land to drop and to become a large tidal marsh. When Whites came, they diked and drained the marsh area in order to farm it. Since then, erosion has revealed the signs of earlier Indian usage of the area.

In 1993-1994, University of Oregon archaeologists led by professors Madonna L. Moss and Jon M. Erlandson studied fifty-two sites on South Coast state park lands. They also collected radiocarbon samples. Working closely with the Coquille Tribe, graduate-student archaeologists Scott Byram and Mark Tveskov paid special attention to fish weir remains on the Coquille River. At what is called the Osprey Weir site on the north bank east of Bullards State Park, they inventoried about 3,000 vertical wood stakes that had been part of a fish weir complex. Some "basketry features" also were found that included spit wood, roots, and cordage used for the basket-like devices placed between the stakes to catch fish. In his report, Scott Byram called the Osprey Weir site the "oldest wood stake fishing weir on the Oregon coast." Together with the fish weir remains at the Philpott site, the Coquille River area is a major archaeological resource that needs to be protected. Radiocarbon dating indicates that the fish weirs in this area are about 1,050 to 1,350 years old.

Indian artifacts from sites along the Coquille River can be viewed in exhibits at the Coquille River Museum in Bandon. Arrowheads, stone tools, fishhooks, baskets, and other artifacts help one to visualize the physical environment of the people who lived along the Coquille River before White people came.

Bullards State Park: Indian-White Conflict

When White people arrived on the South Coast in the early 1850s, centuries of Indian life on the lower Coquille River were disrupted. The Coquille River Indians reacted with violence to the first White intrusions into their territory. An expedition that left Port Orford in August 1851, led by W. G. T'Vault, was attacked by lower Coquille Indians about two miles above the mouth of the river on the north bank. Five men of the expedition were killed. In retaliation, soldiers were dispatched from Port Orford in November to fight the Indians. Captain Tichenor has related that a blockhouse was erected "on the bluff commanding a view of the large Indian village and the [Coquille] river. A howitzer was brought to bear upon the village; shells thrown, clearing the ridge of the natives and causing great terror." Shortly thereafter, a battle took place at the junction of the middle and south forks of the Coquille River between the soldiers and upper Coquille Indians.

By summer 1853, a gold rush to the beach north of the Coquille River was underway. The lower Coquille Indians lived peacefully in their villages near the mouth of the river, although they deeply resented the overrunning of their land by Whites. The gold miners, on the other hand, feared and despised the Indians. In late January 1854, the lower Coquille River became the scene of a savage massacre of an Indian band called the Nasomah.

White miners accused the Indians of "insolence," incidents of theft, and the discharge of a gun by the local Indian chief near the ferry-house. When Sub-Indian Agent F. M. Smith later questioned the chief, he found that the chief had only been shooting at ducks and that the ball from his gun probably had ricocheted. The chief admitted, however, that some of his men had threatened White people, stolen items from them, and used their horses without permission.

As a result of these incidents, a company of about forty miners marched on the Nasomah village at dawn on January 28, 1854. Agent Smith reported that "the Indians were aroused from sleep to meet their death, with but a feeble show of resistance; they were shot down as they were attempting to escape from their homes; fifteen men and one squaw were killed; two squaws were badly wounded. On the part of the white men, not even the slightest wound was received. The houses of the Indians, with but one exception, were fired and entirely destroyed. Thus was committed a massacre too inhuman to be readily believed." Contrary to reports that the Indians were armed to fight, they had only five guns and pistols; only two of them were in working condition.

At least part of the massacre of the Nasomah took place in Bullards State Park. George H. Abbott, who was elected captain of the expedition against the Nasomah, described the massacre site as follows: "The Indian village is in three different parts, situated on both sides of the river, about one and a half mile from the mouth." Abbott divided his force into three elements, one of which attacked each of the village sites.

Over the next two and a half years, sporadic outbreaks of violence between Indians and Whites continued on the Coquille River. But for all practical purposes, the massacre of the Nasomah ended the Indian threat to Whites on the lower Coquille. In the autumn of 1855, according to historian Orvil Dodge, fear of Indian outbreaks in Coos County led to another expedition against the lower Coquille that resulted in four Indians being killed and four being captured and hung. When the Rogue River Indian War of 1855–1856 ended, the remaining Coquille Indians were removed from their native land to the newly created Siletz Reservation farther north on the Oregon Coast.

White Settlers of Bullards State Park

On a hill at the north end of the park there is a small cemetery. The names on the gravestones in this cemetery provide clues to the history of the park since the White settlement of the lower Coquille in the 1850s. These are the names: John Hamblock (1827–1909), Jane Hamblock (1841–1920), John A. Hamblock (1866–1914), Mary E. Hamblock (1860–1874), Robert W. Bullard (1857–1925), Malinda A. Bullard (1862–1941), Lawrence Orvil Bullard (1891–1918), Audrey Evelyn Bullard (1917–1918), Mary M. Long (1810–1879), and Christopher Long (1837–1918).

Gravestone of Mary E. Hamblock (1860–1874) in the Bullards State Park cemetery. Author photo.

The cemetery is a quiet, shaded place hidden by trees from the rest of the park. The lives of the people who are buried here among the evergreen huckleberry and salal span nearly a century of Coos County history. John Hamblock came to Coos County in 1857. Malinda A. Bullard, born in 1862, died in 1941. There are three family names in the cemetery: Hamblock, Long, and Bullard. For a stranger, the mystery is their relationship to each other.

Two of the earliest White people to settle on the lower Coquille were Edward Fahy and John Hamblock. These two young men first visited the Coquille River in 1856, having come up from Port Orford. Fahy was born in Ireland in 1826; Hamblock in Germany in 1828. In 1858, the two men established a small lumber mill on the lower Coquille near Bullards State Park.

Christopher Long came as a young man with his family to Port Orford in 1854. The family came across the plains from Illinois and brought cattle, perhaps the first to come to the South Coast, through Camas Valley. His father, also named Christopher, died in 1855. His mother, Mary M. Long, remarried Andrew Johnson, who was born in Sweden in 1831, and found himself, as Orvil Dodge wrote, "cast away from a vessel at the Coos Bay bar" in 1854. Young Christopher Long had a sister, Jane Ann, born in 1849. She married John Hamblock, and they had four children.

Ferry crossing Coquille River from Bullards Store on the north bank, c. 1925.
Courtesy of Coos Historical & Maritime Museum.

Robert W. Bullard arrived in Coos County in 1877. He came from Winneesheik County, Iowa, and first settled at Arago in the Coquille Valley. He married Malinda A. Hamblock, daughter of John and Jane Ann Hamblock, and together they had six children. It was in 1882 that Robert Bullard established a general store and ferry at the north end of the present bridge over the Coquille River.

Bullards State Park takes its name from the Bullard family that for many years operated a general store and ferry on the southeast corner of the park. For people who lived along the lower Coquille, the Bullard Store was a community center as well as a store. On weekends and holidays, dances were held on the second floor of the building. At Christmas, there was always a festive gathering. Local musicians played fiddles, banjos, and accordions. The ferry that operated from the store was a small scow that could hold a horse team and buggy. The ferry took about ten to fifteen minutes to drift downstream with the tide. It then was pulled back to the north bank by cable.

The Oregon Coast Highway was relocated between Coos Bay and Bandon in 1955. This led to a bridge being built and then to the creation of Bullards State Park beginning in 1962. Prior to 1955, the highway went from Coos Bay to Coquille and then west along the south bank of the Coquille River to Bandon, the route designated today as Hwy 42S.

Bandon Lighthouse at Bullards State Park

Built in 1896 on the north bank of the Coquille River entrance, the Bandon Light (officially named the Coquille River Light) was the last of ten lighthouses to be built on the Oregon Coast. It continued to operate until 1939.

Bandon Light was in operation 1896–1939 on the north bank of the Coquille River.

The Bandon Lighthouse has thick walls of brick that have been plastered and painted white. It is as solid as the offshore rocks south of the Bandon bar. From the south bank of the Coquille River, the Bandon Light gleams whitely in the glare of the summer sun. But it can as easily disappear into fog rolling inland from the sea. Although no longer in use, it has become a symbol of Bandon itself.

Shipwrecks on the Coquille Bar

The Coquille River has a narrow channel and presents a dangerous challenge in bad weather. Ernest L. Osborne and Victor West described the stranding of the *Lila and Mattie* in 1896:

> *On January 22, 1896, the two-masted schooner* Lila and Mattie, *while attempting to cross the Coquille River bar with a light breeze and a strong ebb tide due to a freshet in the river, stranded some three hundred yards north of the north jetty. The lookout at the station had hoisted a danger signal warning the ship of the extremely bad conditions. She did not heed the warning, and while on the bar the wind left the vessel, she fell broadside to the sea, and soon stranded.*

If it hadn't been for the men of the U.S. Life-Saving Service and later Coast Guard, many ships would have been stranded permanently on or near the Coquille bar and battered to pieces by the ocean. It took the life-saving crewmen until February 9 to free the *Lila and Mattie* from its grounding. Lines taken out to the ship in surfboats were tied to anchors, and repeated efforts were made to pull the ship back into deep water and to get her to float again.

Another casualty of the Coquille bar was the schooner *C. A. Klose.* On November 12, 1904, Captain Beadle faced a bad combination of a rough bar and a light breeze. The schooner almost ended at the lighthouse front door. Hung up on the north spit of the river, it was pulled off by means of a hawser attached to the south jetty.

On February 25, 1905, the schooner *Onward*, along with the *Advance* and *Hugh Hogan*, lay off the Coquille River waiting to cross the bar. A stiff northwest breeze made the bar too rough for towing. The schooner *Advance* entered under sail without much trouble. The *Onward* followed about ten minutes later. Then the fastenings of the *Onward*'s centerboard gave way, causing it to drop and catch on the bar. The ship stopped, broached, and its sails lost their wind. Unable to get back out to sea, the schooner was pushed south past offshore Table Rock and then onto the beach by a heavy surf just north of Lookout Point. Efforts to refloat the *Onward* failed, and the ship was abandoned not too many miles as the crow flies from Parkersburg on the Coquille River, where Stein Danielson had built her in 1901.

Wooden steam schooners also had trouble crossing the Coquille bar. The *Fifield* started into the Coquille River on February 29, 1916, but a strong

Oliver Olson wrecked on the Coquille River south jetty in 1953.

northerly current drove it off course and onto the south jetty. The ship floated off the jetty, even though it was heavily waterlogged. But strong waves carried it around to the other side of the jetty and deposited it on the beach near the high water line. Cargo was removed and efforts made to tow the ship off the beach, but to no avail. There the *Fifield* stayed, until the sea finally broke it up.

The wreck of the *Oliver Olson* provided material for an extension of the south jetty on the Coquille River. The *Oliver Olson* was a steel ship 289 feet long, 44 feet wide, and 19 feet in depth built in Portland in 1918. While entering the Coquille River on November 3, 1953 to pick up a load of packaged lumber, it was thrown off course by a strong cross current created by a forty-mile-an-hour wind. The ship struck the outer end of the south jetty. Coast Guard rescuers used a breeches buoy to bring twenty-nine crewmen ashore, but the ship itself was a total loss. Most of the ship's gear was salvaged, its hull cut up for scrap, and what remained of its bottom incorporated into a jetty extension.

After crossing the Coquille River on July 3, the Jedediah Smith expedition continued on up the beach to the vicinity of Whiskey Run, where it camped that night.

Jedediah Smith Campsite 11
Whiskey Run

North from the Coquille River along the beach, the foredune behind the beach gradually rises. Shortly before reaching Whiskey Run, the foredune changes into steep bluffs that overhang the beach. Whiskey Run Creek carves a narrow valley to the sea through this elevated coastal bench. Several miles farther up the beach, the hills of the Seven Devils rise even more precipitously above the ocean.

Directions: At milepost 256.9 on US 101, exit at the Seven Devils State Park sign. Drive 2.8 miles north on Seven Devils Road and turn left toward the ocean (for 1.4 miles) at the Whiskey Run Beach sign. Return to US 101 to continue north to Coos Bay and Charleston, or follow signs to Charleston on secondary roads.

Where Whiskey Run Creek trickles into the ocean, two brothers of French-Canadian and Indian ancestry, John and Peter Groslius, discovered gold, probably in the winter and spring of 1852–53. The first Whites to settle on Coos Bay arrived in the spring through fall of 1853. By 1854, the gold mining on the beach at Whiskey run had attracted a mining population of perhaps a thousand men and a mining camp-town called Randolph sprang up. Pioneer wife and mother Esther Lockhart recalled that "practically everybody deserted Empire City [on Coos Bay] and rushed to the gold mines," including her husband Freeman Lockhart.

The gold at Whiskey Run was panned and sluiced from black sand on the beach, as it was at beach locations further south all the way to Gold Beach. (See earlier section, "Gold Mining on the South Coast.") The gold in the sand had washed down from the Coast Range, mixed with coarser sand and rocks, and then had been thrown back onto the beach by ocean waves.

The gold mining camp-town of Randolph existed for a year or two. Esther Lockhart in a narrative of her life recorded by her daughter Agnes Sengstacken entitled *Destination West* (1942), described the scene: "At Randolph the ocean beach was staked off into 'claims' for miles, and rough boarding houses and log cabins sprang up like magic. Of course all the activities of a frontier mining camp flourished, including the dance hall, the saloon and the poker table, where the gambler played with his cocked revolver beside him."

During the winter of 1854–1855, stormy weather and heavy seas eroded the beach, and the gold-laden black sand disappeared. The gold rush at Whiskey Run ended as abruptly as it began; however, the search for gold in the Whiskey Run area continued, resulting in some significant finds. One pioneer gold miner, Alexander H. Thrift, estimated that about a million dollars worth of gold was recovered in the vicinity of Whiskey Run over a fifteen-year period.

On April 3, 1873, the *Coos Bay News*, an early Coos County newspaper, reported on a revival of Randolph gold mining operations:

In 1866, A. H. Hinch of this county [Coos], and another gentleman discovered an ancient beach, or what is usually known as a Black Sand deposit, one and a half miles east or back, of the present beach, which has been continuously worked up to the present time. These mines are 180 feet above the level of the Ocean; it evidently having receded to that extent [in earlier times]. The deposit varies in depth from one to twelve feet . . . and from three to five hundred feet in bredth [sic], and covered by white sand from forty to fifty feet deep . . . and overgrown by a dense forest . . . and trees or drift of great size are found in the black sand, in a good state of preservation, thus proving that not in the remote past, there was the actual beach of the Pacific Ocean.

The actual location of the first Randolph, or "Old Randolph," is something of a mystery. Emil R. Peterson and Alfred Powers, in their book *A Century of Coos and Curry* (1952), simply noted that after the discovery of gold at Whiskey Run "before long a camp had sprung up along the beach."

Daniel Giles, in his reminiscence of coming to Whiskey Run at age seventeen, recalled pitching "tents on the bluff at Randolph which overhung the beach . . . affording a good view of the ocean." He said that "after a good night's rest the men visited the beach below and could see fine gold rolling along with the sand at every little gushing stream . . . ." Historian Stephen Dow Beckham placed the site of Randolph one-quarter mile south of Whiskey Run Creek. In a report on historic sites, he noted that "the town was on the bluff about seventy feet above the beach. Whip saw pits, broken glass, pieces of clay pipe, and other debris indicate the site."

Confusion about Old Randolph's location also is due to the fact that after a storm in 1854 washed away the remaining gold-laden sand deposits, Randolph folded but the name survived. In 1859, it became an official post office located at the Fahy farm on Fahy Lake. By 1863, the post office had moved to the Coquille River where Bullards ferry was soon to be located with John Hamblock serving as postmaster. Then in 1871, the post office moved a few miles upstream to a spot on the river that is still called Randolph, although there is no longer a post office there.

The Whiskey Run gold rush made a vivid impression on the early settlers of the region who participated in it. They told of seeing gold mixed together with black sand at every little stream they passed. The methods used by the first miners were crude. Shovels served as gold pans, and miners tried to catch the overflow of fine gold flakes with blankets and animal furs. Soon, rocker boxes and sluices were built. Lumber was in short supply, so some of the would-be miners dug pits for sawing logs into lumber, with one man below and the other above. This may have been the county's first lumber business. A story is told that two men built a small "schooner" to haul supplies between Empire City and the mining camp, perhaps also making Randolph the site of the first boat building on the South Coast.

Seven Devils Road-Randolph Trail

The Seven Devils Road continues north from the Whiskey Run road junction. It is narrow and unsuited for wide vehicles. The road takes its name from the series of steep hills and ravines that lie directly south of Cape Arago. Alice B. Maloney suggested that the name probably originated with Hudson's Bay Company explorers. However, it seems likely from pioneer narratives that the name was given to the area by early settlers.

When the Jedediah Smith expedition left Whiskey Run on July 4, it continued to hug the coastline instead of following an Indian trail to South Slough. Harrison Rogers wrote in his journal that the "travelling [was] pretty bad, as we were obliged to cross the low hills, as they came in close to the beach, and the beach being so bad that we could not get along, thicketty and timbered, and some very bad ravenes to cross."

In 1853, a group of men organized as the Coos Bay Commercial Company and came over the mountains from Jacksonville in the Rogue River Valley. After reaching the mouth of the Coquille River, they too "started up the rugged coast over hills that seemed to be crowded out into the waves of the mighty deep, that were afterwards called the 'Seven Devils,'" wrote Captain W. H. Harris, one of the group's leaders.

These early settlers soon discovered an easier route. This became known as the Randolph Trail. It led from Empire City south and east around the hills above the south end of South Slough and followed the traditional route Indians took to the Coquille River. Seven Devils Road follows a later route that skirted Cape Arago along a ridgeline west of South Slough.

The Seven Devils Road-Randolph Trail was an historic route of Indian travel. With the establishment of Empire City and the mining camp of Randolph, the Randolph Trail had a busy traffic of miners and supplies passing back and forth.

Jedediah Smith Campsite 12
Camp Arago

Directions: Cape Arago and other Charleston Recreation Area sites can be reached by turning west off US 101 at milepost 253 at the South Slough Reserve-Charleston Recreation Area-State Parks sign about midway between Bandon and Coos Bay. South Slough Reserve eight miles; Charleston thirteen miles; State Parks sixteen miles.

The Jedediah Smith party camped on Cape Arago the evening of July 4, 1828, a splendid setting to celebrate American Independence Day. By a curious irony, if true, this campsite overlooked the 1579 South Cove anchorage of Francis Drake, a claim that strengthened Britain's bid for the Pacific Coast of North America.

Harrison Rogers left the Jedediah Smith expedition's only observation on this site: "We enc. on a long point, where there was but little grass for the horses. Good deal of elk signs, and several hunters out but killed nothing, the weather still good." We don't even know if the men of the expedition enjoyed the view. Alice B. Maloney has made the interesting observation that "neither Smith nor Rogers makes any mention of looking out to sea for passing ships in all these days directly on the shore."

Francis Drake: South Cove, Cape Arago

In 1579, the English buccaneer and explorer Francis Drake reached the Pacific Ocean in his ship, the *Golden Hind*, on a combined voyage of exploration and harassment of Spanish shipping. After leaving Mexico, he probably followed the prevailing summer winds westward, then north, and finally east and south, bringing him somewhere off the coast

Location: On the south-interior side of the Cape Arago promontory just past the Cape Arago Viewpoint, approximately five miles south of Charleston on the Cape Arago Highway.

of Vancouver Island, Washington, or Oregon. This was the route taken by Spanish galleons returning east from the Philippines to Mexico. Authorities disagree about how far north Drake got; they also disagree about whether he stopped anywhere north of Drake's Bay on Point Reyes just north of San Francisco Bay, where it is believed by most authorities that he took his ship ashore for cleaning and repairs.

In 1977, the South Cove of Cape Arago was dedicated as the place mentioned in one account of Drake's voyage: "we were forced by contrary windes, to run in with the shoare, which we then first descried; and to cast anchor in a bad bay, the best roade we could for the present meete with." The Drake Navigators Guild, Sir Francis Drake Commission of California, and Oregon Historical Society cooperated in this dedication. But did Drake really put in at 42 degrees of north latitude, or farther north at 48 degrees as mentioned in this and other sources? If Drake put in at 48 degrees latitude, then he didn't put in at South Cove. This description of the coastline also has tantalized Drake scholars: "we found the land by coasting alongst it to bee but low and reasonable plaine: every hill (whereof we saw many, but noe verie high) though it were in June, and the Sunne in his neerest approach unto them being covered with snow."

I finally saw "snow" one day while standing on the west ridge of South Slough looking through binoculars at the dunes lying north of Coos Bay. But was it light reflected from the dunes that Drake saw, or an optical illusion created by summer fog? The location of Francis Drake's "bad bay" will remain disputed, but if he didn't take shelter in the lee of Cape Arago, his ship may have sailed past, perhaps even close enough for us to have seen it if we had been standing on the Cape Arago lookout in 1579.

Commemorative plaque honoring British sea captain Francis Drake, who may have anchored briefly in the South Cove of Cape Arago in 1579. Author photo.

Jedediah Smith Campsite 13
Shore Acres

The Jedediah Smith party and herd of horses must have been exhausted by the Seven Devils. The party made only a few miles' progress on July 5, reaching the site of Shore Acres where natural meadows provided "good grass" for the horses. For what seems to have been the first time the expedition made friendly contact with Indians. Harrison Rogers wrote: "Two Inds., who speak Chinook, came to our camp; they tell us we are ten days travell from Catapos [Calapooya] on the wel Hamet [Willamette River], which is pleasing news to us."

This meeting indicates that Coos Bay was the southern boundary of Hudson's Bay Company influence. The Chinook jargon was a limited vocabulary of Indian, English, and French words used in trade and communication between Whites and Indians. Jedediah Smith had stayed at Fort Vancouver on the Columbia River in 1824–1825, so he must have thought that the worst part of the coastal march was over.

Louis J. Simpson and Shore Acres Gardens

Location: Shore Acres Gardens is three miles south of Charleston on the Cape Arago Highway.

In 1906 Louis J. Simpson, the founder of North Bend and the newly promoted manager of the Simpson Lumber Company, purchased what is now known as Shore Acres and much of the rest of Cape Arago as a site for a summer home. Judith and Richard Wagner, in their excellent biography, *The Uncommon Life of Louis Jerome Simpson* (2003), point out that Louis's wifef Cassie named the summer house after a popular play of that name by James A. Herne. The setting of Herne's play was a farm on the coast of Maine within view of a lighthouse. Asa M. Simpson, Louis's father, and the founder of a Pacific Coast lumber empire, was himself from Brunswick, Maine.

The Simpson summer home was a large, three-story building with gambrel roof and shingled exterior. Compared with country estates elsewhere, its size and design were modest. But for the Coos Bay region, it was in a class all its own. Its interior revealed its owner's initial intention to use it as a vacation retreat. The use of native myrtlewood for wall paneling, Navaho rugs on the living room floor, wicker and oak chairs, and a large stone fireplace gave it a rustic appearance. But as historian Stephen Dow Beckham pointed out in his book *The Simpsons of Shore Acres* (1971), the Simpsons continued to enlarge the house and finally made it their principal residence. At the same time, its furnishings became more refined, and it was decorated with many works of European art.

The summer house of Louis J. Simpson and family at Shore Acres, c. 1910.
Courtesy of Coos Historical & Maritime Museum.

The enlarging of the mansion began in 1914. A swimming pool twenty-six by fifty-two feet in size and a Roman bathroom seventy-five feet long were added. A ballroom was constructed on the third floor of the main house that measured thirty-six by seventy-six feet. North of the main house, two concrete tennis courts were built overlooking broken coastal cliffs.

The estate gardens capture our attention now. The State of Oregon has restored the Shore Acres gardens close to their former condition. Simpson took a passionate interest in developing his formal gardens. Hydrangeas were planted first, followed by roses, rhododendrons, and many exotic plants that Simpson imported from distant parts of the world. An oriental garden took form around a large lily pond. This garden then and now included an arched wooden footbridge, stone lanterns, and such common oriental plants as bamboo.

Louis Simpson's life took a tragic turn in 1921. His wife Cassie died of a heart abnormality on April 30. On July 4, a fire started in the main house of the Shore Acres estate. Simpson saw the fire from his gardens and rushed to the house. People inside escaped without injury, but the entire house and all of its treasures burned to the ground.

Simpson remarried and continued to live with his second wife Lela in the gardener's residence. By 1927, a second mansion had begun to rise from the ashes of the first. It spread across a 224-foot expanse of coastal bluff, stood two stories high, and contained seventeen rooms. With gymnasium, and private baths for each bedroom, plans for the second mansion, too, were on a grand scale. The Simpson family began to live in the new home. But two years later, it remained unfinished. The stock market crash of 1929 severely depleted Louis Simpson's fortune, and made it impossible for him to complete the second Shore Acres mansion.

In 1932, Coos County transferred ownership of 134 acres of Simpson's Cape Arago estate to the State Parks Commission. The property had been donated to a local civic organization and then subsequently to the County. And in 1936, according to the Wagners' research, money problems forced the Simpsons to transfer their Shore Acres property to the Bennett Trust Company in settlement of debts. In 1943, following U.S. entry into World War II and closure of the road to Shore Acres and Cape Arago for military reasons, Loius decided to sell the remaining 637-acre Shore Acres property to the State of Oregon for $29,000. The Shore Acres property rejoined the earlier Cape Arago ddonated parcel to create the present Sunset Bay, Shore Acres, Cape Arago state parks. Although Louis's donation and sale of these properties was influenced by financial considerations, Oregon's State Parks Commissioner Samuel H. Boardman deservedly praised him for his generous contributions to the state park system.

Jedediah Smith Campsite 14
Sunset Bay

Location: Sunset Bay is two miles south of Charleston on the Cape Arago Highway.

A short distance down the road from Shore Acres on the way to Charleston is Sunset Bay. This is one of the most photographed spots on the South Coast. It is, in fact, one of the few protected coves of any size on the Oregon Coast. While its popularity is due to its physical beauty, its tide pools, and its fascinating clues to the region's geology, it also has historical importance.

Sunset Bay was campsite fourteen on the Jedediah Smith Trail. Still worn out by their bushwhacking over the Seven Devils, the party made only a few miles on July 6, 1828, transferring their camp from Shore Acres to Sunset Bay. Even the two miles between campsites was a major effort. Harrison Rogers wrote in his journal: "the travelling very bad, mirery and brushy; several horses snagged very bad passing over fallen hemlock."

Imagine the expedition's surprise, however, on meeting with a large reception party of Indians. Rogers wrote: "About 100 Inds. in camp, with fish and mussels for sale; Capt. Smith bought a sea otter skin from the chief; one of them have a fuzill, all have knives and tommahawks. One a blanket cappon, and a number have pieces of cloth."

George B. Wasson, Jr. explained, on the basis of Coquille Indian elders' stories, that the Nasomah, after their flight from the expedition, sent messages of warning to Indians on Coos Bay. There, "a respected Miluk headman"—named Kitzenjinjn—"responded with great military pomp and diplomacy, taking 300 armed men dressed in their finest skins and feathers out onto the coastal headlands near Cape Arago and ceremoniously welcoming the astonished whites."

The expedition spent another day at Sunset Bay working to clear a path for the horses through woods and underbrush between Sunset Bay and what Rogers referred to as "a large river that is in sight about 2 miles distant." The river was Coos Bay.

Whites used Sunset Bay in the late nineteenth and early twentieth centuries as a fishing cove. Some early photographs of the region show small fishing boats pulled up on the beach. In the summer of 1913, Louis Simpson developed a small resort at Sunset Bay complete with three-room cottages, large tents, and a restaurant. A local newspaper reported that "it is an ideal place for the tired out office man or clerk to spend a week or so with his family." It has been such a place ever since.

In the 1940s, Coos County acquired Sunset Bay for failure of the owners to pay taxes. Samuel Boardman happened to see an advertisement in a newspaper advertising it for sale. He rushed to the county courthouse in Coquille, where on February 19, 1948, the forty-eight acres of the state park was deeded to the State of Oregon.

The island that lies on the north side of the entrance to Sunset Bay also has a brief history. It is called Squaw Island. It gets its name from the fact that when Coos Indians were removed from their homeland at the end of the Rogue River Indian War, some Indian women and children hid on the island to avoid capture.

Cape Arago Light: Gregory Point

From a bluff overlooking the ocean that lies between Sunset Bay and Shore Acres can be seen one of the most picturesque lighthouses on the Oregon Coast. The overlook can be reached from the Cape Arago highway or by following the Sunset Bay to Cape Arago trail. The lighthouse is Cape Arago Light.

Cape Arago Light stands just north of Squaw Island on a projecting arm of the cape called Gregory Point. The original lighthouse on the site began operation in 1866 as Cape Gregory Light Station. It was the first permanent

Location: On a bluff just north of Sunset Bay. The lighthouse is closed to the public. Viewpoints between Sunset Bay and Shore Acres Gardens, two to three miles south of Charleston on the Cape Arago Highway.

lighthouse on the Oregon Coast. It was described in the *Coast Pilot* of 1869 as an "octagonal wrought iron tower and lantern, painted white, with the dome of the lantern painted red."

Cape Gregory was known to be a site long used by the Miluk Indians on lower Coos Bay and South Slough. But the first archaeological excavation on Gregory Point took place in 1978. A test pit dug on lighthouse-island, which is separated at high tide from the rest of the point, contained 229 items of aboriginal and Euro-American manufacture. The Indian artifacts included net sinkers, shell scrapers, bone awls, an antler wedge, small clay balls, and other items.

A large number of sea mammal remains were found by archaeologists John A. Draper and Glenn D. Hartmann. These indicated that Indians probably hunted male stellar sea lions on a regular basis, a conclusion that ran contrary to the previously accepted view that they used mainly beached carcasses. The major food source for Indians using the island was shellfish and rockfish, not salmon. The quantity of remains led the two archaeologists to conclude that the island must have been inhabited most of the year.

Archaeologist Reg Pullen has drawn the following conclusion from recent finds:

Gregory Point was first occupied in 500 AD and used until just before the arrival of Euro-Americans in the early 1800s. According to ethnographic information, it was abandoned after raiders from the south burned the village and killed all the residents except one woman who jumped into the ocean to escape death. The residents of Gregory Point lived in plank houses

Cape Arago Light (left) with lighthouse keeper's house (center right) and old life-saving station on the beach below, c. 1910. Courtesy of Coos Historical & Maritime Museum.

scattered throughout the old growth spruce forest that once covered the
point. They pulled their canoes up on the beach at Sunset Bay, and walked
up a trail leading to the village.

An interpretive center to illustrate the history of this early village Might some day be built. A master plan has been developed for a Bal'diyaka Interpretive Center by The Confederated Tribes of the Coos, Lower Umpqua and Siuslaw Indians.

Bal'diyaka Interpretive Center long-range plans envision "a recreated Indian village; an ethnobotany trail; and the Cape Arago lighthouses . . . . The village would contain traditional cedar-planked structures, including a ceremonial house, a dwelling, a children's sleeping house, a sweathouse, a drying house, a woodshed, a windbreak, and a gravehouse." Such an interpretive center would provide a much-needed resource for education in the history of the region's native peoples.

According to anthropologist John Harrington, who did research among the Coos Indians in the early 1940s, a part of the lighthouse reserve was known to old Coos Indians as a village called "Baldiyasa," which translates as "the place where the south wind blows." Local Indians gathered shellfish on the reefs and caught smelt during the spawning season. A part of the lighthouse reserve also was used as a burial ground. After 1866, the federal government forbade the Coos Indians to use the site.

It took over a hundred years for local Indians to regain the right to use the burial ground. Historian Stephen Dow Beckham in his book *The Indians of Western Oregon* (1977) described the victory:

When the Brainard family of Coos Bay wanted to place a tombstone at the
site, the Coast Guard refused. For years Marguerette Therrien Brainard
pressed for permission to place a marker. Finally in 1950 Senator Wayne
Morse obtained a special Act of Congress compelling the Coast Guard to
allow the family to erect a tombstone. Marguerette Brainard continued
to press the rights of the Coos to their ancestral cemetery and finally on
June 12, 1975, the Coast Guard granted an easement to the Coos, Lower
Umpqua, and Siuslaw. Once again the Coos could be buried in the old
village where their ancestors had lived by the sea.

Since 1975, the parcel of land that forms a part of the original burial ground has been used to rebury Indian ancestral remains that have been removed from other sites as a result of archaeological excavations.

Construction of Cape Arago Light came a little over a decade after the first White people settled on Coos Bay. The Coos Bay bar presented a dangerous challenge to coastal schooners. The lighthouse resulted from attention focused on the Coos Bay harbor by United States Coast Survey work between 1861 and 1865, as well as recognition of the need for improved navigational aid at the Coos Bay bar.

To assist in the rescue of passengers and crewmen from wrecked ships, a U.S. Life Saving Service station was built in 1878 in a cove below the lighthouse. It consisted of a small building to house a lifeboat and keeper. Volunteers from Empire City had to come down the bay and across the cape to man the lifeboat in the event of a shipwreck. This life station continued in operation until 1891, when a new station was built on the inside of Coos Bay's north spit about midway between the channel entrance and Empire City.

The remote and exposed location of the Gregory Point lighthouse and life saving station was described by a writer for the *Pacific Coast Pilot* of 1889: "This islet is separated from the main land by a channel about one hundred yards in width at high water. . . . This passage appears to be filled with sunken rocks, and it looks a very bad place from which to launch a boat in heavy weather."

The remains of the original lighthouse still can be seen at a distance from the present lighthouse. A new wooden frame lighthouse was built in 1908; it operated until 1934. In that year, the present lighthouse went up. The tower of the old lighthouse was removed and what remained became the lighthouse keeper's office until it too came down in 1960.

Jedediah Smith Campsite 15
Charleston

The route taken to the entrance to South Slough by the Jedediah Smith expedition was "very bad," according to Harrison Rogers, despite the day's work on the trail. Fallen trees, brush, and ravines made progress slow. But finally on July 8, 1828, the party broke through to the beach at present-day Charleston. There they found a large Indian village, and for the first time were able to stay as guests. Rogers reported: "The river at the mouth is about 1 mi. wide, the Inds. very numerous, they call themselves the Ka Koosh." One writer has noted that the name Kakoosh is close enough to Kuitsch, the name of the Yakonan tribe living on the lower Umpqua River, to make Rogers' rendering of the name questionable.

Rogers also described briefly the trading that went on with the Miluk village at Charleston. He wrote in his journal: "They commenced trading shell and scale fish, rasberrys, strawberrys, and 2 other kinds of bury that I am unacquainted with, also some fur skins. In the evening, we found they had been shooting arrows into 8 of our horses and mules; 3 mules and one horse died shortly after they were shot. The Inds. all left camp, but the 2 that acts as interpreters; they tell us that one Ind. got mad on account of a trade he made and killed the mules and horses." Local Miluk oral history identifies the hostile Indian as a visitor from a lower Umpqua village.

Although Indian villages were located at various sites the whole length of Coos Bay, the entrance to South Slough appears to have had one of the largest concentrations of Coos Indians. The Coos Indians were divided linguistically into two groups: the Hanis and Miluk. Each group spoke a distinct language that the anthropologist Melville Jacobs has compared to the difference between Dutch and High German. The Miluk lived at various places on the east shore of Coos Bay south of Empire, on South Slough, on Gregory Point and Cape Arago, and on the lower Coquille River.

It is not known for sure how long Coos Indians had lived in this region before White people came. An archaeological excavation on South Slough by anthropologist Ron Stubbs indicated that the Miluk lived there at least as early as the 1500s and 1600s. But earlier dates from excavations at other sites on the South Coast suggest that Indians probably lived on Coos Bay and South Slough for perhaps as long as 5,000 years, according to archaeologist Reg Pullen. Pullen has noted that "leaf shaped spearpoints and knives have been found at Crown Point and Valino Island, providing some indications of this earlier occupation." With many changes in the estuary and coastline over thousands of years, archaeological sites of the earliest inhabitants likely have been washed away or covered over by the ocean and sedimentary deposits. Indian shell deposits and fish weirs have been found on South Slough at Crown Point, Younker Point, and the west side of Long Island Point.

Charleston

It has been said that Charleston was called "Charlie's Town" after a Chinaman named Charlie who lived in a shack above the beach. However, Lewis A. McArthur in his book *Oregon Geographic Names* stated that it was "named for Charles Haskell, who is said to have taken up a claim at the mouth of South Slough in 1853." If McArthur is correct, Haskell was one of the earliest claimants on South Slough, along with George Wasson and T. D. Winchester. In any event, there probably were fewer people living at Charleston at the turn of the century than when Jedediah Smith visited the Miluk village located there in 1828.

Directions: Approaching from the south on US 101, take the Charleston Recreation Area turnoff at milepost 253, midway between Bandon and Coos Bay. From Coos Bay at milepost 237.5, follow Charleston Harbor-Ocean Beaches signs from downtown Coos Bay (turn left/west on Commercial Ave.). From North Bend, at milepost 235, follow Ocean Beaches signs from the center of old North Bend (turn right/west on Virginia Ave.

The site of present-day Charleston was a place for weekend and holiday excursions in the early years of the twentieth century. Riverboats on Coos Bay brought passengers to the Charleston beaches for picnics. Then in 1906, Louis J. Simpson began to build his estate at Shore Acres. Traffic to beaches west of South Slough and Charleston increased when Simpson in 1913 opened a resort at Sunset Bay.

When the U.S. Coast Guard erected a life-saving station boathouse at Charleston in 1915 (which now belongs to the University of Oregon Institute of Marine Biology and has been restored for use as a lecture hall), a store went up the following year. But significant growth came after 1924, the startup

Dave Jones store, Charleston, c. 1925. Courtesy of Coos Historical & Maritime Museum.

year for a federally funded project to build a south jetty at the entrance to Coos Bay. Within a year, Charleston had a dance hall, a tavern, and several stores. Dave Jones Locker went up that year. A sawmill was built at the end of Roosevelt Boulevard. Construction workers on the jetty lived in barracks where Institute of Marine Biology classrooms and dormitories are now. In the 1930s, these barracks were turned into a Civilian Conservation Corps (CCC) camp. The CCC young men worked on projects at the new Cape Arago State Park area donated by Louis J. Simpson.

Further development of Charleston was linked to growth of commercial and sport fishing. Offshore commercial fishing out of Coos Bay in the 1920s and 1930s led to the opening of the Hallmark Fisheries plant at Charleston in 1936. In 1937, Al Qualman came from Willapa Bay in Washington State and reintroduced the raising of oysters—the Japanese or Pacific oyster rather than the native Northwest Coast Olympia oyster. Commercial fishing continued to add to Charleston's growth over the new few decades. At the same time, however, logging and farming on South Slough declined, and many families moved out of the area to other places.

Coos Bay Bar

If you happen to be standing on the south jetty when a giant ship comes through the channel entrance, you will feel as if you can almost reach out and touch it. Hundreds of such ships enter and leave Coos Bay each year, as much taken for granted as the coastal rain. But without the two jetties and continuous channel dredging these giant ships couldn't stop in Coos Bay.

Directions: Take the Cape Arago Highway south from Charleston 1.6 miles to the turnoff to Bastendorf Beach Park. Continue past the park to the south jetty, 1.2 miles.

Early settlers recognized the importance of ship transportation in and out of Coos Bay. The *Coos Bay News*, an early newspaper, reported the following good news on April 17, 1873:

> *The opening of steam communication [by the Eastport Steamship Line], twice a month, between Coos Bay and San Francisco [with stops along the coast at Port Orford and Crescent City], makes a new departure in our history as a commercial people . . . Already the tide of travel to Southern Oregon is setting in by this channel [Coos Bay] and we need only a good wagon road to catch the bulk of trade from the counties of Douglas and Josephine. San Francisco is the great center of capital on the Pacific Coast and her capitalists never like to go away from home in search of investments unless they know when they can get back.*

Although considerable tideland has been lost to filling and siltation on the upper bay, the general configuration of the bay is much the same as it was 100 years ago. But the channel entrance to Coos Bay has changed greatly since the first small ship crossed over the bar in 1852 to rescue a complement of U.S. Army dragoons shipwrecked on North Spit. In the early days, the channel entrance was continually shifting, making it difficult to enter without the help of a tug familiar with the waters. Of course the tugs are just as necessary for the giant ships of today.

In the 1890s, federal money made possible the construction of a north jetty. The jetty provided for a channel depth of twenty feet. But heavy seas quickly eroded the jetty and the depth fluctuated to as low as twelve feet. For many years, local leaders tried to get the federal government to finance construction of a south jetty. In an appeal to Congress in 1920, Coos Bay port officials complained that lumber ships with a twenty-five- to thirty-five-foot draft couldn't load and leave Coos Bay. Congress finally responded, and by 1928 Coos Bay had a south as well as a north jetty. This improvement in the channel entrance not only made possible continued growth in lumber exports, it provided a safer entrance for offshore commercial fishermen, leading to the growth of Charleston as a fishing port.

At least sixty ships, and probably more, have been lost in the waters surrounding the Coos Bay channel entrance. In trying to cross the bar, some have been driven southward into the cove between Coos Head and Mussel Reef. Before the south jetty was built, Bastendorff Beach lay under water. Other ships, their rudders broken and out of control, have drifted northward, floundering and finally breaking up in the surf off the north spit of Coos Bay.

Shipwrecks off the Coos Bay Bar

The worst shipwreck ever on the Coos Bay bar occurred on January 12, 1910. The steel steamer *Czarina* started out over the bar. When it was halfway across, high waves washed over it and put out the ship's boilers. The heavy sea carried the helpless ship north off the sand spit of Coos Bay. The captain had anchors dropped to prevent the ship from grounding, but this action doomed the crew and passengers.

The *Czarina* was loaded with coal and lumber. The heavy surf tore loose the lumber, making it impossible for rescuers to reach the ship by boat. The ship lay too far off to reach with a line from shore. The twenty-four crewmen of the ship and one passenger, who had taken to the ship rigging, soon began to drop into the sea from weakness and exposure, as rescuers watched, helpless to aid them. Only one man reached shore alive.

Sailing ships also found the Coos Bay bar difficult to cross. On February 18, 1913, the schooner *Advent* out of Santa Rosalia, Mexico, started to sail into Coos Bay just as the wind died. The ocean current carried the ship south about 600 yards from the channel entrance and about the same distance offshore. A life-saving crew rescued the ship's seven crewmen, but the ship later broke up and washed onto shore.

Wreck of the schooner *Advent* on the south shore of the Coos Bay bar in 1913.
Courtesy of Coos Historical & Maritime Museum.

Wreck of the steamer *Santa Clara* on the south shore of the Coos Bay bar in 1914.
Courtesy of Coos Historical & Maritime Museum.

Another human tragedy occurred on November 2, 1915 when the wooden passenger steamer *Santa Clara*, while trying to cross the Coos Bay bar, struck bottom, damaging its rudder. The ship drifted onto the south spit of the channel entrance. The captain, fearing that the ship would soon break up in the heavy surf, gave an order to lower lifeboats. Two lifeboats capsized before reaching shore, resulting in the drowning of fourteen passengers and crewmen. The remaining passengers and crewmen were helped ashore by Coast Guard rescuers. The next day the ship was high and dry, making it easy for salvagers to board it.

On April 26, 1923, the steamer *Brush* struck Simpson Reef just south of the Coos Bay Bar. The ship's hull cracked, but the Coast Guard rescued its captain, his wife, and the crew. Louis J. Simpson used the ship's lumber cargo that washed ashore to rebuild his Shore Acres home.

In early February 1999 the *New Carissa*, a Japanese-owned 639-foot freighter that grounded on the beach about three miles north of the Coos Bay channel entrance, captured national attention. It had arrived off Coos Bay to pick up a cargo of wood chips, but was delayed from entering the bay by stormy weather. The ship's captain mistakenly dropped anchor one and a half miles from shore, rather than keeping his ship underway at sea. By the morning of February 4, it was too late for the ship's engines to overcome high winds and waves that pushed the ship onto shore.

A helicopter lifted the ship's crew to safety, but the ship contained 400,000 gallons of heavy fuel oil that threatened major ecological damage to nearby off-shore fishing grounds, the Coos Bay estuary, and shorebird habitat. Battered by storm-tossed waves, the ship began leaking oil. Altogether, an estimated 70,000 gallons of fuel oil leaked out of the ship into the sea, turning into pea- and walnut-size balls of tar. Some washed ashore, some went into Coos Bay, but more of the fuel oil swept northward along the coast.

Efforts to pull the ship off the beach failed; so within a week of grounding, the ship was set on fire; then it split apart. Burning consumed 190,000 gallons of fuel oil, but left 135,000 gallons on board the 440-foot bow section. Efforts to pump oil ashore failed. Finally, the tugboat *Sea Victory* got the bow section headed out to sea, but on March 2 gale force winds of another storm snapped the towing cable. The next day the bow section grounded at Waldport, eighty miles north along the coast from Coos Bay, threatening marine life and shorebirds in a new location. Another 2,000 gallons of oil leaked out and washed ashore.

A week later, on March 8, the bow section of the *New Carissa* was again towed seaward. On March 11, U. S. Navy explosives, destroyer gunfire, and a nuclear submarine torpedo combined to sink it, 325 miles offshore and 10,866 feet deep. Despite its initial impact on local fisheries and the hundreds of oiled shorebirds that died from the oil spilled along the Oregon coast, the *New Carissa* shipwreck might have caused much worse ecological damage. As long as the 200-foot stern section remained beached just north of the Coos Bay bar, it would be a reminder of continuing threats to Oregon's coastal environment.

South Slough National Estuarine Research Reserve

Directions: To reach the Research Reserve Visitor Center from Charleston, take the Seven Devils Road south for about four miles. It also can be reached from US 101 by taking the Charleston Recreation Area turnoff at milepost 253 midway between Bandon and Coos Bay.

From the bridge at Charleston it is possible to look south on one of the most historically and biologically interesting parts of the Coos Bay estuary. About two-thirds of South Slough from Valino Island south, and its adjacent upland, is now included within the Research Reserve. It was the first estuarine sanctuary or reserve in the nation when it was established in 1974 to protect a unique environment of birds, plants, and marine life for scientific research and public education. It consists of a little more than 4,000 acres, including 600 tidal, 100 freshwater marsh, and 3,600 upland forest acres.

A good place to view the historic development of South Slough is from the Research Reserve Visitor Center. After looking at exhibits in the visitor center-headquarters and taking in the outside panoramic view, ask for directions to the old Frederickson farmhouse at the southwest end of South Slough.

The impetus for creating the Reserve (originally called an estuarine sanctuary) came in 1970, at a time of growing national and state environmental concern over the loss of wetlands. Governor Robert Straub sought the help of Dr. Ted LaRoe, Chief Scientist with the Office of Coastal Zone Management of the National Oceanic and Atmospheric Administration. LaRoe directed the search for an estuary on the Oregon Coast that could be used as a research site. The Coastal Zone Management Act of 1972 offered a way to protect South Slough from further development. Local citizens and elected representatives actively pursued the selection of South Slough for reserve or sanctuary status. Paul Rudy, director of the University of Oregon's Institute of Marine Biology in Charleston, was a key leader. In 1974, South Slough was chosen over McCaffery Slough on Yaquina Bay, the next in line of twelve possible Oregon Coast sites. Although the land adjacent to the South Slough waterway and wetlands had been logged over and farmed in the past, it was believed that it could be returned to a natural state.

The Miluk Indians' name for South Slough meant a geographical dividing line or land feature. A trail passed from the south end of the slough and over steep hills of the Seven Devils to the beach and on to the Coquille River. Early miners and settlers passing between Empire City and Whiskey run made use of Indian trails. In *Pioneer Trails of the Oregon Coast* (1971) geographer Samuel N. Dicken described two likely routes: "One inland trail from the south took off near the north end of the beach at Five Mile Creek and crossed the hills and [marine] terraces to the east, reaching the southern tip of South Slough." Another trail, easier for pack trains to travel, went farther east and north, dividing near the summit of today's McLain-Libby Drive, one fork going to Empire and the other to Marshfield [Coos Bay].

A large forest fire raged through the South Slough area in 1874, reaching as far to the east as Coalbank Slough. Later residents of South Slough recalled stories about mills on the slough that were destroyed in this fire and later rebuilt. A map published in 1875 showed "Turners Logging Camp" located on the eastside. Pioneer historian Orvil Dodge mentioned that Andrew Wickman had a logging camp on South Slough in 1881. He also noted that at the headwaters of the slough, "large quantities of staves have been manufactured . . . from the very large spruce trees of the forest and a great many men have found lucrative employment."

Twenty-four homesteads are shown on the map of 1875. Census reports reflected the growth of population in the area due to logging and homesteading. Land cleared by logging operations in the 1850s through 1870s made possible the building of small farms on streams leading into South Slough. The diking of marshes by pioneer farmers made additional land available. Logging operations not only made it easier for farms to develop, it also provided local employment and a market for beef, vegetables, and dairy

Andrew Frederickson family homestead overlooking Winchester Creek at the southwest end of South Slough.
Courtesy of South Slough National Estuarine Research Reserve.

products beyond what was needed for family use. Dodge briefly noted that "James O'Shin planted an oyster bed in Coos Bay, near the mouth of South Slough in 1874." But this seems to be the last that is heard of oyster raising on South Slough until Al Qualman planted his oyster beds in 1937.

By the turn of the century, there were several families living on small subsistence farms in the Winchester Creek area. There was a school at the southern end of Long Island Point and a large logging camp that housed upwards of 150 men. The Frederickson family, Swedish-speaking Finns from Gamlakarleby, Finland, established a homestead on South Slough in the late 1890s. The family consisted of five brothers; John, the eldest, arrived on Coos Bay first, followed by his brothers Matt, Victor, Otto, and Andrew. Matt settled first on South Slough in 1898. By 1905, Victor and Andrew joined him on a next-door land parcel. They built the home that is known as the Frederickson farmhouse that still stands today. They divided the house in half with a partition to separate their families, making it into a kind of farmhouse duplex. Eventually, Andrew, his wife Bertha, and their family were the sole occupants, and from this family it passed on to the Research Reserve.

The Frederickson farmhouse stands on a hillside overlooking a large meadow. Winchester Creek meanders through the meadow to South Slough. The meadow is now overgrown with nearly waist high grass, but it was once a pasture. It is an example of tidal marshland that the early settlers reclaimed from its natural state by the construction of dikes on creeks that enter South Slough. A large and extensive dike system also can be seen on the Estuary Study Trail below the new headquarters.

Standing in the meadow below the Frederickson house on Winchester Creek you can see the stumpy remains of an old railroad trestle that kept logging trains above marshy ground. The Smith-Powers Logging Company operated a railroad at the south end of the slough that went back into the hills to the south and east in the direction of Beaver Hill. The railroads that operated on South Slough brought logs out of the hills to the slough below, where they were dumped into the water, tied together, and rafted up the slough and around the bay to one of several mills.

A number of families of Indian ancestry obtained allotments of land on South Slough in the period 1892–1901. Among these were the Wasson, Talbot, Elliot, Younker, Barton, Hanson, Sacchi, and Tanner families. These allotments were made subsequent to the breakup by the federal government of the Siletz Indian Reservation. The land was placed in the trust of the Bureau of Indian Affairs. So many allotments were made on South Slough that it became identified as an Indian area. In the 1950s, when the Coos Indian tribe's trust relationship with the federal government ended, some of these Indian families lost their allotment lands for inability to pay accumulated property taxes to the county. Local timber companies paid the taxes and acquired valuable timberland. Logging on South Slough continued until the establishment of the South Slough sanctuary in 1972.

Three schools located on the east, west, and south sides of the inlet provided places for children to go to school through eighth grade. The schools also doubled as dance halls and community centers. Although a few roads were built down to the slough and between homesteads, the major means of transportation was by boat. Shortly after the turn of the century, a trestle bridge was built across the inlet just north of Valino Island, and another bridge went up at Charleston, which improved transportation across the slough.

Despite the many uses of South Slough land and water over nearly 100 years, the inlet by the 1970s still seemed to be the best preserved of the Coos Bay estuary's many parts. When the South Slough Estuarine Sanctuary was dedicated in the summer of 1980, Stella Frederickson Whittick said, "My dad cleared all this land and now it's really a shame to watch it grow back over like it is." In view of a century of agricultural, mining, fishing, and forest industrial use, it was hard for her to see it return to a more natural state.

Jedediah Smith Campsites 16 and 17
Charleston to Empire to North Spit

Jedediah Smith and his expedition left Charleston on July 9, 1828, but rather than attempt a dangerous crossing of the Coos Bay channel entrance, the expedition crossed the entrance to South Slough somewhere in the vicinity of the Charleston boat basin and bridge. The crossing took placed without difficulty and the expedition proceeded north.

The campsite on July 9 was at the Indian village of Melowitz, according to Alice B. Maloney, who heard of the village from local Indian informants. She doesn't indicate the location of the village, but Harrison Rogers wrote that after traveling about two miles, they "struck another river" and camped. Pigeon Point is approximately two miles north of the Charleston Bridge. But Rogers' comment that they "struck another river" seems to indicate a location closer to Empire. On July 10, Rogers noted that the bay "runs N. and S., or rather heads N.E. and enters the ocean S.W." where it is "about $1^1/_2$ miles wide."

Campsite sixteen was well populated. Rogers wrote: "A great many Inds. live along the river bank; there houses built after the fashion of a shed. A great many Inds. in camp with fish and berris for sale; the men bought them as fast as they brought them."

The next day, July 10, the expedition crossed over the "river" it had reached the day before. The crossing required a swim of about 600 yards, according to Rogers. The Coos Bay harbor channel narrows to about 600 yards at only

The Jedediah Smith expedition crossing the entrance to South Slough in 1828.
Drawing by Kevin Kadar.

one place—Empire. The expedition apparently crossed near where it camped because it crossed early in the morning in canoes. On the other side the expedition found "good grass" and made camp. Therefore, the crossing must have been in the vicinity of Empire, with the Henderson Marsh area on the north spit of Coos Bay the most likely encampment site. The crossing went well, although Jedediah Smith, who had remained on the east shore with five men to swim over the last horses and mules, felt apprehensive. Rogers noted: "He was some what of opinion the Inds. had a mind to attact him from there behaviour, and he crossed over where the swells was running pretty high . . . ." But the Indians who followed the expedition over to the north spit, according to Rogers, acted "pretty shy."

The day's crossing of Coos Bay brought the expedition to the north spit of Coos Bay where they made campsite seventeen. The next day, July 11, the expedition followed a course "N. along the beach of the ocean."

Camp Castaway and the Wreck of the *Captain Lincoln*

The north spit of Coos Bay was the scene of a key event in the later discovery and settlement of the area. The invasion of South Coast beaches by gold miners in the early 1850s made the discovery of Coos Bay inevitable, but the timing was quite accidental. It involved a shipwreck and Robinson Crusoe-like experience by U.S. Army dragoons, or mounted riflemen.

On January 3, 1852, at 2 a.m. in the dark, early hours of a new day, the schooner *Captain Lincoln* ran aground on a sand bar—off the

Location: On the north spit of Coos Bay east of Empire-Barview and north of the Coos Bay channel entrance. Exact location unknown. To reach the north spit, turn west off US 101 at milepost 232.7 onto the Horsfall Beach/Oregon Dunes access road, approximately two miles north of North Bend.

entrance to Coos Bay. Aboard the transport were about thirty men and supplies headed for Fort Orford.

The *Captain Lincoln* had developed a leak shortly after departing from Benecia, California. Pumps were manned to keep the ship afloat, but rough seas made it impossible for the ship to reach anchorage at Port Orford. The captain made a desperate decision to run in close to shore and try to beach the ship rather than go down at sea. By this time, the ship floundered off Coos Bay. Philip Brack described the forced landing on Coos Bay's north spit. "We seemed to strike a bar that was about 200 yards from shore," he said, "but the huge breakers lifted our trembling vessel over into deeper water, but she settled down to the bottom and for awhile the breakers rolled over her decks." When the tide receded, the *Captain Lincoln* was high and dry on a beach.

The location of the shipwreck was described by Henry H. Baldwin, another member of C Troop, 1st Dragoons, as being two miles north of "Kowes" or "Kowan" bay. Pioneer historian Orvil Dodge concluded from Philip Brack's account that the wreck occurred on the ocean side of north spit "nearly opposite the present site of Empire City." Captain Morris S. Miller, Assistant Quartermaster, visited the site and reported its location and that of Camp Castaway:

> The camp was near the point where the wreck had occured, on the sand-spit lying between Kowes river and the Pacific—a very dreary position, the sand being miles in extent in both directions, and blown by the wind in clouds, penetrating every canvass covering, and besprinkling every article of food while cooking-the only protection being a ridge of sand hillocks, behind which the camp was situated.

The men of C Troop quickly moved supplies from the ship to shore. Baldwin's account provided a few more physical details of the campsite that might be used to establish its approximate location. "Two large lakes a few yards distant furnished excellent water, and was close by," he said. "The schooner's large cook's galley was hoisted ashore and placed on a commanding point or ridge overlooking the camp."

Shelters made from the ship's spars and sails were erected to protect the men and supplies from the weather. Almost as soon as the men had established camp, Indians from nearby villages across the bay arrived to investigate and to trade or barter. As so frequently happened in contacts between Indians and Whites, something was found to be missing—in this case a revolver. An Indian was apprehended, tied to a pole on which the United States flag had been raised, and given twenty-five lashes with a "raw-hide." C Troop had been dispatched to Fort Orford for the purpose of intimidating South Coast Indians; therefore it was taken for granted that any hostile act by local Indians ought to be treated severely.

After this initial incident, however, relations with the local Indians were friendly. Baldwin wrote that the "old chief, named, Hunness" came on his second visit with "a long pack-train of squaws laden with fish of all kinds, wild geese, ducks, elk and venison." In return, the Indians were given "hardtack, rice, tobacco and lots of old dragoon pants, shell jackets, capes, skirts, boots and shoes, which pleased them extremely well, especially the jackets, which were decorated with grand yellow lace and a multitude of bright brass buttons."

News of Camp Castaway reached several White outposts. Baldwin related that within a few weeks, several Americans and a Hudson's Bay Company officer visited them from the Umpqua River and from Randolph, just north of the Coquille River, to offer assistance. Through correspondence with headquarters in Benecia, California, Lieutenant Stanton informed Assistant Quartermaster Miller that wagons could move supplies from Camp Castaway to the Umpqua River, where he hoped to find buyers for salvaged supplies.

While awaiting Captain Miller's arrival, Lieutenant Stanton attempted to find out whether a boat or ship could get into Coos Bay. He wrote to Captain Miller that he "had a whale-boat run off through the breakers, in order to bring her round into the river." He added that "the mate who was with her tells me he found a good channel all the way in, with from five to six fathoms water and no breakers."

On April 25, Captain Miller reached Camp Castaway after swimming a pack train of twenty mules across the "Kowes river," or lower Coos Bay. When he learned that Lieutenant Stanton had been unable to find a buyer for the ship's supplies, he proceeded to the Umpqua River and chartered the schooner *Nassau* to go to Coos Bay to pick up the supplies and return them to Fort Orford. Captain Miller wrote that "the schooner was to enter the river and be moored to the west bank; the stores were then to be hauled across the sand point by teams."

Captain Miller already had sent wagons to the Umpqua on the brig *Fawn*. At Winchester Bay, the mules he brought with him from Fort Orford were hitched to the wagons and driven down the beach to Camp Castaway, where the transfer of supplies from the camp to the *Nassau* took place. The *Nassau* sailed without mishap to Fort Orford, where supplies were offloaded, and then to Benecia with Captain Miller and the crew of the wrecked *Captain Lincoln*.

During his two-month stay on the South Coast, Captain Miller had an opportunity to observe the Indians from Fort Orford to the Umpqua River. In his report, he wrote as follows about them:

> *There has been but little intercourse as yet between the Indians and the whites along the route from Fort Orford to Kowes river, and the use of ardent spirits is still unknown to them. They evinced throughout the most friendly disposition, aiding us readily with their canoes in crossing the rivers, bringing wood and water to the campfire, and considering themselves amply remunerated for these services by a small quantity of hard bread.*

> *They are full of curiosity with regard to the whites, particularly desirous of procuring clothing, and much disposed to barter; offering even their children in trade. In the vicinity of Fort Orford they are aware of the value of coin, but in other places their currency is small shells strung together, and called "sirvash." They are humble and peaceably disposed, being armed entirely with the bow and arrow; and, in my opinion, no difficulty need be apprehended from them, unless it originate in aggressions of the whites.*

Captain Miller's observation about the possibility of White aggression was prophetic. On the whole, the wreck of the *Captain Lincoln* seems to have turned out to be a brief, happy adventure for C Troop and local Coos Bay Indians. But it brought the attention of White gold miners, settlers, merchants, and sea captains to Coos Bay, as well as the rest of the South Coast. Within a few years, Indians and Whites on the South Coast were at war and the possibility of living together in peace ended forever.

Empire

Location: An incorporated district of the city of Coos Bay that can be reached via Commercial Ave., Newmark Ave., or Virginia Ave. (North Bend). Follow signs to Charleston and Ocean Beaches. From the Empire boat launch, one can see where the Jedediah Smith expedition probably crossed Coos Bay to North Spit.

A chart of Coos Bay showing channel depths makes it easy to understand why the first White people from the Umpqua River and from Jacksonville chose Empire (City) as the site of the first White settlement. Once over the Coos Bay bar, it is the first site along the lower Coos Bay channel that provides a water depth near shore adequate for anchorage of ships. At Empire, the lower Coos Bay channel reaches its narrowest point. Channel depth at dockside in Empire is about twenty-three to twenty-six feet at mean low water level, nearly the same as in the late nineteenth century. Elsewhere along the east shore of lower Coos Bay, extensive tidal mudflats are exposed at low tide, which makes ship anchorage and navigation near shore impossible.

In the early days, Empire City was a welcome oasis in the wilderness. Esther Lockhart in her narrative of pioneering on Coos Bay wrote of arriving at Empire City in the fall of 1853 and putting up at the town's "hotel." "On reaching Empire City," she wrote, "which consisted of one cabin and a rude hotel, we went at once to the latter place, kept by our genial friend Frank Ross, where we feasted on fresh salmon, clams and roasted wild ducks and geese."

Empire City wharf looking across the Coos Bay channel to the north spit.
Reprinted from *Harper's New Monthly Magazine* (Oct. 1856).

The old Southern Oregon Improvement Company sawmill at Empire City, c. 1898.
Courtesy of Coos Historical & Maritime Museum.

Empire City became the seat of Coos County government and remained so until 1896, when voters chose Coquille as the new location. Henry H. Luse built a sawmill at Empire City in 1855. In 1883, the Southern Oregon Improvement Company bought out Luse and built an even larger sawmill on the site of Luse's original mill. The mill closed ten years later and remained closed for many years. The old mill stood below the bluff next to the boat launch site. In 1942, it reopened and operated for a number of years thereafter as the Cape Arago Lumber Company.

A surviving landmark of late nineteenth-century Empire (City) is the Tower House on the corner of Newmark Avenue and Fourth Street built in 1872 by Dr. Charles W. Tower. This is a distinctive-looking two-story, six-bedroom house with porthole and pointed-arch windows, eastside veranda, and a steeply pitched roof in the Gothic Revival style. Dr. Tower and his wife moved from the house to Marshfield in 1874, when the house became the Patrick Flanagan home. The Tower House and the Pioneer (Wagner) House in Powers are the oldest surviving buildings in Coos County. The Tower House is on the National Register of Historic Places.

Downtown Coos Bay: Historic Buildings

A fire in 1922 along the railroad tracks on Front Street destroyed the heart of Coos Bay's old business district. The city of Coos Bay then was called Marshfield, until residents voted in 1944 to change the name to Coos Bay, after a vote on consolidation with North Bend failed to pass.

Location: A three-block square area between Commercial Ave. and Curtis Ave., Coos Bay waterfront and Third Street.

Many other older buildings in downtown Coos Bay have been razed to make way for urban development of the downtown area. However, there still are buildings within a few blocks of the Bay Area Chamber of Commerce visitor center that illustrate several major architectural styles of the first three decades of this century.

The Chandler Hotel at the corner of Second Street and Central Avenue was the hub of a new business district that developed away from Front Street after the turn of the century. When it opened for business in 1909, the Chandler Hotel represented a major step forward for the growing town of Marshfield. The hotel's French Renaissance, Mansard-style roof represented a touch of continental and big-city architecture. Five stories in height, the hotel towered above other downtown buildings. In the style of the late nineteenth-century Renaissance Revival, its lower story contrasted with the design of the three stories of hotel rooms and the upper-level attic story.

On the eve of the hotel's opening, Jesse Allen Luse, owner-editor-reporter of *The Sun* weekly newspaper, described the hotel's interior features:

> *On the main floor is found the lobby, office, cigar store and news stand, writing room buffet, grill, ladies reception room and cafe. They are arranged with due regard for the convenience of guests and uniquely furnished. The old Mission style of architecture prevails and our native woods are seen to perfection. In the lobby early English furniture, upholstered in red leather is found. With massive pillars it gives an expression of splendor to the eye and one is almost bewildered with the grandeur, which he has found. A local telephone system connects every room with the office and a switch board is there to connect you with long distance if necessary.*

The Chandler Hotel was an example of local businessmen pooling their capital to promote the commercial future of their town. The lack of a first-

Chandler Hotel on Central Avenue and Second Street, Coos Bay, c. 1912.
Courtesy of Coos Historical & Maritime Museum.

Elks Club Building (Security Bank Building in 1998) on Second and Anderson streets, Coos Bay, built in 1920. Chandler Hotel rear-left. Author photo.

class hotel was considered a major shortcoming. A Chicago architect initially was hired to design the building, but delays led to reassignment of its design to a Portland, Oregon architectural firm that designed the Chandler Hotel to look like Portland's Cornelius Hotel. The Chandler Hotel was named in honor of William S. Chandler, a major investor who had just resigned as manager of coal mining and railroad interests on Coos Bay.

Next door to the old Chandler Hotel building at the corner of Second and Anderson streets is a two-story building that originally was built as the Temple of Marshfield B.P.O.E. Lodge #1160. The building was completed in 1920. In 1998, it was the headquarters of Security Bank, the firm responsible for its restoration. The distinctive exterior feature of the building is its arched, second-story, brick-framed windows. Coos Bay Architect Steve Clay, who supervised the building's restoration, has explained that the building represents a "stylistic blend" of Commercial or Chicago Style on the ground floor and Neo-Classic or Georgian Revival on the upper floor.

The Elks Club Building was the last of a series of buildings that William S. Chandler helped finance in Marshfield. Chandler came to Coos Bay in 1899 as a mining engineer. He soon was involved in a variety of business ventures and became a wealthy man. He helped finance construction of the Chandler Hotel (1908), First National Bank Building (1909), Coke Building (1910), and Irving Block (1910), all located within a block of each other. He also donated the land on which the Elks Club Building was built, and he loaned $66,000 for its construction.

The principal architect in Chandler's architectural ventures was his son and namesake, William G. Chandler, who graduated from the University of Oregon with an engineering degree in 1907. The younger Chandler had a unique opportunity to develop a series of nearly contiguous buildings. Steve Clay has noted that "in each building that W. G. Chandler designed there was a sense of permanence and a variation in the exploration of some of the different architectural styles of the day."

Together, the Chandler Hotel and Elks Club buildings bracket a period of important growth in the downtown of Marshfield. Their construction coincided with a major expansion of forest industrial manufacturing on Coos Bay.

In addition to the Chandler Hotel and old Elks Club buildings, two nearby buildings out of the 1920s and 1930s deserve attention. One is directly across the street from the Chandler Hotel. When completed in 1928, it became headquarters for the Coos Bay Bank. It is a fine example of Classic Revival architecture with Greek anthemion ornaments on its parapet, Ionic columns, and Roman-style round-arched windows on the ground level. In 1998, it was the location of the Bank Brewery.

The second building is located a half-block west of the Elks Club building on Anderson Street. It was built in the 1930s as a federal office building and for many years housed the Coos Bay post office; in 1998 it was home of the Coos Art Museum. The building nicely illustrates several architectural styles of the period. It is classical in its simple rectangular form. The classical motif is carried through in the simple detail of the entablature, or area just below the cornice or roofline, as well as in the fluted decorative areas between the windows. These are stylized pilasters, and the way they are treated identifies the building with the popular architectural style of the 1920s and

Interior decoration of the Egyptian Theatre, Coos Bay, built in 1925. Ward Robertson photo.

1930s called Art Deco. The lobby area of the building illustrates several prominent Art Deco motifs—the chevron pattern of the small panels on the wall opposite the main entrance, the decorative molding, and the shiny brass railings on the stairway leading to the second floor that are shaped in a rounded sunburst pattern.

The Art Deco or Modernistic style originated with the 1925 Paris exposition of decorative and industrial arts. The Art Deco style is identified by the use of zigzag lines, chevrons, vertical stripes, sunrise patterns, and other geometric forms to achieve decorative effects on the interiors and exteriors of public and commercial buildings. Art Deco designers also incorporated stepped towers and vertical projections into building facades. They sometimes used the Egyptian obelisk for decorative effect. The obelisk can be seen as a design motif in Oregon's coastal bridges.

Two blocks south of the Bay Area Chamber of Commerce office on Broadway is an even more exotic-looking architectural treasure, the Egyptian Theatre. The exterior looks like the front of any other small town theater, except for the Egyptian motif on its sign. But inside, one finds a lavish display of theater decoration.

The Egyptian Theatre opened for business in 1925. It was built during the Egyptian craze that followed the discovery of Tutankhamen's tomb in 1922. Hollywood's Egyptian Theater opened that year and was called "Hollywood's first movie palace." Egyptian theaters began to be built in many places, including Marshfield. In the lobby at the foot of each of two stairways are large statues of seated Pharaohs. The walls and columns of the theater are lavishly painted with Egyptian hieroglyphs.

A crowd of about 1,700 people attended the opening of the Egyptian Theatre. Jesse Luse of *The Sun* described the fanfare:

The first-nighters stormed the ramparts of the Egyptian theatre on opening night and many hundreds were turned away. It was surprising, indeed, to see the crowd that had assembled for the initial performance. L. J. Simpson welcomed the patrons in behalf of the amusement managers, as he knows how. He spoke in laudatory terms of Harry Noble and the Coos Bay Amusement Company for giving to Southwestern Oregon this unparalleled

Original stage backdrop for the Egyptian Theatre; a forested landscape with a snow-covered mountain in background. Can-can dancers center stage.
Ward Robertson photo.

and magnificent theater. There were present representatives of the leading motion picture concerns of the Pacific coast, and many distinguished film stars sent congratulations. That all are proud of the new edifice was given unquestionable endorsement by the great turn out for the opening event. While the exterior is anything but pleasing to the eye, a most unique and modern electric sign of gigantic proportions points the way to the entrance, and, once within the patron is dazzled with the varicolored paintings, wrought in Egyptian splendor by the artists brush—a thing of beauty and a joy forever. The decorations are exquisite, and would cause the Pharos of old to stand in amazement as they gazed on their enfolding charm and beauty.

At the sixtieth anniversary of the Egyptian Theatre's opening, local vaudeville singers, dancers, and comedians, along with Portland organist Paul Quarino, took theatre-goers back to the 1920s. The highlight of the program for anyone interested in the interior decoration of the theatre was the use of five original stage backdrops. Two were of Egyptian scenes: a temple interior and a desert landscape with pyramids in the background. Another backdrop featured a forested landscape with a snow-covered mountain, perhaps Mt. Hood, as its central focus. Two others illustrated woodland and a terrace.

The B. F. Shearer Company of Seattle did the interior decoration of the theatre. The company already had decorated thirty-six other theaters on the Pacific Coast in the early 1920s before it did the Egyptian Theatre in Marshfield. A *Coos Bay Times* reporter noted that Carl Berg, the man in charge of decoration, "has spent considerable time in research work regarding Egyptian decorations and symbols and architecture." The reporter explained that: "The winged sun represents the overshadowing deity which takes care of all things of mankind on earth. The scarab is our American tumbling bug which has a very deep spiritual meaning in their philosophy."

In a curious way, the Egyptian Theatre was more than an exotically decorated theatre. It symbolized an ancient civilization that Americans in the 1920s could admire. The same *Times* reporter wrote: "The Egyptians were a most scientific people, their priests being the wisest men of their age. How well they planned their work and understood nature is marvelous even to the present age." In Egyptian civilization, Americans of the 1920s discovered an inspiration for science, art, and entertainment.

In 2006, the Egyptian Theatre was purchased by the City of Coos Bay's Urban Renewal Agency, ending its long run as a commercial theater. It will be missed as a landmark first-run movie house, but its life will continue as a venue for showing historic films and staging community programs.

Coos Bay Boardwalk

With the flags of many nations flying overhead, the Coos Bay Boardwalk is a festive place. Here, one can walk on the site of early Marshfield's wharf that provided a place to dock for incoming coastal steamers and smaller boats,

Location: Downtown Coos Bay on the waterfront opposite the Bay Area Chamber of Commerce visitor center.

the so-called "mosquito fleet." With its combination of semi-enclosed and open space, the boardwalk offers both an unobstructed view of upper Coos Bay and photographic exhibits of Coos Bay history, economic activity, and natural features. In one of the shed-like enclosures built and placed at different angles to mimic the unplanned arrangement of early wharf structures, visitors can view an old riverboat. And at the right time, one might even be lucky enough to see a replica of Robert Gray's *Lady Washington* of the late eighteenth century, or even a replica of Francis Drake's *Golden Hind* of the late sixteenth century, in port on a visit.

The Coos Bay (then Marshfield) waterfront was a busy place. Front Street, just north of the Boardwalk along the railroad tracks, was the main street of Marshfield until the 1920s. For three blocks north it was lined with businesses—hotels, banks, saloons, restaurants, printing shops, barber shops, houses of prostitution, and other commercial enterprises. From Central Avenue to Alder Street stretched a long wharf that allowed for the unloading of passengers and freight.

At the turn of the century, Front Street still was built over tidal mudflats, before it was filled in with dredge spoils to make a foundation for the railroad tracks. The street and buildings on either side of Front Street were

Marshfield waterfront at the turn of the century; coastal steamers and riverboats at the wharf. Courtesy of Coos Historical & Maritime Museum.

supported by pilings and the street was planked. Young boys made rafts and floated among the pilings underneath the town's main businesses and thoroughfare. In those days, Marshfield was a rough, backwoods, coastal town. One writer commented in 1906 that "Front Street in Marshfield is suggestive of a backwoods mining camp."

From the Marshfield wharf, one could look south toward Isthmus Slough and see coal bunkers where ships took on coal for transport to San Francisco or Portland. Smoke and steam from lumber mills rose into the air. And on all sides, there were ships and boats of every size and purpose from steam-driven, stern paddle-wheel boats to sailing schooners to small riverboats used to deliver milk from Coos River dairy farms.

Marshfield Sun Printing Museum: Coos Bay

Location: 1049 N. Front St., about five blocks north of the Coos Bay Boardwalk.

The Marshfield Sun Printing Museum is another architectural and historic survival. In this curious-looking, five-sided, two-story, wood-frame building, Jesse Allen Luse, the grandson of Henry H. Luse, who established the first sawmill at Empire City, printed and published *The Sun* weekly newspaper from 1911 until he died in 1944. Luse actually began publication of the paper in another location on Front Street as early as 1891. At the time of Luse's death, *The Sun* was the longest continuously published weekly newspaper in Oregon.

The Sun Museum, with its Washington Hand Press and Chandler & Price Platen Press, its walls lined with type cases, its marble-top imposing tables, and its other printing equipment, keeps alive the look and feel of a turn-of-the-century newspaper and job printing shop. On the building's second floor are photographic exhibits of early Marshfield and the "Mosquito Fleet" of riverboats that operated on Coos and Coquille rivers.

As a young man of twenty-one years, Jesse Allen Luse published the first issue of *The Sun* newspaper on February 12, 1891. He continued to publish *The Sun* until June 16, 1944—a newspaper career of slightly more than fifty-three years. In the day of the small weekly newspaper, when *The Sun* got its start, publication of a newspaper had to be combined with job printing. Luse was a printer as well as a newspaper editor and publisher, and he admired other newspapermen who weren't afraid to get their hands smeared with printer's ink.

Visitors to Luse's old printing and newspaper shop step back in time. The press used to print *The Sun* is a Washington Hand Press that stands in the far right corner of the museum. The Washington Hand Press was patented in 1821 by Samuel Rust of New York. It is a flat-bed, hand-operated press that looks much like presses used in Benjamin Franklin's time a century earlier, except that it is lighter in design and made of iron instead of wood. Because it was lightweight, the Washington Hand Press became the standard press for frontier newspapers in the American West. Few of these presses have survived.

The second most important item of printing equipment in the museum is a Chandler-Price platen press. The jobbing platen press was an American invention. It was developed in the early nineteenth century to handle the printing of business stationery, handbills, business cards and forms, and the like. This jobbing platen is a variation of the Franklin or Gordon Press of 1856, designed by George Phineas Gordon, a New York printer.

In the *Sun* building today, with its old printing equipment, wood stove, and smell of printers ink, it is possible to imagine what it used to be like on Front Street. A train still rumbles past the building at least twice a day, right down the center of Front Street along the track that the first train to Marshfield followed when it arrived from Eugene in 1916.

Washington Hand Press in the Marshfield Sun Printing Museum on North Front Street, Coos Bay. Claude O. Coffman photo.

Isthmus Slough: Mill Sites

On entering the city of Coos Bay from the south (just past Bunker Hill Elementary School), one can see a large woodchip pile, perhaps a ship taking on a cargo of chips, and the remains of what once was the largest lumber manufacturing facility on Coos Bay. This is where the C. A. Smith Lumber Company built its mill in 1907–1908. The mill later became the Coos Bay Lumber Company mill, and finally, until its closure a few years ago, the Georgia-Pacific Corporation mill and plywood plant. A modern but much smaller Georgia-Pacific sawmill has been built on the site, the only sawmill in Coos Bay today.

Location: On the eastside of US 101 from Coos Bay south and then east on Hwy 42 toward Coquille.

If you want to get a closer look, take the turnoff to Allegany and stop at either end of the Eastside Bridge that spans Isthmus Slough. Isthmus Slough reflects the continuing business of log exports from the region with its rafts of logs tied to the shoreline. But it also is a graveyard of abandoned forest-industry artifacts: pieces of machinery, holding pens for logs, conveyors for bringing logs out of the water, and the like.

The first mill on upper Coos Bay was Asa Simpson's mill at North Bend, started in 1856. It was not, however, the first mill on the South Coast. That credit goes to H. B. and Edward Tichenor, nephews of Captain William

E. B. Dean and Company sawmill on Isthmus Slough.
Lithograph reprinted from A. G. Walling, *History of Southern Oregon* (1884).

Tichenor, and I. F. Neefus, who started a mill at Port Orford in 1852. On Coos Bay, the construction of the Pershbaker mill in 1867 led to the growth of Marshfield. By 1885, E. B. Dean & Company had built a mill on the east bank of Isthmus Slough just south of the present bridge. Between the 1900 and 1910 census, Marshfield grew from 1,391 to 2,890 people because of the arrival of the C. A. Smith Lumber Company and Smith-Powers Logging Company. The C. A. Smith mill was the first big mill in the region, and the beginning of a new chapter in forest industry on the South Coast.

Hundreds of small mills like the old E. B. Dean & Company mill appeared and disappeared over the years, up and down the South Coast. Ownerships changed frequently; wild fluctuations in the lumber market made it hard for them to survive for long. The same was true of larger forest industrial companies. But after the turn of the century, the forest industrial giants took over the West Coast, taking advantage of the last stands of old-growth timber in the United States.

In the years that followed, forest industry evolved from the milling of rough lumber to more sophisticated manufacturing processes. At first, the C. A. Smith Lumber Company operation consisted of a large lumber manufacturing plant. But by World War I, the company had experimented with the manufacture of both veneer and pulp. In the 1920s and 1930s, these new processes led to the appearance of many new plants in the Coos Bay region. Veneer was used to make battery separators for automobiles and in the construction of airplanes. In the 1930s, plywood manufacturing also began.

Log storage on Isthmus Slough. Author photo.

The most obvious fact about the location of forest industrial enterprises on Isthmus Slough was their access to water. Water access was essential to the early lumber mills. It was the only means of transportation in the early days. Mills were built at the water's edge in the vicinity of logging operations. Logs were pulled to the water with oxen until the 1890s; then steam donkeys and logging railroads replaced them. But most logging railroads ended on a nearby slough or river, and most logs continued to be rafted to the mills. In earlier years, the logs stored on Isthmus Slough would have been processed into lumber, veneer, or plywood. Today they probably await shipment to China, Japan, and other Pacific Rim countries for processing.

Isthmus Slough: Coal Mines

Like many aspects of the timber industry in the region, the evidence of early coal mining is invisible. Today there are no coal bunkers, no steam schooners waiting to be loaded with coal, not even any coal mines in the vicinity of Coos Bay that are still in operation. But once there were, and periodically geologists and business entrepreneurs revive hopes of new coal mining ventures.

Coal mines once dotted the landscape of Coos County. A 1943–1944 survey identified seventy-two coal mines in the Coos Bay region, of which eleven were located in the vicinity of Isthmus Slough. One of these, the Southport Mine off Isthmus Slough, was one of the larger mines in the region. In the 1870s, towns along Isthmus Slough like Henryville and Utter City sprang up overnight in anticipation of coal mining prospects. Occasionally an old coal mine entrance is rediscovered as a result of logging, but otherwise the only evidence of these old mining operations and towns are photographs and maps that bear witness to their once-important place in the region's economy.

Coal miners at the entrance to the Beaver Hill Mine.
Oregon Historical Society, #OrHi 38865.

The first railroad tracks in the region connected coal mines with nearby towns and wharves for incoming coal ships. One such railroad connected the Newport Mine on Coalbank Slough with Coos Bay along a two-mile track. Another five-mile section of railroad was built between the mining towns of Utter City and Carbondale on Isthmus Slough and Beaver Slough. In 1893, the Coos Bay, Roseburg & Eastern Railroad was completed, linking Marshfield with Coquille and Myrtle Point. It brought coal from the Beaver Hill Mine, opened in 1894, to coal bunkers on Coos Bay.

Early coal mining ventures often failed. The Henryville Mine, located midway between the turnoff to Sumner and Coaledo, just beyond Davis Slough, open in 1874. After investors spent $200,000 for trestle, bunkers, mine shafts, coal cars, and miners' quarters, their false hopes were abandoned in 1876. It was reopened several times later, but without success.

Of all the coal mines on Isthmus Slough, the Southport Mine, which opened in 1875, proved to be most productive. It still was operating during World War II. The entrance to the Southport Mine lay just a half-mile south and west of the Sumner turnoff. In a fifty-five-acre area, 250,000 tons of coal were mined by World War II. Mine shafts ran upwards of 2,000 feet into the hills. The Southport coal veins were part of the same coal bed that made the even larger Newport Coal Mine on Coalbank Slough and the Beaver Hill Mine on Beaver Slough so productive.

The Newport and Beaver Hill mines operated with varying degrees of success until the early 1920s, when competition from fuel oil and gas shut out their market. The best indicator of the importance of coal to the economy of the Coos Bay region is not the dollars and tons of coal exported but the number of people who lived in the major coal mining communities. In their heyday, the Newport or Libby and Beaver Hill communities each supported about five hundred people.

Coos County Historical Society Museum: North Bend

In 1906 (year of the San Francisco earthquake), the intersection of Sherman and Virginia avenues, and the North Bend waterfront a few blocks east, seemed likely to become the future business center on Coos Bay. Louis J. Simpson, son of early "Old Town" North Bend milltown founder Asa Simpson (and soon-to-be builder of a new Shore Acres summer home), had just created the new North Bend. The Coos Bay Commercial Club, organized by Simpson, had

Location: The museum is located at 1220 Sherman Ave. in Simpson Park on the west side of US 101 next door to the Visitor Center, just before leaving North Bend.

just been organized and quartered in "The Castle Building" (renamed Winsor Building) on the southeast corner of Sherman and Virginia. The building had a castle-like third-floor structure that symbolized the business status aspired to by local businessmen. On the downhill east corner (of Sheridan and Virginia) of what was called the "brick block" stood the new First National Bank building.

In the vicinity of Sherman and Virginia avenues at the end of the twentieth century, antique and collectibles businesses put one in touch with the past rather than the future. The manufacturing businesses on the waterfront—box factory, milk condensary, sash and door factory, woolen mill—have long since disappeared. Log export operations have replaced these earlier businesses. It's difficult to imagine the commercial optimism that existed in 1916 when

The Castle Building (renamed Winsor Building) on the southeast corner of Sherman and Virginia avenues in North Bend, c. 1906. Courtesy of Coos Historical & Maritime Museum.

a railroad from Eugene finally reached Coos Bay and a mock wedding celebration was staged at the Sherman-Virginia Avenue intersection joining the futures of Miss Coos County and Mr. Eugene Lane.

In 2006 the Coos Historical and Maritime Museum was still the major historical attraction in North Bend. Architectural plans for a new museum facility have been drawn up but await funding. In the meantime, the museum building located in Simpson Park (donated in 1916 by Louis Simpson) contains a treasure of historic artifacts: old photographs, musical instruments, baby carriages, office equipment, household utensils, women's clothing, children's toys, maps, journals, business ledgers, school readers, family Bibles, ship models, doctors' tools, world war souvenirs, Indian artifacts, and more.

The highlight of the museum is its collection of Native American artifacts. This consists of over 400 stone, bone, and antler pieces, and more than 200 baskets. Some of these items are from the collection of ship's captain James Magee and his wife Sarah. Captain Magee brought back souvenirs from his trips around the world—exotic shells from the South Pacific and statues from Indian and Japan. His wife Sarah collected Indian baskets and hats made by South Coast Indian women. Items from the Magee Collection, together with baskets and stone tools from the Molly and Charles Fahy Collection, provide a rich illustration of Native American cultural life.

Locomotive No. 104 stood at the museum entrance for many years, but it has been moved to a new historic railroad display site in Coos Bay developed by the local Oregon Coast Historical Railway Association (at 744 N. 1st St., on US 101 northbound at the railroad switching area just south of the main business district). Locomotive No. 104 is a 1922 steam engine built by Baldwin Locomotive Works in Philadelphia, Pennsylvania. It began hauling logs in 1923 for the Coos Bay Lumber Company. It continued its service until 1954, pulling log cars from Powers to Isthmus Slough. The locomotive is 59 feet 9.5 inches long and weighs seventy-three tons. It could pull forty to fifty cars on a level grade. It is a giant historical artifact and reminder of the Coos Bay region's forest industrial heritage.

Locomotive No. 104 began its logging service in 1923 for the Coos Bay Lumber Company. It is on display at the Oregon Coast Historical Railway Association in Coos Bay..

The Coos Historical and Maritime Museum also has a large collection of photographs relating to logging and lumber milling. The history of railroading in Coos County is well illustrated by photos from the Slattery Collection, named for Jack Slattery who operated a local photo shop and copied photographs on Coos County history for over forty years. The collection covers every topic from logging, coal mining, shipbuilding, and maritime transportation to the people, houses, and businesses of the region's towns.

Wherever people lived in Coos County, they were never far from a river, inlet, or bay. For early Native Americans and later White settlers, the waterways of the region provided food resources and routes of transportation. Rotating museum exhibits highlight this theme of "Tidewater Highways."

Until the 1930s, the main means of travel in the Coos Bay-Coquille River region was by boat. And the primary way of getting to and from the region was by coastal steamer between Coos Bay or Bandon and Portland or San Francisco.

Ships have played a major role in the history of the South Coast and some of the most distinctly local artifacts in the museum are those related to their history. Maritime artifacts include ship nameplates, signal guns, steering wheels, models of boat hulls, and the like.

The museum has a research library that is open for use by appointment. The library contains important records of early ships and coastal shipping. Family Bibles reflect the importance of religion in people's lives. A large number of early maps contain essential information about early towns, coal mines, logging camps, and overland routes. Medical books contain lore on how to treat illnesses. And many manuscripts and scrapbooks, such as one containing clippings and memorabilia of Louis J. Simpson's campaign for governor of Oregon in 1918, reveal important personal insights into the region's history.

Coos Bay to Heceta Head

McCullough Memorial Bridge over Coos Bay

Location: At milepost 234 on leaving North Bend.

The construction of McCullough Bridge was a dividing line in the region's history between a frontier era of dependence on sea transportation and a modern era of land transportation connections with the rest of Oregon and the other Pacific Coast states. Land connections of a sort had existed from early times down the Umpqua River and the beach between Winchester Bay and Coos Bay. After 1872, travelers also could reach Coos Bay over the Coos Bay Wagon Road. The Southern Pacific Railroad completed a railroad line to Coos Bay in 1916. But in a symbolic as well as a real sense, the South Coast was isolated, a "far corner" as Stewart Holbrook once wrote.

One has to go back to June 6, 1936, when McCullough Bridge was dedicated, to recapture a sense of what it meant to the region. A *Coos Bay Times* headline read: "Coast Span Brings Reality to Dream of Decade." Beneath a picture of the bridge, the newspaper highlighted the bridge's importance. "Coos Bay's completed bridge—a useful monument to the engineers and statesmen of Oregon, who in the most severe economic depression of their generation, had courage and skill sufficient to thrust this sixth longest bridge in the world across the finest bar harbor on the Oregon coast."

McCullough Bridge under construction in 1935.
Courtesy of Coos Historical & Maritime Museum.

McCullough Bridge was the last of five coastal bridges built in the 1930s as a result of efforts to put Americans back to work through the construction of public buildings, bridges, dams, and other facilities. In late 1932, after Franklin D. Roosevelt was elected president to succeed Herbert Hoover, the state highway department persuaded Oregon's Governor Joseph Meier to make construction of a system of coastal bridges the state's number one public works project. In addition to the bridge at Coos Bay, coastal bridges also went up over Yaquina Bay at Newport, Alsea Bay at Waldport, Siuslaw River at Florence, and Umpqua River at Reedsport. The building of the Coos Bay bridge came after a decade of greatly increased automobile traffic. The number of cars transported by the *Roosevelt Ferry* across Coos Bay on July 4, 1922 totaled thirty-three. By July 4, 1935, the *Roosevelt Ferry* carried 1,976 cars. In that same period, passenger traffic increased from 172 to 6,955 persons.

By July 30, 1934, construction of McCullough Bridge had begun. McCullough Bridge cost $2,143,000 to build, the most costly of five bridges, whose total cost was $5,602,000, a sum almost equal to what the Oregon legislature appropriated in 1917 to build the state's first highway system. Thirty percent of the bridge's cost was paid for by the federal government's Public Works Administration, and the rest through the sale of bonds by the State of Oregon.

The design engineer for all five coastal bridges was Conde B. McCullough. His name was attached to the largest of the five bridges, the bridge over Coos Bay. If you examine the plaques at either end and on either side of the bridge, you will discover that the bridge in fact has two names. One reads: "McCullough Bridge/Conde Balcom McCullough/Bridge Engineer & Assistant State Highway Engineer 1919–1946." The other reads: "Coos Bay Bridge/Federal Emergency Administration of Public Works/Project No. 982." Originally named the Coos Bay Bridge, it was renamed in honor of McCullough in 1947 following his death the previous year.

As the largest of the coastal bridges, the bridge over Coos Bay symbolically is the capstone of McCullough's bridge-building career. McCullough served as Bridge Engineer for the Oregon State Highway Department from 1919 to 1932, then became Assistant Highway Engineer. Louis F. Pierce in an article on McCullough has pointed out that of the 3,200 bridges still being used in Oregon in 1980, 900 were built under McCullough's direction in the period 1919–1946. In 1933, the John McLoughlin Bridge at Oregon City, designed by McCullough, was awarded first prize as the most beautiful steel bridge of its class by the American Institute of Steel Construction. Bridge historian David Plowden has called the McCullough-designed coastal bridges "the most interesting concentration of concrete bridges in America."

In building the Oregon Coast bridges, McCullough borrowed the ancient stone arch as a major architectural element. He borrowed European techniques of utilizing concrete to construct arches. And he borrowed currently fashionable Art Deco ornamentation to add visual interest to those

The newly completed McCullough bridge in 1936. Courtesy of Rollie Pean.

parts of the bridges visible from the highway. (See discussion of Art Deco style in "Downtown Coos Bay: Historic Buildings.")

McCullough Bridge, technically a cantilever truss bridge, was a major engineering feat. It was claimed that the Coos Bay and Yaquina Bay bridges contained the largest arch spans in the world supported on wooden pilings. Each arch span measured 265 feet in length. The bridge is just over a mile in length (5,336 feet). Its main or channel span is 793 feet in length with adjoining anchor spans of 457 feet 6 inches in length. The clearance above high water is 120 feet with a 527-foot opening. Seven concrete and steel arches, varying in length from 151 to 265 feet, form the support structure of the north end of the bridge, and six support the south end roadway, varying from 170 to 265 feet in length.

From an engineering point of view, what lies beneath the water unseen by even the most curious bridge lover is even more important than the superstructure. Beneath each of the main piers, 608 wooden piles were driven down in the sandy bottom of the bay. Each pile extends thirty-five feet beyond what is called the "seal," a point thirty-six feet below mean sea level. The pilings, the bridge's engineers claimed, would last longer than the bridge itself, even though they were untreated.

Shortly after the coastal bridges were finished, a friend asked McCullough what he thought about covered bridges. His answer was surprising for a man who had just completed a mile-long bridge of major proportions.

Personally, I am all for the old covered bridge. It wasn't wide enough nor strong enough to carry the loads, it is true, but it was long enough to reach from one bank of the river to the other, which is all that a bridge is supposed to do anyway. Ninety-nine and seven tenths percent of the people who travel over the rivers now would be a lot better off if they stayed at home in the first place. They simply travel the roads and burn up more gas so that we can build more roads for them to burn up gas on. It is a vicious circle. The whole thing is the responsibility of the engineers. If we only knew the truth, the decline of ancient Babylon and the complete dissolution of Sodom and Gomorrah were probably dated from the time when they formed the first engineering society.

McCullough had good reason to question the effects of bridge building on automobile use. Shortly after the Rogue River Bridge's completion, there was a significant increase in traffic flow compared to earlier use of the ferry. But McCullough's good-humored skepticism about the wisdom of so much contemporary road and bridge building didn't keep him from applying his best creative engineering skills to his work.

Umpqua River Lighthouse and Coastal Visitor Center: Winchester Bay-Salmon Harbor

Six ships wrecked at the mouth of the Umpqua River between 1850 and 1857, when a lighthouse finally was erected on the river's south bank, the first lighthouse to be built on the Oregon coast. At that time, the Umpqua River was an important route of transportation for goods going to the gold mining areas in southern Oregon. Unfortunately, the lighthouse was built on the sandy beach near the harbor entrance. When a heavy winter storm hit the coast in 1861, the foundation of the lighthouse washed away and the structure collapsed.

Requests for funds to build a new lighthouse were ignored. For three decades, ships made do as best they could. At least two ships wrecked off the bar because navigational aids still

Directions: At milepost 217, just north of the Winchester Bay Wayfinding Point (an overlook of the Umpqua River entrance), turn west off US 101 at the Umpqua Lighthouse State Park sign. Follow the loop road approximately 0.4 miles, then turn left on the Lighthouse Road loop. The Umpqua Lighthouse and Coastal Visitor Center is just a few hundred yards past Lake Marie. From Salmon Harbor at milepost 215.5, the Coastal Visitor Center is about 1.6 miles off the south shore road.

showed the first lighthouse. The bar was no less hazardous than before. It underwent major changes with each passing storm. One day the channel might be at one location, and two weeks later it might be as much as three-quarters of a mile north or south.

Congress finally appropriated funds for a new lighthouse in 1893. The present lighthouse first flashed its protective light in 1894. It is a plain, tapered conical tower that reaches a height of sixty-five feet. With its 210,000 candle-power beam, it can be seen from eighteen to twenty miles out at sea. Its heavy masonry walls and rock foundation make it look impervious to the worst of coastal storms. Originally, two lighthouse keepers' homes stood on either side of the lighthouse. The simple Victorian beauty of their crossed gables and wraparound front porches, which now can be seen only in old photographs, contrasts sharply with the cement block architecture of today's Coast Guard quarters.

In recent years, the light in the lighthouse has been repaired and restored to operating condition. Its Fresnel lens consists of nearly 1,000 hand-cut glass prism pieces that focus light into twelve beams. The lens was made in Paris in 1890. A brass carriage system underneath the lens enables it to turn.

The Umpqua River Lighthouse was one of ten lighthouses constructed on the Oregon Coast between 1866 and 1899. Like many of the other lighthouses, it is on the National Register of Historic Places.

Opposite the Umpqua River Lighthouse is an ocean overlook called the Umpqua River Whale Watching Station. Outdoor exhibits identify different types of whales, with special attention given to the characteristics of the gray whale, the most frequently sighted species.

A short distance from the Umpqua River Lighthouse stands the former U.S. Coast Guard Umpqua River Station. Built in 1939, this building once served as an administration building and barracks. The Coast Guard used the building until 1971. It is now the Coastal Visitor Center, with museum exhibits and the sign-up point for summer tours of the lighthouse.

Outside the Visitor Center there is a thirty-six-foot Coast Guard rescue boat that was built in 1932 and operated for forty-six years. In high seas that might capsize the boat, it could right itself in forty-five seconds due to its rounded, buoyant design. It could range up to 200 miles off the coast. The boat was restored as a Boy Scout Eagle Service Project by Roseburg Troop 225.

The Umpqua River Station is a good example of Colonial Revival architecture. It is a rectangular, two-story building with side gable roof and three projecting dormers. The building has wing extensions and a porch with eight paired columns that support a flat upper porch with balustrade. The upper balustrade repeats the paired column motif of the lower porch. The iron railing of the lower porch has two center sections on either side of the stairs that incorporate the nautical symbol of a compass circle. In its restored condition, with white shingles, red roof, green shutters and window trim, the Umpqua River Station nicely reflects the order, discipline, and simple dignity of its Coast Guard heritage.

Inside, the Umpqua River Station's former mess room, day room, bedroom,

Umpqua River Light. Author photo.

U.S. Coast Guard Umpqua River Station (now Coastal Visitor Center). Author photo.

office, and dining-living room have been converted into three historical exhibit rooms. Exhibits focus on the building of the lighthouse, water transportation on the lower Umpqua River, the Life-Saving Service, and the "Gray Whale's Odyssey."

Transportation on the lower Umpqua is well illustrated with photographs of early sternwheelers that operated on the river. One of these was the *Eva of Gardiner*, known simply as the sternwheeler *Eva*. The *Eva* was a paddle-wheel steamer with its wheel on the stern. The *Eva* operated on the lower Umpqua from Scottsburg to Gardiner and Winchester Bay between 1894 and 1916. The coming of the railroad from Eugene put her out of business. One can see the *Eva*'s large, mint-condition bow-light on display along with the steamer's nameplate. Photographs show the *Eva* loading and unloading passengers on the south beach of the Umpqua River at Winchester Bay. Passengers continued south to Coos Bay on a stage drawn by a paired four-horse team. The sternwheelers *Eva* and *Restless* carried upwards of sixty people along with freight.

Sawmilling history of the lower Umpqua is depicted in photographs of an historic Gardiner sawmill. There also are many interesting photographs of sailing schooners and other kinds of ships entering the Umpqua River, which always had the potential for a dangerous bar crossing.

White Settlement on the Lower Umpqua River

From the Umpqua River Station it is only a short drive to the Umpqua River bar at Winchester Bay. At the entrance to the Salmon Harbor marina, one can look out across to the Umpqua River's north spit. This is a good place to reflect on the experience of a young sea captain who played a role in the early White settlement of the Umpqua River and who kept a journal in which he described the Umpqua River landscape and its people.

On August 2, 1850, Captain Albert Lyman, age twenty-four, arrived off the mouth of the Umpqua River in the schooner *Samuel Roberts*. He wrote in his journal: "The coast here is of high sandy hills with fir trees on the summits. A line of breakers showed where the bar of the river was situated." After lying offshore two days awaiting favorable winds, Captain Lyman piloted his ship across the Umpqua River bar.

Captain Lyman had left San Francisco on July 8 with a group of thirty-four men, all of whom, including Lyman, were shareholders in a company called the Klameth Exploring Expedition. Their purpose was to explore and establish settlements on the Rogue River (referred to as the Klameth River on early maps). When their exploration of the country near the mouth of the Rogue River proved disappointing, they sailed north to the Umpqua River. At the same time, three men were exploring down the Umpqua River to its mouth. By coincidence they met the *Samuel Roberts* and the exploring expedition. One of these men was Levi Scott who had established a land claim at what soon would become Scottsburg.

Lower Umpqua Indians approached the *Samuel Roberts* in canoes. Captain Lyman observed that "they appeard very different from the indians of the Klameth [Rogue River] having seen much more of the whites. They were most of them provided with shirts, coats & pants & were much more respectful in their demeanor." Captain Lyman also commented that their canoes were "very gracefully shaped and are made from a log of wood though very light and handy."

After anchoring the schooner upstream near what was to become Scottsburg, Captain Lyman continued on by canoe to the Hudson's Bay Company's Fort Umpqua, which lay across the river and a little upstream from present-day Elkton. He described Fort Umpqua as follows: "There was formerly a great business carried on here in furs with the indians, but at present it does not amount to much. Mr. Gagnier is assisted by one white man and a few Kanakas [Hawaiians] and indians. He cultivates about 50 acres of land and raises wheat & corn, potatoes & most all kinds of garden vegetables. He has a few apple trees which bear well. Mr. Gagnier has an indian wife and one son."

Meanwhile, other members of the expedition had been exploring the Umpqua River too. By August 27, when the *Samuel Roberts* weighed anchor to return to San Francisco, four townsites had been laid out. Captain Lyman wrote that one had been located "at the mouth of the river called Umpqua, one at the head of navigation called Scottsburg, one near the fort called Elkton, and one at the forks of the river 30 miles from the fort called Winchester."

After returning to San Francisco, Captain Lyman had a difficult time rechartering his schooner. In early November he sold it. But his thoughts kept returning to Oregon. Lyman was talented at sketching, and his journal for October 1850 contains several sketches of the Umpqua River Indians. In late November, he returned to Oregon, but this time as a ship's passenger rather than as a captain. He spent three weeks at sea amusing himself by reading the tragedies of "Shakespier." The weather was appropriately stormy. "My pen would fail in the attempt to discribe the magnificence of the scene as we crossed the bar," he wrote. "But few times in a sailors life time do they ever witness as grand a sight. The heavy sea broke entirely across the bar. On each side for a long distance was there one sea of rageing foam breaking & rolling in with terrific grandure."

Lyman stayed briefly in Scottsburg, but soon established a land claim near Elkton. By spring he had planted "some cabage, watermelon, squash, turnip & beans & pease." Come September, however, homesickness had overcome him. "Have made up my mind to go home to my parents and brothers who have long been wishing to embrace me once more," he wrote in his journal. "Yes, I will surrender all my hopes in Oregon and fly to those who are dear to me and who are acheing to see me."

Lyman sold his claim, and by December 18, 1851, had crossed over the Umpqua bar for the last time on his way to San Francisco and his home in Connecticut. Before he left, Lyman described the fledgling settlements along the lower Umpqua River. He noted that "at the mouth where Umpqua City is located Doct Paine has a zink house & severall others are erected & being built in that neighborhood." Some people had taken claims upriver. "One company," he wrote, "has taken a claim a few miles above Umpqua City which they call New Providence. The crew of the Bark Bostonian which was lost here have taken an island near New Providence where they have a zink house." Several log cabins, frame houses, and zink buildings had been erected at Scottsburg. He estimated that there were about twenty claims between Scottsburg and Elkton.

Although his stay on the South Coast was brief, Albert Lyman's journal and sketches are among the best sources we have on Indian life and early White settlement on the Umpqua River.

Fort Umpqua: North Spit of the Umpqua River

Location: The Fort Umpqua site is unmarked and inaccessible by road. For information on how to reach the north spit of the Umpqua River by foot or ORV, ask at the Oregon Dunes National Recreation Area headquarters in Reedsport on US 101 at milepost 211.5.

The north spit of the Umpqua River once was the location of a military fort. The site of old Fort Umpqua shows on maps as Army Hill. A large sand dune rises above the shore of the spit where the Umpqua River turns north. A correspondent for *Frank Leslie's Illustrated Magazine* described Fort Umpqua in 1858: "It occupies a sandy situation [two miles and a half from the river mouth], and is well protected from all of the coast winds by a thick growth of pines and encircling timbered sand hills." The fort was built in the fall of 1856 beside what was left of the small settlement of Umpqua City that sprang up in the fall of 1850. This fledging town soon was outflanked by the upriver settlement of Scottsburg. After 1856, Umpqua City consisted of only a small hotel and store.

In 1856, the old Umpqua City site seemed an ideal place for a southern boundary outpost to prevent Indians from leaving the Siletz Indian Reservation to the north and returning to their homes south of the Umpqua River. The Siletz Reservation had just been established for Indians who had survived the Rogue River War of 1855–1856. The Coos, Lower Umpqua, and Siuslaw Indians, however, were kept on a reserve in the vicinity of Fort Umpqua itself.

About 700 Indians lived in the vicinity of Fort Umpqua for nearly three years under the watchful eye of U.S. Army regulars. In 1859, the surviving members of the Coos, Lower Umpqua, and Siuslaw Indians—about 460 in number by that time—were forced to march up the coast to a new reservation site at Yachats. Fort Umpqua, however, continued to operate with a small number of soldiers until it was closed in 1862.

The fort consisted of about forty acres on which soldiers had built a hospital, laundry, bakery, blockhouse, buildings for officers and enlisted men, warehouses, and miscellaneous outbuildings. At its peak of occupation,

Fort Umpqua on the north spit of the Umpqua River.
Reprinted from *Frank Leslie's Illustrated Magazine* (Apr. 24, 1858).

Lower Umpqua Indian plank house.
Reprinted from *Frank Leslie's Illustrated Magazine* (Apr. 24, 1858).

the fort held 167 soldiers. Major John B. Scott lived there with his wife and daughter; and the post surgeon, Edward P. Vollum, also lived there with his wife. The fort was built near the water's edge, and its activity would have been visible from the south shore of the Umpqua River.

For the officers, women, and soldiers who lived there, Fort Umpqua was a rainy, boring, squalid little outpost. The Indians forced to live nearby suffered from food shortages, White diseases, prostitution, and alcoholism. Nearly a third of them died in the three-year period they were at Fort Umpqua.

The correspondent for *Frank Leslie's Illustrated Magazine* who visited the Indian settlement near Fort Umpqua in 1858 described how the Indians were living. He observed that they still lived in cedar plank lodges in winter, but used the White people's canvas tents in the summer. Inside their homes, the Indians used traditional woven mats and skins for beds, but many also had tables and chairs, as well as non-Indian dishware. Under White influence they were giving up the ornamentation of children's noses with "bead and pearl appendages." Head flattening was less common than before. White clothing had replaced traditional fiber skirts and capes, and nudity.

Traditional burial practices, however, still were in use. The correspondent wrote that "the dead are buried in a rough box, a few feet below the surface, with all of the clothing and trappings on. An inverted canoe sometimes covers the grave, and over the whole a gable-shaped hut is built of part of the lodge of the deceased. . . ." The correspondent found the three days and nights of mourning that accompanied a burial with their "monotonous and dismal howling" to be most "piteous," adding to his awareness of the "melancholy tale of extinction of the red man" which the Fort Umpqua Indian settlement presented.

In the spring of 1864, Corporal Royal A. Bensell, Company D, Fourth California Infantry, assigned to the Alsea Indian Reservation subagency at Yachats, was ordered south with ten other men, soldiers and packers, to hunt for Indians who had fled the reservation. On his way south, Bensell passed by the site of Umpqua City, or what was left of it. "Stopt at Umpqua City consisting of a small grocery and a large untenanted Hotel," Bensell wrote in his journal. "Here originaly stood Fort Umpqua. . . . The remains of the garrison can be seen ready for shipment to Scotsberg. . . . The Officers Quarters were expensive buildings. Some neat conservatories still stand, monuments of useless extravagance."

The "expedition," as Bensell called it, continued on to Coos Bay. For nearly a week (April 29–May 4), he and the other soldiers hunted for Indians around the bay and up Coos River. They rounded up forty-six Indians in all—men, women, and children—and took them back up the coast to Yachats. They met resistance on Coos Bay from local White people. Bensell wrote: "The lumbermen up these bayous and Sloughs are the roughest of men. Nearly all are married to Squaws or else have a written obligation that [they] will marry rather than allow the Ind Agt to deprive them of their concubines. They conceal the Indians, warn them, and otherwise enhance the difficulties of catching the red devils." Bensell estimated that there were some sixty Indians living on the Coos and Coquille rivers prior to the roundup. Despite his dutiful soldiering, however, Bensell seemed to realize that hunting down Indians was a dirty business. He wrote: ". . . this rowing after Siwash is no part of a soldiers duty."

Although nothing remains today of the Fort Umpqua site on the north spit of the Umpqua River, it is a spot on the map of the South Coast that serves as a grim reminder of the destructive effect that White settlement had on the region's native inhabitants.

Oregon Dunes National Recreation Area: Coos Bay to Florence

Location: Oregon Dunes National Recreation Area headquarters is located at the north end of Reedsport (milepost 211.5) on US 101; the dunes stretch from Coos Bay to Florence.

The unique geological feature of the South Coast is its long strip of coastal dunes, stretching from Coos Bay to the Siuslaw River. The Oregon Dunes National Recreation Area (NRA) was created by the U.S. Congress in 1972 as an administrative unit inclusive of the coastal dunes and adjacent lands. The Oregon Dunes NRA contains 32,150 acres and just over thirty-eight miles of ocean beach line. Some of the dunes reach heights of 300 feet and extend for nearly a mile in length. The headquarters for the Oregon Dunes National Recreation Area is located in Reedsport at the north end of town on Highway 101. While public interest in the Oregon Dunes focuses on its geology and ecology, it has played an important role in the history of the South Coast.

The Oregon Dunes NRA consists of federal, state, and private land holdings. The largest portion of the dunes and adjacent lands lie within the Siuslaw National Forest, which was set aside by President Theodore Roosevelt in 1907. In 1958, Oregon U.S. Senator Richard Neuberger proposed establishing an Oregon Dunes National Seashore to be administered by the National Park Service. After a decade of debate, Oregon U.S. Representative John Dellenback proposed the establishment of a national recreation area under the administrative control of the U.S. Forest Service. The major difference between the two proposals was that Rep. Dellenbeck's proposal allowed private ownership of land to continue within the recreation area.

Although the Oregon Dunes is a geological wonder, it also provides a unique habitat for plants and animals. It is inhabited by ten species of wildlife that are endangered or candidates for such status, including the bald eagle, osprey, snowy plover, common egret, and white footed vole.

The historic importance of the Oregon Dunes derives from its geographical location and features. Three major coastal rivers flow out of the Coast Range through the dunes to the sea: the Coos, Umpqua, and Siuslaw. Several smaller creeks also have carved paths through the sand: Tenmile Creek, Tahkenitch Creek, and Siltcoos River. The major rivers, especially, were locations of early Indian and later White settlements. The Umpqua and Siuslaw rivers served as transportation routes from inland to the sea.

Most of the major historic sites in the Oregon Dunes area have been described elsewhere in this book: Camp Castaway, Umpqua Lighthouse, Fort Umpqua, Umpqua City, and Umpqua Indian Reservation (1856–1859). But the major historic use of the dunes has been as a route of transportation. For the most part, coastal Indians stayed within narrowly defined territories along coastal rivers. But when they wanted to trade or war with one another, coastal beaches provided easier routes of travel than forest trails. Most transportation was by river or beach. White settlers in the early years adopted Indian transportation routes and modes of transportation. The only ready-made roads for horses or horse-drawn wagons and stages were the beaches, and even early roads didn't replace them.

The first settlers on Coos Bay brought their families down the Umpqua River by boat and then followed the beach to a point south of Horsfall Beach where they first crossed the dunes of Coos Bay's north spit and then crossed the bay by canoe to Empire City. This route continued to be followed right up to 1916. In that year, a railroad line from the Willamette Valley, that followed the Siuslaw River to Florence and then headed south along the eastern edge of the Oregon Dunes, reached Coos Bay. The first settlers at Florence came down the Siuslaw River. A stage line soon ran between the Siuslaw and Umpqua rivers. The Umpqua River, the largest of the South Coast rivers and the easiest to navigate, became the major route between the coast and inland valleys.

One of the first operators of a stage line along the shoreline of the Oregon dunes was Henry "Hank" Hudson Barrett. Born of English-Scotch parents in Rochester, New York in 1826, he came to California in 1849, worked in the gold fields for a while, and then came north to Coos Bay in the 1850s. He started a stage line between Coos Bay and the Umpqua River, and then he added a line from the Umpqua River to Florence. Barrett's Landing was a place name on the south beach of both the Umpqua (at Winchester Bay) and Siuslaw rivers. Barrett's was not the only stage line. Jarvis, Cornwall, & Company were operating a stage from Coos Bay to the Umpqua River in 1886. When Barrett died in 1905, his sons continued the stage line until the railroad finally brought the stage transportation era on the South Coast to a close.

Barrett's stage was little more than an open wagon with a canopy over it. It had wide tires to track through the sand. One or two pairs of horses pulled the wagon. The travel schedule was irregular because of the necessity of crossing coastal streams at low tide. But one could leave Florence, Gardiner, or Coos Bay one day and come back the next. A stage ride along the beach sounds like fun, but it meant more hardship than fun for early travelers. Oregon historian Frances Fuller Victor wrote sourly of a ride from Gardiner to Coos Bay: "The beach road is wearisome, with the perpetual roll of the

Horse-drawn stage waiting to meet the steamer *Eva* at Winchester Bay.
Courtesy of Coos Historical & Maritime Museum.

broad tires over unelastic wet sand, and the constant view of a restless waste of water on one hand, with dry, drifting sand between us and the mountains on the other, varied only with patches of marsh and groups of scraggy pines at intervals."

The arrival of the automobile on the South Coast offered a rival means of conveying passengers south and north along the beach from the Umpqua River. Vern Gorst and Charles King started the first auto stage line on the South Coast. They began in the auto stage business by operating a line between Jacksonville and Medford in the Rogue River Valley. Then in 1912 they moved their business to Coos Bay, where they began by shuttling passengers between North Bend and Marshfield (Coos Bay) for twenty-five cents a ride, challenging local boat taxis.

In 1914, Vern Gorst, an inveterate inventor and pioneer in aviation, took a Curtiss airplane engine and a propeller, mounted them on a Hupmobile chassis, added pontoons, and created probably the first amphibious auto. Gorst called it "The Fast Freight to Florence." Inspired by his own creation and the idea of operating a beach auto stage line, Gorst and King purchased six Model-T Fords and began carrying passengers from Coos Bay to the steamer landing at Winchester Bay. Gorst, later in the 1920s, organized the Pacific Air Transport Company that carried federal mail from Los Angeles to Seattle. By 1927, Gorst's new airline was carrying passengers as well as mail, quite a flight of the imagination beyond Gorst's earlier beach-stage business.

The beach auto stage line was a novel but short-lived experiment. The shoreline of the Oregon Dunes presented unique problems for early autos. In places where the sand was particularly soupy, a raised road surface made of planks mounted on wood supports was built. If the auto stage slipped off the planks, passengers had to help lift it back on. On several occasions, freak waves washed over the autos, and on one such occasion, the auto had to be winched out of the sand. Tenmile Creek presented a particular challenge. A horse-drawn wagon was used to pull auto stages across its two- or three-foot depth. But it was the coming of the railroad in 1916 that killed the beach auto stage as surely as the sternwheeler *Eva*'s business.

Although the Oregon Dunes National Recreation Area was established in recent time, human interference with natural dune-making processes since 1900 has radically changed the Oregon Dunes. About 1910, non-native European beachgrass was planted near rivers and roadways to stabilize the dunes. This has resulted in dramatically increased growth of vegetation. Aerial photographs taken in 1939 showed that vegetation covered about 20% of the dunes, but by the 1990s, vegetation had expanded its coverage of the dunes to about 80%.

In 1998, the Oregon Dunes NRA began a project to restore the natural processes of dune creation. An area adjacent to the Oregon Dunes Overlook, midway between Reedsport and Florence, was selected for vegetation removal by mechanical and manual means, prescribed burning, and follow-up herbicide application. One of the major objectives of this project and its extension to other parts of the dunes will be to improve wintering and nesting habitat for the snowy plover, which has been listed as threatened by both the State of Oregon and the U.S. Fish and Wildlife Service. The snowy plover needs open, sandy beaches for nesting and rearing its young. The encroachment of vegetation makes it easier for predators to get close to nesting sites and to eat snowy plover eggs. In 1997, it was estimated that there were 141 adult snowy plovers on the Oregon Coast as a whole, and 19 within the Oregon Dunes NRA (with the same number of nesting sites). Removal of dunes vegetation and restriction of human entry into snowy plover nesting areas will contribute to snowy plover population recovery.

Historic uses of the Oregon dunes in this century have threatened the continued existence of the dunes and beaches for human beings and wildlife. In one human generation, the dunes seem to have lost their capacity for self-renewal.

Umpqua Discovery Center: Reedsport

Directions: At the north end of Reedsport (Oregon Dunes National Recreation Area headquarters at milepost 211.5), turn right/east off US 101 at the Drain/Eugene/East 38 sign. Continue 0.4 miles to 3rd Street and turn left; follow Discovery Center signs to the waterfront. Entering Reedsport from the east on Hwy 38, turn right at 3rd Street. Admission fee.

The Umpqua Discovery Center, located on the historic waterfront area of Reedsport, highlights the natural and human history of the lower Umpqua River. Housed in a modern museum building with an extensive ground-level waterfront boardwalk and an upper observation-level quarterdeck, the Center provides a dramatic scenic overlook of an historic river area.

The Southern Pacific Railroad Bridge that figured prominently in Reedsport's development rises above the river a hundred yards or so to the west of the Discovery Center. It opens and closes to allow fishing boats or trains to pass through. There was no town of Reedsport until the Pacific Great Western Railway Company began to build a line through western Douglas County in 1912 (the same year Reedsport was named as a post office site). By then, the company had been purchased by the Southern Pacific Railroad. In 1916, the railroad line from Eugene to Coos Bay had been completed, and Reedsport, as a hub of South Coast rail construction, had become a growing new town.

The town was named for Alfred W. Reed of Gardiner, whose son, Warren P. Reed, was heir to thousands of acres of property on which Reedsport took shape. Warren P. Reed developed the town, much as Louis J. Simpson developed North Bend a decade earlier. Photographs of the new town's waterfront from the railroad bridge east to Rainbow Slough show an extensive dock and wharf area with fish canneries, riverboats, and marine supply and navigation company businesses. In the 1920s, the town expanded

Reedsport in 1938 looking north toward the historic waterfront, railroad bridge, and Umpqua River-Smith River junction. Courtesy of Coos Historical & Maritime Museum.

farther south of the river into the present-day east Reedsport business and residential district.

Exhibits in the Discovery Center offer glimpses of these and other aspects of lower Umpqua River history in visitor-operated slide programs on early Indian people, maritime history, and river towns. Photographs of the Umpqua River floods of 1927 and 1964 provide insight into the natural hazards of Reedsport's riverside location. But many Center exhibits focus on the natural history of the Umpqua River. These exhibits provide a good introduction to birds, marine animals, and Roosevelt elk that can be seen three miles east of Reedsport on Hwy 38 at the Dean Creek Elk Viewing Area. Roosevelt elk and other wildlife were important to local Kalawatset Indians. They used elk antler bones for such utensils as wedges, scrapers, digging tools, and spoons; they used elk hides to make items of clothing; and they used elk meat for food. The Discovery Center draws attention to these and other wildlife resources used by Native Americans and early White settlers.

On my first visit to the Discovery Center I was fortunate to be able to watch artist Peggy O'Neal beginning work on the murals for the award winning exhibits "Tidewaters and Time," "Paradise of the Past," and "Early Explorers." These life-like murals present vivid images of the early history of the Lower Umpqua River. A reconstructed plank house shows how early Native Americans lived. The natural and human sounds that accompany these and other exhibits help one to relive the past. They contribute to the Discovery Center's successful integration of natural and human history.

Jedediah Smith Campsites
18 to 20
Winchester Bay to Smith River

About a quarter mile north of the Oregon Dunes National Recreation Area headquarters on US 101 is Bolon Island. To get to Bolon Island, cross the Umpqua River Bridge, one of the five major coastal bridges completed under Conde B. McCullough's engineering direction in 1936. (See "Rogue River Bridge: Gold Beach" and "McCullough-Bridge: Coos Bay" for more information.)

This is the least significant of the four major South Coast bridges. But for the bridge enthusiasts, it too offers several distinctive features. Like McCullough's other bridges, it incorporates the decorative motifs of the Art Deco or Modernistic style, which can be seen in its twin towers with their recessed vertical lines. It also presents the traveler with Gothic arch openings. Together with the Siuslaw Bridge, it is unique because of its moveable swing drawspan openings that permit through boat traffic.

From Bolon Island, one can look northeast to the junction of Smith River and Umpqua River. At a campsite located across from Bolon Island, the Jedediah Smith expedition made some fatal errors.

On July 10, 1828 at Empire, Jedediah Smith and his men swam their horses across Coos Bay to the north spit, where they camped that night before continuing up the beach to the mouth of the Umpqua River the next day. There, late on July 11, the expedition came upon an Indian village of seventy to eighty people on the south bank of the river at Winchester Bay. Despite the reputation for hostility to Whites that the Umpqua Indians had gained with the Hudson's Bay Company, the expedition at first found them to be friendly.

The Jedediah Smith expedition proceeding north along the beach from Coos Bay to the Umpqua River in 1828. Drawing by Kevin Kadar.

The next day, July 12, the men of the expedition crossed the Umpqua River, coming ashore near the site of Umpqua City. They proceeded north around the bay and camped in the vicinity of Gardiner. Some of the Indians they met the day before accompanied them, and one of them, according to Harrison Rogers, "stole an ax and we were obliged to seize him for the purpose of tying him before we could scare him to make him give it up." Captain Smith, Rogers continued, "put a cord round his neck, and the rest of us stood with guns ready in case they made any resistance, there was about 50 Inds. present but did not pretend to resist tying the other." This was the worst moment on the expedition's coastal march. The action resulted in recovery of the axe, and the rest of the day passed peacefully enough in trade for "land and sea otter and beaver fur." Rogers even noted that the Indians brought them berries.

On July 13, the expedition left camp near present-day Gardiner and continued on around the east side of the bay about four miles until it reached the mouth of the Smith River, where camp was made that evening. In what was to be the last entry in his journal, Harrison Rogers wrote: "50 or 60 Inds. in camp again to-day (we traded 15 or 20 beaver skins from them, some elk meat and tallow, also some lamprey eels). The traveling quite mirery in places; we got a number of our pack horses mired, and had to bridge several places. A considerable thunder shower this morning, and rain at intervals through the day. Those Inds. tell us after we get to the river 15 or 20 miles we will have good travelling to the Wel Hammett or Multinomah, where the Callipoo Inds. live."

Jedediah Smith commemorative roadside marker. Author photo.

The morning of July 14, Smith left camp with two other men to look for a route east to the Willamette Valley. He warned Harrison Rogers not to let the Kalawatset Indians, with whom they had been trading, into camp. Rogers, however, apparently disregarded Smith's warning. Unknown to the men of the expedition, the Kalawatsets had been on the verge of attacking them since the previous day (July 12) when one of their tribesmen had been seized and bound for having stolen an axe. Then, as the Kalawatsets later told the story, two incidents provoked them to attack and kill all but one of the men Smith had left behind. A chief who had earlier opposed attacking Smith's party was insulted by being forced to dismount from one of the expedition's horses. The Kalawatsets also alleged that Harrison Rogers had tried to force an Indian woman into his tent. When the Indian woman's brother resisted, they said that Rogers knocked him down.

At some time later in the morning, when the men of the expedition were cleaning their rifles, the Kalawatsets jumped upon them with knives and axes. One man, Arthur Black, fled into the woods and eventually made his way up the coast until some Tillamook Indians guided him to Fort Vancouver. Several others apparently ran away from the camp, because only eleven skeletons were found by Hudson's Bay Company's Alexander McLeod three months later; but they were never heard from again.

Jedediah Smith and the two men with him had gone upriver. After turning back downstream toward camp, they were fired on by Kalawatsets from the riverbank. Smith escaped their fire and reached the opposite bank of the river. He climbed a hill from which he could see the camp, but it looked deserted. Having decided that nothing could be done for the rest of his men, Smith and his remaining two men headed north. As had Arthur Black, they eventually reached the Tillamook Indians, who showed them the way to Fort Vancouver, where they arrived on August 10, two days later than Black and nearly a month after the Umpqua massacre.

The location of the Smith expedition massacre is not clearly indicated in Harrison Rogers' last notes. But Indians informed a surveyor, Harvey Gordon, under contract with the United States government in 1857–1858, that the campsite and location of the massacre was at a spot on the north bank of the Smith River channel opposite the west tip of Perkins Island. Alice B. Maloney believed from her investigations that the campsite was on one of the islands at the mouth of the Smith River.

Years after the massacre occurred and White settlers arrived in the area, stories appear to have located the site on the south bank of the Umpqua River at the beach. Some years ago, an older resident of Gardiner whose father was proprietor of the town's hotel in 1889 recalled hearing such tales. He wrote: "From time to time old pioneers came to the bar-room to play cards and talk about the happenings in the lower Umpqua region. The three important topics of conversation were the Jedediah Smith massacre, the first cargo boat wrecked at the mouth of the Umpqua, and the flood at Scottsburg in 1861. In conversations about the Smith affair, it was always mentioned as having taken place at the mouth of the Umpqua."

Whatever the value of these pioneer stories in other respects, Harrison Rogers' diary leaves no doubt that the Smith expedition crossed the Umpqua River and made its way along the north shore to the vicinity of the fork of the Smith and Umpqua Rivers. Harvey Gordon's report seems to establish the most likely location of the massacre site on the north bank of the Umpqua River at its junction with the Smith River.

Scottsburg and Gardiner

Travelers going north on Highway 101 pass through the town of Gardiner as they leave the Umpqua River. Those going east on Highway 38 to the Willamette Valley drive through Scottsburg. Both towns deserve mention as historic landmarks.

Location: Scottsburg is 17 miles east of Reedsport on Hwy 38; Gardiner is at milepost 209.4 on US 101.

The gold rush in southern Oregon that led to exploration for gold along the South Coast from the Chetco River north to Whiskey Run stimulated interest in the Umpqua River as a transportation route inland. Levi Scott staked a claim to land at the head of tidewater in 1850 that became the town of Scottsburg.

In its first year, the town acquired some fifteen businesses devoted to trade in goods brought upriver by boat for transfer inland. The original town had a lower waterfront street that washed away. What remains today offers little evidence of the once-flourishing town of several hundred people and streets filled with the sounds and smells of horse and mule pack trains loading supplies for the mines on either side of the Siskiyous. It is reported that some pack trains numbered as many as 500 animals.

The most visible sign of community existence today is the cozy little postage-stamp-size post office that sits snuggly beside Highway 38. The establishment of the Scottsburg post office dates back to October 8, 1851. Several older buildings are reminders of an earlier day. One of these, the

Drain stage meeting stern-wheeler *Eva* at Scottsburg.
Courtesy of Coos Historical & Maritime Museum.

remains of the last Hedden's Store, the first having been established by Cyrus Hedden in 1851, brings back fond memories to older natives of the Umpqua Valley. Harold Minter in his book on the Umpqua Valley recalled that an earlier Hedden's Store was a place of rich smells—"cigar smoke, contending with the hearth of the 'Bonanza' heating stove, which provided tobacco chewers with a target. . . . Shelves of current brands of pepper, cinnamon, cloves, sage, allspice. . . . [together with] wooden syrup buckets, vinegar barrels, kerosene containers, binding twine, new harness, and coal tar. . . ."

For years, Scottsburg was a major jumping-off place for people going on to the South Coast. Travelers came by stage or horseback from Drain to Elkton to Scottsburg and then caught a riverboat or steamer to Winchester Bay. There they transferred to a beach stage that took them south as far as Coos Bay. Scenic Highway 38 between Reedsport and Scottsburg wasn't completed and opened for travelers until 1923. The forbidding, moss-draped rock bluffs finally had to make room for the automobile.

While Scottsburg was the point of entry to the South Coast from inland Oregon, Gardiner was the point of departure for those leaving the South Coast by way of the Umpqua River. The town was started in 1850 when the schooner *Bostonian* wrecked on the Umpqua River bar and the ship's trade goods were salvaged and removed to the site that became the town. The new settlement acquired a customs office the following year.

Gardiner grew over the next several decades into a small mill, shipbuilding, and salmon cannery town. By the 1880s, it had several hundred people. One local historian of the town has called the period 1880–1916, the "Golden Age of Gardiner." "All the houses were painted white," he wrote, "and the Gardiner people were all tremendously proud of the appearance of their new town . . . ."

Gardiner was the major town at the mouth of the Umpqua River until Reedsport, which became a post office site in 1912, began to develop as a

Gardiner mill, docks, and town, c. 1900. Courtesy of Douglas County Museum.

result of the construction of a Southern Pacific Railroad line south to Coos Bay. International Paper Company opened a pulp plant at Gardiner in the early 1960s. In the plain-lined but solidly built architecture of Gardiner's older homes and church and their neatly painted white exteriors, we see evidence of the town's New England roots.

Gardiner now is a National Historic District with sixty-four historic structures. One of these is the Wilson Jewett House, built in 1908, that stands on the east side of US 101. Douglas County researcher Ella Mae Young has pointed out that Wilson Jewett gets credit for "creating the 'White City by the Sea' image of Gardiner by donating lumber and white paint to rebuild the city after fires in 1880, 1911, and 1915."

Jessie M. Honeyman Memorial State Park and the Civilian Conservation Corp (CCC)

This state park is named after Jessie Millar Honeyman (1852–1948), who was eighty-nine years old in 1941 when the park was dedicated in her name. She was president of the Oregon Roadside Council, a citizens group that supported roadside beautification and park development. State Park Historian W. A. Langille wrote that she was "a most unusual and loveable character, who brought from the highlands of Scotland a love and keen appreciation of the beauty of nature."

Location: At milepost 193.4, about three miles south of Florence on US 101.

The development of the coastal highway opened up the area adjacent to Lake Cleawox and Woahink Lake. In what is surely one of the most beautiful settings on the Oregon Coast, young unemployed men were employed in one of the first programs created under President Franklin Roosevelt's New Deal launched in 1933 in response to the Great Depression. These workers in the Civilian Conservation Corps (CCC) began in 1935 to construct the park facilities. CCC workers built structures at Honeyman that now are on the National Register of Historic Places: the stone-and-log Cleawox Lake bathhouse (1938), now a concession building; the caretaker's house and garage (1936–37), now the park office; and several rustic shelters (1937).

The first CCC camps in Oregon were set up in 1933 near Gold Beach in Curry County and Benson Park in Multnomah County. Unemployed single and married men ages eighteen to twenty-five years were organized into camps of about 200 men each, including supervisors and staff. In the state park camps, the National Park Service provided technical support and shared supervision of the men with the U.S. Army. By 1935, there were CCC camps on the South Coast at Humbug Mountain, Cape Sebastian, and Coos Head (Charleston). A 1935 summary of projects included: firebreaks; reduction of fire hazards; roadside and trailside clearing; building of truck and foot trails; campground clearing and construction of latrines, tables, and stoves; laying of water pipelines; and reforestation.

Swimming area at Cleawox Lake in Honeyman State Park with CCC-built bathhouse (now Honeyman Park Lodge) in the background, c. 1940s. Courtesy of Oregon State Archives.

CCC workers at Honeyman did all of these things. The bathhouse and caretaker's house involved stone construction, which is a distinctive feature of so many CCC projects in Oregon. The shelter kitchens were of rustic, native materials, local stone and cedar. At Honeyman, CCC workers also built 266 feet of stone walls, cleared seventy-two snags and sinker logs from the lakes, and moved or planted 39,896 trees and shrubs, which contribute so much to the beauty of Honeyman to this day.

Honeyman State Park is the best example on the South Coast of the work accomplished during the Great Depression by the CCC camps. The work went on from November 1935 to June 1940. It was a small part of an enormous national CCC contribution to the nation's "infrastructure." From 1933 to 1937, CCC workers across the country built: 3,247 bridges, 960 cabins, 13,959 shelters and towers, 538 sewage systems, 5,392 miles of foot and horse trails; and they planted more than 300 million trees in reforestation projects.

Other CCC camps were operated on the South Coast under the direction of the U.S. Forest Service and Oregon Department of Forestry. CCC work on Oregon's first state forest, the Elliott State Forest, has been described in Jerry Phillips' book, *Caulked Boots and Cheese Sandwiches* (1996), a well-researched, anecdotal "Forester's History." Camp Walker (1933–1937) was established on upper Scholfield Creek east of Reedsport. The "CCC boys" of

Camp Walker built roads and trails, ran survey lines, strung telephone wire, constructed lookouts, and worked on many other projects. It was reported in 1934 that Camp Walker had 180 men, "all from Oregon and all literate," in CCC Company #981. According to Phillips, upwards of 1,000 CCC men worked in the Elliott State Forest from 1933 to 1941. A number of "side camps, spike camps, or stub camps" were set up away from Camp Walker for individual projects. Camp Reedsport (1933–1941), located on the present high school site, became the main CCC camp for work from Reedsport to Coos Bay after Camp Walker closed in 1937. In that year, CCC men built an airport or landing field at Lakeside.

Other New Deal programs also were employers of last resort in the 1930s. The Civil Works Administration (CWA) employed upwards of 500 men in various county and municipal projects. Hundreds more were employed by the Works Progress Administration (WPA) in building coastal bridges. As late as 1938–1939, WPA and other federally funded public works projects employed upwards of 1,400 men and women in Coos County.

These various work programs helped to ease the devastating effect of the Great Depression on the South Coast economy. In the Coos Bay region, only half as many lumber mills were operating when the CCC and other federal programs began as were operating in 1929; only a third as many people were employed. Although job opportunities had improved greatly by the late 1930s, many people continued to be employed in government programs as late as 1939.

After retiring in 1950, Samuel H. Boardman reflected on his experience with the CCC camps during the 1930s:

> *Throughout the entire state I had at one time seven CCC camps working in the parks and at this peak period there were twenty-seven National Park inspectors touring the camps and the parks office. One became a bit "edgy" at times. I recall a two-year period when the blue prints were worn out through the various agencies discussing the proper stresses of a foot bridge crossing the Rogue River at Casey State Park [above Shady Cove]. In sheer desperation, to save the budget setup for the bridge, I traded the Casey Bridge for a privy at Honeyman Park.*

Siuslaw Pioneer Museum

The Siuslaw Pioneer Museum is located in the old Florence School building built in 1905. It offers a rich display of artifacts relating to late nineteenth and early twentieth century coastal history

The exhibits in the museum have been organized according to topic: logging, farming, ships and shipwrecks, and the like.

Location: Florence, east of US 101 in "Old Town" at the corner of 2nd and Maple S treets, behind the Chamber of Commerce and City Hall.

Each topic has its own exhibit area. There also is an Indian artifact room and a room dedicated to wartime photographs and memorabilia. The museum houses the Jensen Galley of Historical Photos, a collection of local history photographs.

The museum offers several excellent, short slide programs that introduce visitors to the history of the Siuslaw River and the town of Florence. There also is a slide program on shipwrecks.

Among the Indian artifacts are two large dugout canoes. Indian baskets illustrate the skills of local Indian women in earlier days. The museum has many Euro-American tools used in logging and farming as well as household furnishings. Hundreds of photographs illustrate all aspects of White settlement of the Siuslaw River area. The museum has a gift shop and a library for people interested in genealogical and historical research.

A visit to the museum provides a good background for a drive along the Siuslaw River to Mapleton or for a walk along the main street of "Old Town" Florence on the waterfront, a popular tourist stop. "Old Town" can be seen from the Siuslaw River Bridge upstream and on the north bank of the river.

Florence and Siuslaw River

The northernmost historic town on the South Coast is Florence. It lies at the north end of the Oregon Dunes National Recreation Area on the north bank of the Siuslaw River. One of five bridges designed by State Highway Engineer Conde McCullough and built in the 1930s joins Florence to the north end of the Oregon Dunes.

Location: At milepost 190 on US 101.

The Siuslaw River Bridge is the fourth major bridge on the South Coast designed by Conde B. McCullough, bridge engineer with the Oregon State Highway Department (1919–1946). This bridge, at 1,568 feet, is modest in scale but repeats the design motifs of other bridges McCullough designed. As in the Umpqua River Bridge, McCullough uses a bowstring-type concrete arch to hold up the bridge deck or roadway. Ornate pylons or obelisks stand at the entrances to the bridge. The bridge's decorative features are in the Art Deco or Modernistic style. (See "Downtown Coos Bay: Historic Buildings" for information on the Art Deco style.) This bridge, like the Umpqua River Bridge, is a drawbridge that opens for the passage of boats.

To the east of the bridge along the north bank of the Siuslaw River stand several blocks of "Old Town" Florence. In the early 1970s, its buildings were dilapidated and run-down. Fifteen years after a renewal began, *Eugene Register Guard* newspaper reporter Larry Bacon wrote: "$425,000 would probably have bought most of the property along the street. Nobody called it Old Town then. Bay Street was a collection of rundown empty buildings, a couple of bars, an old movie theatre, and a garage . . . ."

North entrance to the Siuslaw River Bridge with Art Deco pylons in foreground and bridge center. Courtesy of Rollie Pean.

When some youthful entrepreneurs bought the Kyle Building and turned it into a wallpaper-making business, things began to happen. Other people began to buy old buildings and restore or remodel them. "Old Town" was born and became what it is today, an example of historic restoration and recreation. Like Old Town Bandon, it illustrates the important role played by historic landscape in the new tourist economy of the South Coast.

The dominant historic building in Old Town is the building formerly owned by William Kyle. It was constructed in 1901 and operated as a general merchandise store by Kyle and his sons until 1941, when ownership of the building changed hands. Across the street from the Kyle building is an old train depot built in 1913 to be a warehouse. It was located in Mapleton and moved to Florence in 1976. On nearby Maple Street are several other buildings dating from around the turn of the century. One originally was the office of the Florence Telephone Company. The Johnson House dates from 1892. The Calison Building, built in 1904–05, used to be the Florence schoolhouse. A fire destroyed part of the upper story in 1910 and another fire in 1953 eliminated the upper story altogether. The schoolhouse once had a belfry rising above its second floor.

The first White people settled on the lower Siuslaw in the 1880s. The area once was part of a coastal Indian reservation until it was opened up for White settlement in 1876. In 1882, there were three houses in Florence. The town was incorporated in 1893, and by 1901 Florence had a population of about 300 people, a school, two hotels, and several merchandise stores.

South approach to the Siuslaw River Bridge with "Old Town" Florence on the right.
Courtesy of Rollie Pean.

Florence developed in the 1880s along with the growth of sawmills and salmon canneries on the Siuslaw River. The first cannery was built in 1877 near the mouth of the river, and the first sawmill was built the year after. O. W. Hurd built a cannery at Acme (Cushman) in 1882. William Kyle built another one in 1884 on Bay Street in Florence. He also opened a general merchandise store. Still another cannery went up in 1887. Chinese workers were brought from Astoria to work in the canneries. Hurd began operation of a steamboat between Florence and Mapleton in 1884. The first coastal steamer to cross the Siuslaw bar was the *Alexander Duncan*, which put into the estuary in 1877. The *Mary D. Hume* was the second recorded steamer to cross the bar, carrying out 900 cases of salmon in 1883.

The town of Florence acquired its name because of a shipwreck, according to a story told by early residents. The nameplate of the sailing ship *Florence* floated ashore. One day in the early 1880s, when a hotel built by Thomas Safly was designated to be a post office, the *Florence*'s nameplate was nailed over the door and Florence became the name of the town.

The town grew in the 1890s due in part to government financed jetty construction. There also was a rival town on the south bank called Glenada, where the Barrett stage line from Gardiner met the Siuslaw River. Whisman Brothers' stage line ran from Glenada to Eugene. Glenada consisted of a sawmill, hotel, church, and about a dozen houses. Railroad construction from Eugene to Coos Bay in the period 1912–1915 stimulated further growth of Florence and Glenada.

Heceta Head Lighthouse

The Heceta Head Lighthouse (205 feet above the ocean) perches on a precipitous headland (1,000 feet in height) that separates the South Coast of Oregon from the northern coastline.

Location: At milepost 178.3 on US 101, about 12 miles north of Florence.

The lighthouse was almost an afterthought. It was not built until 1894, long after the pioneer period of the South Coast had ended. But in 1889, the U.S. Light-House Board decided that it needed "a coast light . . . to divide the dark space between Cape Arago and Cape Foulweather."

Heceta Head is named for the Portuguese explorer-navigator Don Bruno de Hezeta, who, in service to Spain, explored the Northwest Coast in 1775. Hezeta's log recorded his sighting of the Columbia River entrance as well as this dramatically scenic headland.

The British-made light that first flashed from Heceta Head on March 30, 1894 was a technical wonder. James A. Gibbs in *Oregon's Seacoast Lighthouses* (1994) captured the poetry of its almost medieval construction: "The sparkling creation of glass and brass had to be assembled piece by piece and was composed of eight panels, each prism two inches thick, for a total of 640 prisms. The lens rode on brass chariot wheels. The carriage turned by clockwork as weights descended down through the trunk of the tower about 35 feet. Keepers had to rewind the weights with a crank handle at

Coast Highway visitors in the early 1950s viewing Heceta Head Lighthouse in the distance. Courtesy of Oregon State Archives.

intervals to keep the two-ton apparatus revolving." In the early days, the lamp burned coal oil.

The lighthouse was a remote eleven miles from Florence over primitive roads, until coastal highway construction began in the 1920s. The Cape Creek Bridge, a tunnel, and an improved road made the lighthouse accessible, when the Roosevelt Highway (now US 101) was completed in 1932. Electricity came to the lighthouse in 1934.

In 1963, Heceta Light became automated. In 2000 the Oregon State Parks took over ownership and responsibility for the lighthouse. The former keeper's quarters, known as Heceta House, is an interpretive center as well as a bed and breakfast. Despite the passing of the era of lighthouse keepers, Heceta Light continues to perform its function of protecting ships at sea.

Jedediah Smith's Route to Fort Vancouver

After the massacre of the Jedediah Smith expedition on July 14, 1828, Smith and three other men of the expedition who escaped made their way north to Fort Vancouver, arriving there on August 10. Arthur Black made his own way up the coast. His exact route is unknown. Smith and two of his men took a different route. According to a map believed to be based on an original map drawn by Jedediah Smith himself, the route from the massacre site took the three men a short distance east and then north across the Smith, Siuslaw, Alsea, and Yaquina rivers a considerable distance inland from the ocean. They probably reached the coast in the vicinity of the Siletz River. From there they were led by Tillamook Indians northeast to the Yamhill River and eventually to Fort Vancouver.

On reaching Fort Vancouver, Smith and his men made a full report to Dr. John McLoughlin, chief factor of the Hudson's Bay Company. McLoughlin ordered Alexander McLeod, who had explored the lower Umpqua River two years earlier and traveled as far south as the Rogue River, to try to recover the furs and horses taken by the Kalawatsets, or lower Umpqua Indians. McLeod's party, accompanied by Jedediah Smith, arrived at the mouth of the Umpqua River on October 28. McLeod wrote in his journal: "Fine Weather . . . Proceeded to the Sea . . . Stoped at the entrance of the North Branch, where Mr Smiths Party were destroyed, and a Sad Spectacle of Indian barbarity presented itself to our View, the Skeletons of eleven of those Miserable Sufferers lying bleaching in the Sun."

From Alexander McLeod's report to Governor Simpson, it would appear that the Kalawatsets felt multiple grievances before they finally attacked the party. One near-attack even seems to have been quieted down by cooler heads. The next day, when the Indian who was chiefly responsible for speaking out against the attack was humiliated by being forced to dismount from one of the expedition's horses, tempers flared again. Governor Simpson also noted in another letter that Alexander McLeod had been informed by the Kalawatsets that Harrison Rogers, "in Smith's absence, attempted to force a Woman into his Tent, whose Brother was knocked down by Rogers while endeavouring to protect her . . . ." Although this act seems inconsistent with what we know about Rogers from his journal, the truth will never be known.

Alexander McLeod was remarkably successful in recovering the Jedediah Smith expedition's furs and horses. The Kalawatsets had traded the stolen goods north and south along the coast. Altogether some 700–800 beaver and otter skins and about forty horses were recovered in addition to several rifles, cooking pots, traps, clothes, beads, and other items. The most important items recovered, however, were the journals of Jedediah Smith and Harrison Rogers.

Thus ended the Jedediah Smith expedition's exploration of Oregon's South Coast. It was a tragic end to a trailblazing expedition. But the knowledge gathered from this exploration survived and contributed to increasing American interest in the Oregon Country.

In the summer of 1829, Jedediah Smith rejoined his partners Jackson and Sublette. The following year, the three men sold their company, and Smith left the western mountains for a farm in Ohio. He immediately took steps to publish the story of his travels. He contracted with Samuel Parkman to help him in preparing his journals for publication. He also worked on a map of his travels. At the same time, he helped finance his two brothers, Peter and Austin, in a new business venture with his former partners Jackson and Sublette. They planned to transport trade goods to Santa Fe.

As the time neared for his brothers' trade caravan to head southwest in 1831, Smith decided to go along. Apparently, he couldn't resist participating in a new adventure. On May 27, while on his way to Santa Fe, he left the main party to search for water. Comanche Indians attacked and killed Smith near the Cimarron River.

Jedediah Smith was only a little over thirty-two years of age at the time of his death. He was only twenty-three when he first started in the fur trade. But in the ten years of his career as a fur trader and mountain man, he built a reputation as one of the great explorers of the American West.

Within several decades of his death in 1831, Jedediah Smith was largely forgotten. The discovery and publication of a portion of his journals by Maurice S. Sullivan in 1934 has led since that time to increased knowledge and appreciation of his contributions to exploration of the West. The publication of Dale L. Morgan's biography of Jedediah Smith in 1953 and another book about his mapping of the West by Morgan and Carl I. Wheat in 1954 (along with still another book by Wheat on mapping the Trans-Mississippi West) established his reputation as a major American explorer. The publication in 1977 by George R. Brooks of Jedediah Smith's narrative of his 1826 southwest expedition has further enhanced Smith's reputation, in particular as an ethnographer.

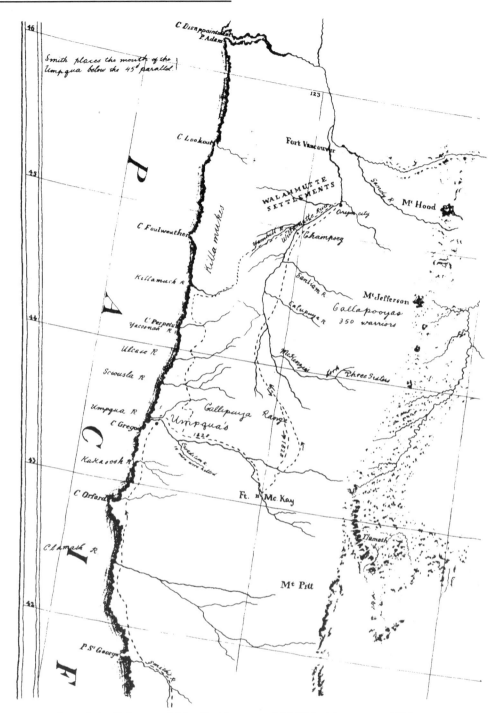

A portion of the Frémont-Gibbs-Smith map of 1845 in Morgan and Wheat, *Jedediah Smith and His Maps of the American West* (1954) showing the Jedediah Smith route along the Oregon Coast to the Umpqua River and then to Fort Vancouver. Tracing from facsimile reproduction by Kevin Kadar.

In 1836, the American Albert Gallatin published a map of North America showing the location of Indian tribes. It showed evidence of having been influenced by a map Jedediah Smith had been working on at the time of his death. In 1839, David H. Burr, Geographer to the House of Representatives, published a map that clearly was based on one by Jedediah Smith. Morgan and Wheat in describing the Burr map noted that "here are Smith's travels developed in considerable detail, with Smith's own legends and place names carefully laid down." This map shows Jedediah Smith's route through northern California and up the coast to the Umpqua River. Morgan and Wheat called the Burr map "an American cartographic milestone."

The pioneer ethnographer of the Oregon Country, George Gibbs, had access to a map with information from Smith's explorations soon after he reached Oregon in 1849. In his 1851 journal of travels in northern California, he referred to "the manuscript map of Oregon and California, by Jedediah S. Smith, which was, till lately, the best source of information as to this part of the country." It is on this basis that Jedediah Smith has come to be viewed as one of the preeminent explorers of the American West.

Appendix
Jedediah Smith's Relations with Indians

The tragic end of the Jedediah Smith expedition near the mouth of the Umpqua River raises questions about the expedition's relations with Indians. How did the expedition treat the Indians they met along the way? Who was to blame for the trouble they had? How can it be explained that of the estimated ninety-four men killed while in the employ of American fur companies in the period 1823–1829, twenty-nine of them died while under Smith's command?

In recent years, writers looking at the Jedediah Smith expedition from an Indian point of view have been highly critical. George B. Wasson, Jr., in "The Memory of A People: The Coquilles of the Southwest Coast" (in *The First Oregonians* (1991), has written that Coquille elders recalled how terrifying the expedition seemed to their people. They smashed their canoes to keep them from being used by the expedition "and hid among the trees to watch in awe as the white men tore up the Indians' plank houses to make a raft on which to cross the tidewater." Anthropologist Roberta L. Hall in *People of the Coquille Estuary* (1995) commented that the elders must have confused this event with what happened at the Rogue River. But nevertheless, she concluded, "the insensitivity with which Smith and his men treated native people was clear long before the party reached the Coquille [River]." Hall noted that Alexander McLeod on his trips to the South Coast treated the native people respectfully because he wanted to trade with them. By contrast, Smith and second-in-command Rogers "seemed unaware that they were visitors in a land occupied by people whose customs differed from their own."

Another writer, Beverly H. Ward, whose marriage to Eugene Edward Mecum in 1924 joined her life with that of a family of Coquille and Coos Indian background, has told an equally critical story of the Jedediah Smith expedition. Her book *White Moccasins* (1986) combined oral tradition with information from historical documents. She wrote:

> The [Jedediah Smith] brigade pushed up through the Indians' trails, and the horses and mules tramped over the Indians' fire pits while turning the villages into shambles. When the men reached the rivers, they tore down the Indians' houses and used the cedar planks to build rafts. When they made camp, some of the horses and mules strayed. They fell into the Indians' elk pits, and the Indians shot them with arrows.

> The Coquilles left their villages. They sent the women and children up river in canoes, and some hid in the brush.

Later, at the Umpqua River, Ward continued:

The Umpquas had traded with the Hudson's Bay men, and some had met [David] Douglas [British botanist] on his trip [with Alexander McLeod], but Smith's men were different. Most of the men had Indian women that they took along to use as guides, although they were left behind on this long trip. The women-hungry men tried to force their attentions on the Umpqua women when they came to trade. When some of their tools disappeared, they blamed the Indians. They poked fun at the chief when he tried to ride a horse, and one thing led to another. The white men had sealed their fate.

To put the question of the Jedediah Smith expedition's relations with the Indians of Oregon's South Coast in perspective, one should place them in the context of Smith's relations with Indians before he reached the South Coast. The narrative and journals of Jedediah Smith and Harrison Rogers present a picture of Smith trying to make and keep peace with the Indian tribes he met. On his first southwest expedition in 1826, he established peaceful relations with the Ute and Mojave Indian villages on his route and attempted to arrange a peace treaty between the Ute and Snake Indians. On the trail in northern California and Oregon, whenever the expedition met Indians or approached a village, efforts were made to show by means of sign language that the expedition meant no harm. Smith nearly always tried to give gifts of freshly killed meat or trinkets to the Indians who came to his encampments. The expedition also paid for food it received from Indians with trade goods.

On his first southwest expedition to California in 1826, Smith passed through Indian villages without more difficulty than the theft of a horse. He had more trouble in the spring of 1827 while looking for a pass over the Sierra Nevada. On the American River, he encountered the Maidu—hundreds of them, he wrote, "wilder than antelopes running and screaming in every direction." On two occasions he ordered several of his men to fire on Indians, killing two on one occasion and "more" on the other. With apparent feelings of guilt and self-justification, Smith wrote of the incident: "I endeavored to convince them of my disposition to be friendly by every means in my power but to no purpose."

On his second trip to California in the summer of 1827, Smith met disaster at the hands of the Mojave Indians. Their attack was entirely unexpected, since Smith's expedition had stayed with them the previous year without trouble. Smith wrote in explanation: "I have good reason to believe that the Amuchabas [Mojave Indians] were instructed to kill all Americans coming in that direction; but let that be as it may the fact that they [the Spanish in California] punished an indian for being friendly to me would readily convey the idea that they would reward them [Mojave Indians] if they were enemies." In fact, a bad experience with other White fur traders from the Southwest may have been equal motivation for the attack.

The Indians encountered in northern California the next spring were friendly. Some of these Indians, Smith commented, were among those who had been hostile the previous spring. Groups of fifty to sixty Indians usually showed up when the expedition made its camps. But as the expedition moved north, the Indians became more frightened. On March 1, 1827, Smith and some of his trappers came upon an Indian lodge. The Indians fled, but Smith and his men rode their horses after them. They stopped one Indian woman and quieted her with "some presents." But an Indian girl of ten or eleven fell while trying to escape. Smith dismounted to see if she was hurt and found her dead. The incident shocked him. In his diary he wrote:

> *Could it be possible thought I, that we who called ourselves Christians were such frightful objects as to scare poor savages to death. But I had little time for meditation for it was necessary that I should provide for the wants of my party and endeavor to extricate myself from the embarassing situation in which I was placed. I therefore to convince the friends of the poor girl of my regret for what had been done covered her Body with a Blanket and left some trifles near by and in commemoration of the singular wildness of those Indians and the novel occurrence that made it appear so forcibly I named the River on which it happened Wild River.*

The expedition moved north along the Sacramento or Buenaventura River, as it was called by the Spanish, to the Yuba and then to the Feather River. Smith found Indians to be "numerous" in the river valley. He remarked: "If Missionaries could be useful in Civilizing and Christianizing any Indians in the World their efforts should be turned towards this valley." The Indians were friendly and the soil and climate ideal. But the Indians' way of life-seemed to Smith to need improvement:

> *A great many of these Indians appear to be the lowest intermediate link between man and the Brute creation. In the construction of houses they are either from indolence or from a deficiency of genius inferior to the Beaver and many of them live without any thing in the shape of a house and rise from their bed of earth in the morning like the animals around them and rove about in search of food.*

When the expedition crossed over the mountains west of present-day Red Bluff to the headwaters of the Trinity River, the Indians they met were hostile. Some Indians along the Trinity River shot arrows at Smith's horses and refused to respond to his efforts to get them to stop, so he ordered his men to fire their rifles at them. After one incident in which nine horses and two mules were injured, he wrote that the Indians "in all probability paid for the damage they had done me by the sacrafice of two or three of their lives." The following day, the Indians continued to follow the expedition, yelling from nearby hills. Smith made signs to show that he wanted to talk with them. When these efforts failed, he fired at them again, as he wrote, "to intimidate them and prevent them from doing me further injury . . . ."

As the expedition neared the forks of the Trinity and Klamath rivers, it entered the country of the Hupa Indians. The Hupa were peaceful. They visited the expedition's camp and traded skins, eels, and roots for awls and beads without incident. But striking out to the west into the territory of the Chilula Indians, Harrison Rogers and Thomas Virgin ran into trouble. Some Chilulas shot arrows at their horses and Virgin killed one of them.

There was no more trouble as the expedition left the Trinity and continued along the Klamath River into the land of the Yurok. Harrison Rogers noted that "they appear friendly and say nothing about the Ind. that Mr. Virgin killed . . . ." The Yurok helped the expedition cross the river and guided it a short distance downstream. Near the mouth of the Klamath River, the expedition camped near another Yurok village. There, some Yuroks came to trade fish for beads. But one member of the expedition, Peter Ranne, a Frenchman, made several of them angry. Harrison Rogers believed that Ranne tried to take their fish without paying for them, and that when they threatened him, he fired his rifle to drive them off.

A few days later, after camp visits by the Yuroks, the expedition discovered that an axe and drawing knife were missing. In retaliation, Smith took an Indian hostage and forced him to accompany the expedition for two hours as it proceeded northward. When none of the hostage's friends came after him to give back the knife, Smith turned the Indian loose.

It seems likely, based on Native American oral tradition, that news of these hostile incidents preceded the expedition as it traveled up the northern coast of California and into Oregon. Fear generated by this news may account for the empty villages the expedition found in Oregon, a fact that Smith and Rogers' journals document. Governor George Simpson of the Hudson's Bay Company, in a letter to Jedediah Smith following the Umpqua River massacre, wrote of "a report that had preceded you from Indians that your party had been conducting themselves with hostility towards the different Tribes you passed in your way from the Bona Ventura [Sacramento River] (for which it appears there were some grounds) . . . ."

Theft was a major source of conflict between Whites and Indians. However, Jedediah Smith responded quite favorably to the Utes in 1826. He wrote: "They appear to have very little disposition to steal and ask for nothing unless it may be a little meat. As stealing and Begging are the most degrading features in the Indian character and as their prevalence is almost universal to be exempt from them is no ordinary merit." He also praised the Indians in the Sacramento Valley for their honesty and lack of thievery.

But theft turned out to be a major problem for the Jedediah Smith expedition on the South Coast. In fairness to Smith, it must be noted that the Hudson's Bay Company explorer and fur trader Alexander McLeod also had a problem with theft when he came to the coast in 1827. Camped about four miles up the Rogue River, his party discovered that a small hatchet had been stolen. McLeod's journal entry regarding this incident deserves to be quoted at length because of the comparison it offers with the actions of Jedediah Smith. McLeod wrote as follows in his journal:

. . . after our search made in which the remainder of the natives joined, to no avail we had recourse to other means and detained half dozen of them for some time, till a message was delivered to the principal characters, signifying our intentions of recovering the stolen article, or else ample remuneration made us in return in a short time, three Chiefs with about sixty followers made their appearance, and informed us that our suspicions were well-founded, but that the offender was out of reach and some days would elapse before the article could be recovered, to bring the case to a termination, they offered us a hostage and gave us up the services of an Indian of their tribe till our return when they would recover the stolen article and restore it, this settlement was acceded to, and both departed us with our hostage on our return and the Indians to their dwellings . . . we availed ourselves of the opportunity this circumstance offered of intimating to them our abhorence of thieving and indeed it was [not so much] the value of the article as the act to have passed it over in silence might not only leave a bad impression but actuate them to further aggression . . . .

Smith and McLeod clearly took the attitude of most Whites that theft by Indians, however petty, had to be punished.

Jedediah Smith's experience with the problem of theft also deserves comparison with the experience of the Lewis and Clark expedition. Once Lewis and Clark reached the Columbia River, theft became a major problem. James P. Ronda in *Lewis and Clark Among the Indians* (1984), on Lewis and Clark's relations with Indians, commented:

From The Dalles down to the coast, Lewis and Clark were troubled by repeated incidents of theft. Those thefts posed two quite distinct problems. Plainly the expedition could not afford to lose tools, weapons, and valuable trade goods. But on another level, the explorers found persistent theft a habit hard to understand. Differing concepts of property, notions of communal sharing, increased commercialization of native life, and theft as an attention-getting tactic were all explanations that did not occur to the ethnographers in the expedition.

After an attempt by Chinook Indians to steal their guns, Ronda noted, "Clark bluntly informed the Indians that anyone seen near the baggage would be shot."

The Jedediah Smith expedition had few opportunities to communicate with South Coast Indians until it reached Cape Arago and Coos Bay. There, relations seemed fairly amicable, although a trading transaction at Charleston with a lower Umpqua Indian started trouble for the expedition with the Umpqua River Indians. On reaching the Umpqua River, another incident of theft provoked a harsh response similar to the action taken earlier at the mouth of the Klamath River in California. A lower Umpqua or Kalawatset was taken hostage and tied up until a stolen axe was returned. What finally brought about the massacre of the expedition is a more complicated question.

From Alexander McLeod's report to Governor Simpson, it would appear that the Kalawatsets felt multiple grievances before they finally attacked the party. One near-attack even seems to have been quieted down by cooler heads. The next day, when the Indian who was chiefly responsible for speaking out against the attack was humiliated by being forced to dismount from one of the expedition's horses, tempers flared again. Governor Simpson also noted in another letter that Alexander McLeod had been informed by the Kalawatsets that Harrison Rogers, "in Smith's absence, attempted to force a Woman into his Tent, whose Brother was knocked down by Rogers while endeavouring to protect her . . . ."

The truth of this charge will never be known. Only twice does Harrison Rogers' journal provide any insight into his attitude toward Indian women. On one occasion while at the mission of San Gabriel in California, he refused the advances of an Indian woman who put him off by her boldness. Rogers wrote: "I must say for the first time, I was ashamed, and did not gratify her or comply with her request, seeing her so forward." But despite his refusal, this journal entry suggests that he was not averse to sleeping with Indian women, only with one as brazen as this one. Later, while traveling through Hupa country, he remarked that one squaw was "a very good featured woman . . . ." These journal entries provide some basis for believing that Rogers may have acted as the Kalawatsets said he did. But we can't be sure. In general, Rogers appears to have been an intelligent, levelheaded leader for whom an attempted rape on the eve of departing the Umpqua River would have been out of character.

One of the leading scholars of Jedediah Smith's life, Maurice S. Sullivan, concluded in 1936 that "since the long-forgotten journals of McLeod have come to the attention of students . . . the Kalawatsets have been freed from blame for the massacre of Smith's men." The killing of fifteen men, however, hardly seems any more justified than the lack of good judgment shown by Jedediah Smith and his men. In retrospect, it would appear that the Jedediah Smith exploring expedition might have avoided its tragic end that resulted from the accumulated injuries to the Kalawatsets' sense of pride. At the end of the twentieth century, we have a far stricter, ideal standard of respect for cultural differences than Jedediah Smith demonstrated either in thought or action.

Sources of Information

The sources used in the writing of this book have been organized topically, approximately in the order of their use in the text. Sources particular to a site or section of the South Coast appear under the heading "Individual Sites." The reader also should look under other topic headings for related sources (e.g., under "Indian Culture and Indian-White Conflict" for sources related to Gold Beach-Rogue River). Descriptions of individual sites also are based on the author's personal observation of sites and miscellaneous sources (newspaper articles, documents, and the like) that have not been included here. This is not intended to be a complete bibliography on Oregon South Coast history; however, an effort has been made to include relevant recent publications.

General

Bancroft, Hubert Howe. *The Works*, Vol. XXVII, *History of the Northwest Coast*, Vol. 1, 1543–1800 (New York, 1967) (1884).

Dodge, Orvil. *Pioneer History of Coos and Curry Counties* (Bandon, 1969) (1898).

"Historical and Genealogical Research Sources for Oregon's South Coast," prepared by Steve Greif and the Coos County Historical Society (2005) at www.cooshistory.org/micro.html

McArthur, Lewis A. *Oregon Geographic Names*, 4th ed., rev. and enl. by Lewis L. McArthur (Portland, 1974).

"Oregon Coast: Mile-By-Mile Guide to Highway 101," [Promotional Brochure; milepost guide] (May/June 1998).

Peterson, Emil R. and Alfred Powers. *A Century of Coos and Curry* (Coquille, 1952).

Walling, A. G. *History of Southern Oregon* (Portland, 1884).

Geology

Allen, John Eliot and Ewart M. Baldwin. *Geology and Coal Resources of the Coos Bay Quadrangle*, Oregon Bulletin No. 27, State of Oregon, Dept. of Geology and Mineral Industries (Portland, 1944).

Allen, John Eliot. "Jetties Altering Vast Sand Dunes Along Coast," *Oregonian*, Jan. 10, 1985, p. D2.

Allen, John Eliot. "New Map Details Offshore Deposits," *Oregonian*, Nov. 21, 1985, p. D1.

Baldwin, Ewart M. *Geology of Oregon* (Ann Arbor, MI, 1959).

Beckham, Dow. *Stars in the Dark: Coal Mines of Southwestern Oregon* (Coos Bay, 1995).

Brooks, Howard C. and Len Ramp. *Gold and Silver in Oregon*, Bulletin No. 61, State of Oregon, Dept. of Geology and Mineral Industries (Portland, 1968).

Dott, R. H., Jr. *Geology of the Southwestern Oregon Coast West of the 124th Meridian*, Bulletin No. 69, State of Oregon, Dept. of Geology and Mineral Industries (Portland, 1971).

Lund, Ernest H. "Oregon Coastal Dunes Between Coos Bay and Sea Lion Point," *Ore Bin*, 35 (May 1973), 73-92.

Ramp, Len, Herbert G. Schlicker, and Jerry J. Gray. *Geology, Mineral Resources, and Rock Material of Curry County, Oregon*, Bulletin No. 93, State of Oregon, Dept. of Geology and Mineral Industries (Salem, 1977).

Exploration

Cook, Warren, L. *Flood Tide of Empire: Spain and the Pacific Northwest, 1543–1819* (New Haven & London, 1973).

Cutter, Donald C. "Spain and the Oregon Coast," 29–46, in Thomas Vaughan, ed. *The Western Shore* (Portland, 1975).

Davies, K. G., ed. *Peter Skene Ogden's Snake Country Journal* 1826–27 (London, 1961).

Elliott, T. C. "Vancouver's Journal," *Oregon Historical Quarterly*, XXX (Mar. 1929), 34–41.

Elliott, T. C. "Captain Cook on the Oregon Coast," *Oregon Historical Quarterly*, XXIX (Sept. 1928), 270–273.

Gough, Barry M. "The Northwest Coast in Late 18th Century British Expansion," 47–80, in Thomas Vaughan, ed. *The Western Shore* (Portland, 1975).

Hezeta, Bruno de. *For Honor and Country, The Diary of Bruno De Hezeta*, Translation and annotation by Herbert K. Beals (Portland, 1985).

Holmes, Kenneth L. "Francis Drake's Course in the North Pacific, 1579," *Geographical Bulletin*, 17 (June 1979), 5–41.

McArthur, Lewis A. "The Pacific Coast Survey of 1849 and 1850," *Oregon Historical Quarterly*, XVI (Sept. 1915), 262–265.

Pethick, Derek. *First Approaches to the Northwest Coast* (Seattle & London, 1979).

Schlesser, Norman Dennis. *Fort Umpqua: Bastion of Empire* (Oakland, OR, 1973).

Thwaites, Reuben Gold, ed. *Original Journals of the Lewis and Clark Expedition, 1804–1806*, Vol. 6 (New York, 1969; reprint) (1905).

Archaeology

Aikens, C. Melvin. *Archaeology of Oregon* (Portland, 1993).

Atwood, Kay and Dennis J. Gray. *People and the River: A History of the Human Occupation of the Middle Course of the Rogue River of Southwestern Oregon*, Vol. I, Prepared for USDI-Bureau of Land Management, Grants Pass Resource Area, Medford, OR, 1995.

Connolly, Thomas J., et al. *The Standley Site (35DO182): Investigations into the Prehistory of Camas Valley, Southwest Oregon*, University of Oregon Anthropological Papers, No. 43 (Eugene, 1991).

Deich, Lyman. A pre-preliminary report of excavations carried out during the 1982 field season by the U.S. Bureau of Land Management, the Oregon Archeological Society, and the Rogue Valley Archeological Society for the State of Jefferson Conference, Feb. 17–18, 1983.

Draper, John A. and Glenn D. Hartmann. *A Cultural Resource Evaluation of the Cape Arago Lighthouse Locality, Gregory Point, Oregon* (Corvallis, 1979).

Draper, John A. An analysis of lithic tools and debitage from 35CS1: a prehistoric site on the southern Oregon coast, An unpublished Master of Arts in Interdisciplinary Studies thesis, Oregon State University, Mar. 10, 1980.

Gray, Dennis J. *The Takelma and Their Athapascan Neighbors: A New Ethnographic Synthesis for the Upper Rogue River Area of Southwestern Oregon*, University of Oregon Anthropological Papers, No. 37, Eugene, 1997.

Greengo, Robert E., ed. *Prehistoric Places on the Southern Northwest Coast* (Seattle, 1983).

Griffin, Dennis. Archaeological investigation at the Marial site: Rogue River Ranch 35CU84, Richard E. Ross, Principal Investigator, Department of Anthropology, Oregon State University, Corvallis, 1983.

Hall, Roberta L., et al. *People of the Coquille Estuary: Native Use of Resources on the Oregon Coast* (Corvallis, 1995).

Joyer, Janet. "Messages in Stone," *Southern Oregon Heritage*, 2 (Fall 1996), 30–34.

Lalande, Jeff. "The Indians of Southwestern Oregon: An Ethnohistorical Review," *Anthropology Northwest*: Number 6 (Corvallis, 1991).

Leatherman, Kenneth E. and Alex D. Krieger. "Contributions to Oregon Coast Prehistory," *American Antiquity*, 1 (1940), 19–28.

Minor, Rick, Stephen Dow Beckham, and Ruth L. Greenspan. *Archaeology and History of the Fort Orford Locality: Investigations at the Blundon Site (35CU106) and Historic Fort Orford* (Eugene, 1980).

Minor, Rick and Kathryn Toepel. "Excavations at Tahkenitch Landing," *Current Archaeological Happenings in Oregon*, 10 (Mar. 1985), 8–10.

Oregon South Coast Archaeology Research: http://nwdata.geol.pdx.edu/seagrant/Archaeology/OR_Coast_Dates_Program; http://oregonstate.edu/dept/anthropology/SeaGrantWeb/index.html

Pullen, Reginald John. The identification of early prehistoric settlement patterns along the coast of southwest Oregon: survey based upon amateur artifact collections, An unpublished Master of Arts in Interdisciplinary Studies thesis, Oregon State University, Dec. 4, 1981.

Pullen, Reg[inald John]. "Stone Sculptures of Southwest Oregon: Mythological and Ceremonial Associations," 120–124, in Nan Hannon and Richard K. Olmo, eds. *Living With the Land: The Indians of Southwest Oregon* (Medford, OR, 1990).

Ross, Richard E. "Prehistory of the Oregon Coast," 554-59, in *Handbook of North American Indians, Vol. 7, Northwest Coast*, vol. ed. Wayne Suttles (Washington, DC, 1990).

Ross, Richard E. Excavations on the lower Coquille River, Coos County, Oregon, A report submitted to Oregon State Parks and Recreation, 1976.

Ross, Richard E. Preliminary archaeological investigations at 35CU9; Port Orford, Oregon, A report submitted to Oregon State Parks and Recreation, 1977.

Ross, Richard E. and Sandra L. Snyder. "The Umpqua/Eden Site (35DO83): Exploitation of Marine Resources on the Central Oregon Coast," 80–101, in Kenneth M. Ames, ed. *Contributions to the Archaeology of Oregon* 1983–1986 (Portland and Salem, 1986).

Indian Culture and Indian-White Conflict

Arneson, James. "Property Concepts of 19th Century Oregon Indians," *Oregon Historical Quarterly*, 81 (1980), 391–422.

Baun, Carolyn M. and Richard Lewis, eds. *The First Oregonians: An Illustrated Collection of Essays on Traditional Lifeways, Federal-Indian Relations, and the State's Native People Today* (Portland, 1991).

Beckham, Stephen Dow. *Requiem for a People* (Norman, OK, 1971. Reprinted Corvallis, OR, 1996).

Beckham, Stephen Dow. *Indians of Western Oregon* (Coos Bay, 1977).

Beckham, Stephen Dow, Rick Minor, and Kathryn Anne Toepel. *Cultural Resource Overview of the Eugene BLM District, West-Central Oregon* (Eugene, 1981).

Beckham, Stephen Dow. "History of Western Oregon Since 1846," 180-88, in *Handbook of North Americans, Vol. 7, Northwest Coast*, vol. ed. Wayne Suttles (Washington, DC, 1990).

Boyd, Robert T. "Demographic History, 1774-1874," 135-48, in *Handbook of North Americans, Vol. 7, Northwest Coast*, vol. ed. Wayne Suttles (Washington, DC, 1990).

Douthit, Nathan. *Uncertain Encounters: Indians and Whites at Peace and War in Southern Oregon 1820s-1860s* (Corvallis, 2002).

Drucker, Philip. "The Tolowa and their Southwest Oregon Kin," University of California Publications in American Archaeology and Ethnology, 36 (1936), 221–300.

First Nations Collection, Southern Oregon Digital Archivees, The Library, Southern Oregon University, at www.soda.sou.edu

Hall, Roberta L. *The Coquille Indian: Yesterday, Today and Tomorrow* (Lake Oswego, OR, 1984).

Hall, Roberta. "Language and Cultural Affiliations of Natives Residing Near the Mouth of the Coquille River Before 1851," *Journal of Anthropological Research*, 48 (1992).

Hall, Roberta and Don Alan Hall. "The Village at the Mouth of the Coquille River," *Pacific Northwest Quarterly*, 82 (July 1991), 101–108.

Harrington, John P. The Indians of the Oregon Coast, The ancient and original inhabitants, as recorded in the John P. Harrington Collection of the Smithsonian Institution National Anthropological Archives, Unit #l: Introduction, compiled by Jim Thornton (Coos Bay, 1978?).

Miller, Jay, and William R. Seaburg. "Athapaskans of Southwestern Oregon," 580-88, in *Handbook of North Americans, Vol. 7, Northwest Coast*, vol. ed. Wayne Suttles (Washington, DC, 1990).

Nielson, Vernon. "Indian Tribes of Curry County," *Oregon Historical Quarterly*, XXXII (Mar. 1931), 24–26.

Ord, Edward O. C. *Ord's Diary in Curry County, Ore.*, 1856 (Transcribed by H. J. Newhouse from the original manuscript in the Bancroft Library, University of California, Berkeley).

O'Donnell, Terrence. *An Arrow in the Earth: General Joel Palmer and the Indians of Oregon* (Portland, 1991).

Ronda, James P. *Lewis and Clark Among the Indians* (Lincoln, Neb. and London, 1984).

Sapir, Edward. "Notes on the Takelma Indians," *American Anthropologist*, New Series 9 (1907), 251–275.

Spier, Leslie. "Tribal Distribution in Southwestern Oregon," *Oregon Historical Quarterly*, 28 (1927), 358–365.

Schwartz, E. A. *The Rogue River Indian War and Its Aftermath, 1850–1980* (Norman, OK and London, 1997).

Suttles, Wayne, ed. *Handbook of North American Indians*, Vol. 7, Northwest Coast (Washington, D.C., 1990).

Victor, Frances Fuller. *The Early Indian Wars of Oregon* (Salem, 1894).

Ward, Beverly H. *White Moccasins* (Myrtle Point, OR, 1986).

Walsh, Frank K. *Indian Battles Along the Rogue River 1855–1856* (Grants Pass, OR, 1972).

Youst, Lionel. *She's Tricky Like Coyote: Annie Miner Peterson, An Oregon Coast Indian Woman* (Norman, OK and London, 1997).

Zenk, Henry B. "Siuslawans and Coosans," 572-79, in *Handbook of North Americans, Vol. 7, Northwest Coast*, vol. ed. Wayne Suttles (Washington, DC, 1990).

Zucker, Jeff, Kay Hummel, and Bob Høgfoss. *Oregon Indians Culture, History and Current Affairs: An Atlas and Introduction* (Portland, 1983).

Jedediah Smith

Adams, Tom. "Bibliography of Articles Relating to Jedediah Strong Smith," *Pacific Historian*, 19 (Spring 1975), 69–72.

Brooks, George R. *The Southwest Expedition of Jedediah S. Smith: His Personal Account of the Journey to California 1826–1827* (Glendale, Calif., 1977).

Camp, Charles L., ed. James Clyman, *American Frontiersman*, 1792–1881 (Portland, 1960).

Chase, Don M. and Doris H. "Bibliography of Sources Relating to Jedediah Strong Smith," *Pacific Historian*, 7 (Aug. 1963), 149–162; (Nov. 1963), 105–115.

Dale, Harrison Clifford, ed. *The Ashley-Smith Explorations and the Discovery of a Central Route to the Pacific 1822–1829* (Glendale, CA, 1941).

Davis, Lee. "Tracking Jedediah Smith Through Hupa Territory," *American Indian Quarterly*, 13 (Fall 1989), 369-89.

Fung, Leslie G. "Jedediah Strong Smith: Escapist or Capitalist," *Pacific Historian*, 21 (Spring 1977), 70–78.

Gale, Frederick C. "Jedediah Smith Meets Indians and Vice Versa," *Pacific Historian*, 10 (Spring 1966), 34–38.

Garber, D. W "Jedediah Strong Smith Fur Trader from Ohio: A Postscript," *Pacific Historian*, 22 (Spring 1978), 9–25.

Maloney, Alice B. "Camp Sites of Jedediah Smith on the Oregon Coast," *Oregon Historical Quarterly*, XLI (Sept. 1940), 304–323.

Moore, Wert E. "Location of Umpqua Massacre," *Pacific Historian*, 4 (Nov. 1960), 144.

Morgan, Dale L. *Jedediah Smith and the Opening of the West* (Lincoln, Neb., 1964; reprint)(1953).

Morgan, Dale L. and Carl I. Wheat. *Jedediah Smith and His Maps of the American West* (San Francisco, 1954).

Morgan, Dale L. "Jedediah Smith Today," *Pacific Historian*, 11 (Spring 1967), 35–46.

Oregon Historic Trails Report, compiled by Karen Bassett, Jim Renner, and Joyce White (Oregon Trails Coordinating Council, Salem, 1998), 87–98.

Pollard, Lancaster. "Site of the Smith Massacre on July 14, 1828," *Oregon Historical Quarterly*, XLV (June 1944), 133–137.

Rich, E. E., ed. *The Letters of John McLoughlin . . . First Series*, 1825–38 (London, 1941).

Smith, Alson J. *Men Against the Mountains: Jedediah Smith and the Great South West Expedition of 1826–29* (New York, 1965).

Sullivan, Maurice S. *The Travels of Jedediah Smith, A Documentary Outline Including the Journal of the Great Pathfinder* (Santa Ana, Calif., 1934).

Sullivan, Maurice S. *Jedediah Smith: Trader and Trailbreaker* (New York, 1936).

Sullivan, Maurice S. Letters to Alice Bay (Mrs. Michael Collinbroke) Maloney, Sept. 7, 18, 29, 1934. Coos Bay Public Library.

Sunder, John E. Bill *Sublette: Mountain Man* (Norman, OK, 1959).

Wasson, George B., Jr. "The Memory of A People: The Coquilles of the Southwest Coast," 83–87, in *The First Oregonians* (Portland, 1991).

Wood, Raymond F. *Monuments to Jedediah Smith* (Stockton, CA, 1984).

State Parks, Bridges, and Architecture

Armstrong, Chester H. *Oregon State Parks: History 1917–1963* (Salem, 1965).

Atly, E. Shellin, C. B. McCullough and the Oregon Coastal Bridges Project, Unpublished student paper, University of Oregon Department of Architecture, June 3, 1977.

Boardman, Samuel H. Samuel H. Boardman Collection, Oregon State Archives, 92A-31, 5 boxes.

Boardman, Samuel H. "Oregon State Park System: A Brief History," *Oregon Historical Quarterly*, 55 (Sept.1954), 179–234.

Blumenson, John J. G. *Identifying American Architecture: A Pictorial Guide to Styles and Terms, 1600–1945* (Nashville, Tenn., 1977).

Clark, Rosalind L. *Architecture Oregon Style* (Portland, 1983).

Coos Bay Times, June 1, 1936.

Gemeny, Albin L. and Conde B. McCullough. *Application of Freyssinet Method of Concrete Arch Construction to the Rogue River Bridge in Oregon* (Salem, 1933).

Hadlow, Robert W. *Elegant Arches, Soaring Spans: C. B. McCullough, Oregon's Master Bridge Builder* (Corvallis, 2001).

McAlester, Virginia and Lee. *A Field Guide To American Houses* (New York, 1984).

McCullough, Conde B. "How Oregon Builds Bridges," *Oregon Motorist*, 10 (Feb. 1930), 13–15, 27–28.

McCullough, Conde B. "Western Practice Utilizes New Types," *Civil Engineering*, 2 (Sept. 1932), 549–553.

McCullough, Conde B. "Remarkable Series of Bridges on Oregon Coast Highway," *Engineering News-Record*, Nov. 14, 1935, pp. 677–678.

Merriam, Lawrence C., Jr. and David G. Talbot. *Oregon's Highway Park System 1921–1989: An Administrative History* (Salem, OR, 1992).

National Register of Historic Places Inventory, Nomination Form, Temple of Marshfield, B.P.O.E. Lodge #1160, Coos Bay, Oregon, Submitted by Samuels & Clay Architects, Coos Bay, July–Aug. 1982.

Official Souvenir Program, Coos Bay Bridge Celebration, June 5–7, 1936, North Bend.

Oregon Department of Transportation, Environmental Section. Miscellaneous files on Historic Highway Bridges of Oregon.

Pierce, Louis F. *Esthetics in Oregon Bridges—McCullough to Date* (Portland, 1980).

Plowden, David. *Bridges: The Spans of North America* (New York, 1947).

Smith, Dwight A., James B. Norman, and Pieter T. Dykman. *Historic Highway Bridges of Oregon* (Salem, 1986).

Wrenn, Tony P. and Elizabeth D. Mulloy. *America's Forgotten Architecture* (Washington, D.C., 1976).

Shipwrecks and Lighthouses

Gibbs, James A., Jr. *Sentinels of the North Pacific* (Portland, 1955).

Gibbs, James A. (with Bert Webber). *Oregon's Seacoast Lighthouses* (Medford, OR, 1994).

Grover, David H. *The Unforgiving Coast: Maritime Disasters of the Pacific Northwest* (Corvallis, 2002).

[*New Carissa*] *Oregonian*, miscellaneous daily news articles, Feb. 5, 1999 to Mar. 12, 1999.

"Oregon Coast Lighthouse Back in Service," *Oregonian*, Jan. 24, 1985.

Oregon Lighthouses at www.unc.edu/~rowlett/lighthouse/or.htm

Osborne, Ernest L. and Victor West. *Men of Action: A History of the U.S. Life-Saving Service on the Pacific Coast* (Bandon, 1981).

Webber, Bert. *Silent Siege: Japanese Attacks Against North America in World War II* (Fairfield, WA, 1984).

West, Victor. Chart of Shipwrecks [Coos Bay]. Coos County Historical Society Museum, North Bend, OR.

West, Victor. "Shipwrecks of the Southern Oregon Coast," 7 vols. loose-leaf notebooks with photographs, Southwestern Oregon Comunity College and North Bend public libraries.

West, Victor and R. E. Wells. *A Guide to Shipwreck Sites Along the Oregon Coast* (North Bend, 1984).

Transportation

Alley, William. "Air Minded City: Commercial Aviation Comes to the Rogue Valley," *Southern Oregon Heritage*, 3, No.1 (1997), 25–29.

Dicken, Samuel N. *Pioneer Trails of the Oregon Coast* (Portland, 1971).

Gorst, Wilbur H. *Vern C. Gorst: Pioneer and Granddad of United Air Lines* (Coos Bay, 1979).

Smith, Dwight A., James B. Norman, and Pieter T. Dykman. *Historic Highway Bridges of Oregon* (Salem, 1986).

Forests and Forest Industry

American Forests, April 1982.

Beckham, Stephen Dow. *Swift Flows the River: Log Driving in Oregon* (Coos Bay, 1990).

Collingwood, G. H. and Warren D. Brush. *Knowing Your Trees* (New York, 1974).

Davies, John. *Douglas of the Forests: The North American Journals of David Douglas* (Seattle, 1980).

Griffith, John. "Nucor Offers Hope for Coos Bay," *Oregonian*, Feb.26, 1998, D1.

Griffith, John. "Hoping to Grow Money on Trees," *Oregonian*, Mar.27, 1998, D2.

Lansing, William A. *Seeing the Forest for the Trees: Menasha Corporation and Its One Hundred Year History in Coos Bay, Oregon 1905 to 2005* (Eugene, 2005).

Peattie, Donald Culross. *A Natural History of Western Trees* (New York, 1952).

Phillips, Jerry. *Caulked Boots and Cheese Sandwiches: A Forester's History of Oregon's First State Forest "The Elliott"* (1912–1996) (Coos Bay, 1997).

Port Orford Cedar: An American Wood (Washington, DC, 1973).

Robbins, William G. *Hard Times in Paradise: Coos Bay, Oregon, 1850–1986* (Seattle and London, 1988).

Silvics of Forest Trees of the United States, Agricultural Handbook, No. 271
(Washington, D.C., 1965).

Zobel, Donald B. "Port Orford Cedar: A Forgotten Species," *Journal of Forest
History*, 30 (Jan.1986), 29–36.

Individual Sites

General

Beckham, Stephen Dow. The Oregon seaboard: an inventory of historical and
archaeological sites, A report submitted to the Oregon Coastal Conservation
and Development Commission, Florence, Ore., Nov. 1972.

Beckham, Stephen Dow. Coos County inventory historic sites and buildings, A
report prepared for the State Historic Preservation Office, Oregon State Parks,
Salem, Ore., 1976.

Beckham, Stephen Dow and Rick Minor. Cultural resources overview of the
Coos Bay BLM District, A final report submitted to the Coos Bay District, U.S.
Bureau of Land Management in fulfillment of contract YA-512-CT9-135, Lake
Oswego, Ore., July 15, 1980.

Chetco Valley

Olsen, Edward G. *Then Till Now in Brookings-Harbor: A Social History of the Chetco
Community Area* (Brookings, 1979).

Lundquist, William. "White Gold: The Roots of the Lily Bulb Industry on the
South Coast," *Southern Oregon Heritage*, 3, No.1 (1997), 35–37.

Gold Beach-Rogue River

Arman, Florence with Glen Wooldridge. *The Rogue: A River to Run* (Grants Pass,
1982).

Bastasch, Rick. *Waters of Oregon: A Source Book on Oregon's Water and Water
Management* (Corvallis, 1998).

Brinckman, Jonathan. "U.S. Set to Call Coho Threatened," *Oregonian*, Aug. 4,
1998, A1.

Curry County Echoes, 1973.

Dodds, Gordon B. *The Salmon King of Oregon: R. D. Hume and The Pacific Fisheries*
(Chapel Hill, NC, 1959).

Grey, Zane. *Tales of Fresh Water Fishing* (New York, 1928).

Griffith, John. "Salmon Plan May Cut Logging Revenue," *Oregonian*, Mar.5, 1998,
D2.

"Historic Status Sought for Coastal Span," *Oregonian*, Jan. 31, 1982.

Hume, R. D. *Salmon of the Pacific Coast* (Gold Beach, 1975) (1893).

Jackson, Carlton. *Zane Grey* (New York, 1973).

Jacobs, Steven E. and Cedric X. Cooney. "Oregon Coastal Salmon Spawning
Surveys, 1994 and 1995," *Information Reports*, Number 97-5, Oregon
Department of Fish and Wildlife, Portland, May 1997.

Korbulic, Mary. "Romancing the Rogue: Zane Grey's Fickle Love Affair with the
Rogue River," *Table Rock Sentinel*, 12 (Nov./Dec. 1992), 3–11.

Pampush, Geoff. "Only Oregonians Can Save Salmon," *Oregonian*, Aug. 4, 1998,
B11.

Meier, Gary and Gloria. *Whitewater Mailmen: The Story of the Rogue River Mail
Boats* (Bend, OR, 1995).

Sterling, Julie. "As Rough As It Gets," *Oregonian*, April 5, 1998, T1-T2.

Wild Flyer, Fall 1996; Summer 1997.

Klamath-Siskiyou Ecoregion

Frissell, Christopher A. Ecological benefits of wildland protection: The proposed Copper Salmon Wilderness proposal in southwest Oregon, Open File Report Number 97- , Flathead Lake Biological Station, The University of Montana, Polson (1997?).

Trail, Pepper. "Recognizing Paradise: The World Discovers the Klamath-Siskiyou Ecoregion," *Jefferson Monthly* (Feb. 1998), 8–11, 15.

Wallace, David Rains. *The Klamath Knot* (San Francisco, 1983).

White, Georganne. "Natural History in Our Own Backyard," *The Point Orford Heritage Society News*, 4 (Feb. 1998), 3–5.

Humbug Mountain-Port Orford

Reinhart, Herman Francis. *The Golden Frontier: The Recollections of Herman Francis Reinhart 1851–1869*, Edited by Doyce B. Nunnis, Jr. (Austin, TX, 1962).

Masterson, Patrick. *Port Orford: A History* (Wilsonville, OR, 1994).

"Port Orford's History in its Architecture," Port Orford Promoter's Brochure (Port Orford, n.d.).

Bandon-Coquille River

Beckham, Curt. *The Night Bandon Burned* (Myrtle Point, 1985).

Beckham, Dow. *Bandon By-The-Sea* (Coos Bay, 1997).

Bennett, George. "A History of Bandon and the Coquille River," *Oregon Historical Quarterly*, 28 (Dec. 1927), 310–357; 29 (Mar. 1928), 20–50.

"Coquille Historical Buildings," [Promotional Brochure] (Coquille, 1998).

Hall, Roberta. "Language and Cultural Affiliations of Natives Residing Near the Mouth of the Coquille River Before 1851," *Journal of Anthropological Research*, 48 (1992), 165–184.

Hall, Roberta and Don Alan Hall. "The Village at the Mouth of the Coquille River," *Pacific Northwest Quarterly*, 82 (July 1991), 101–108.

Hall, Roberta L., et al. *People of the Coquille Estuary: Native Use of Resources on the Oregon Coast* (Corvallis, 1995).

Linke, Kay and Art Dobney. "Background: Coquille River Lifeboat Station," *Port of Bandon*, July 29, 1985.

Osborne, Ernest L. *Wooden Ships and Master Craftsmen* (Bandon, 1978).

Stone, Boyd. *You Are the Stars: History of the Coquille Area* (Coquille, 1995).

Walling, A. G. *History of Southern Oregon* (Portland, 1884).

Wasson, George B., Jr. "The Memory of A People: The Coquilles of the Southwest Coast," 83–87, in *The First Oregonians* (Portland, 1991).

Webber, Bert. *Silent Siege: Japanese Attacks Against North America in World War II* (Fairfield, WA, 1984).

Welch, George. "Early Day Riverton," *Bandon Western World*, June 15, 1967.

Wooldridge, Alice H., ed. *Pioneers and Incidents of the Upper Coquille Valley* (Myrtle Creek, 1971).

Myrtle Point

Beckham, Curt. *Myrtle Point Beginnings* (Myrtle Point, 1986).

Hermann, Binger. *The Baltimore Colony and Pioneer Recollections* (Myrtle Point(?), 1956).

"Reflections of Our Past," A brochure consisting of photographs and maps of historic buildings in Myrtle Point, Ore., sponsored by local businesses, 1982(?).

Powers

Stevens, Victor. *The Powers Story* (Myrtle Point, 1979).

Coos Bay Wagon Road:

Eickworth, Clara. Miscellaneous notes on the Coos Bay Wagon Road, A photocopy of an unpublished manuscript in the author's possession.

Laird, Ivan. Interviewed by Lloyd Lyman, May 21, 1975, *Living History* Tape #449, Southwestern Oregon Community College Library Collection.

Metcalfe, Joanne Perrott. "The Coos Bay Wagon Road," *Coast Magazine*, 1 (Sept. 1979) and 2 (Oct. 1979).

Cape Arago-Shore Acres-North Spit:

Beckham, Stephen Dow. *The Simpsons of Shore Acres* (Coos Bay, 1971).

Beckham, Stephen Dow. "The Cape Arago Lighthouse," Parts 1, 11, *Coos Historical Quarterly* (Winter; Spring 1984), n.p.

[Camp Castaway] 32nd Cong. 2d Sess., House Docs., Vol. I, Pt. 2, 1852-53, H. Doc. 1, pp. 103–122.

Draft Environmental Impact Statement for the Bal'diyaka Interpretive Center at Gregory Point on the Oregon Coast in Coos County, Sept. 1995, Prepared by SRI/Shapiro, Inc. for U.S. Dept. of the Interior Bureau of Land Management, Coos Bay District and the Confederated Tribes of Coos, Lower Umpqua and Siuslaw Indians.

Wagner, Judith and Richard. *The Uncommon Life of Louis Jerome Simpson* (North Bend, 2003).

Wasson, George B., Jr. "The Memory of A People: The Coquilles of the Southwest Coast," 83–87, in *The First Oregonians* (Portland, 1991).

Charleston-South Slough

Butler, Barbara. "The emigration of Scandinavian settlers and their influence on the South Slough region," University of Oregon Institute of Marine Biology student paper, Spring 1985.

Caldera, Melody J., ed. *South Slough Adventures: Life on A Southern Oregon Estuary* (Coos Bay, 1995).

Clark, Erme and Bruce Euje. "A look at the re-emerging Ferrei ranch salt marsh," University of Oregon Institute of Marine Biology student paper, Spring 1980, Book I.

Gilmore, Janet C. *The World of the Oregon Fishboat: A Study in Maritime Folklife* (Ann Arbor, MI, 1986).

Hudson, Mary E. "Historical land use of South Slough," University of Oregon Institute of Marine Biology student paper, Spring 1979, Book III.

Hutchinson, Susan and Mary Henrickson. "The history of Charlies' town as told by its pioneers," University of Oregon Institute of Marine Biology student paper, Spring 1974, Book II.

Kirkpatrick, Jane. *A Gathering of Finches* (Sisters, OR, 1997) [a historical novel].

Qualman, Alfred A. Interviewed by Lloyd Lyman, Mar. 21, 1975 *Living History* Tape #402, Southwestern Oregon Community College Library.

Qualman, Alfred A. *Blood on the Half Shell* (Portland, 1983).

Coos Bay-North Bend

Beckham, Stephen Dow. *Coos Bay, The Pioneer Period 1851–1890* (Coos Bay, 1973).

Beckham, Dow. *Swift Flows the River: Log Driving in Oregon* (Coos Bay, 1990).

Case, George B. "A History of the Port of Coos Bay, 1852–1952," Marshfield Sun, Annual ed. 1984.

Douthit, Nathan. *The Coos Bay Region 1890–1944: Life On a Coastal Frontier* (Coos Bay, 1981).

Douthit, Nathan. "The Marshfield Sun and Its Editor Jesse Luse," *Marshfield Sun,* 2d annual ed. (1979), reprinted in *The Kemble Occasional* (Fall 1982), 1–5.

Drabble, Dennis. "Return of the Egyptian," *Preservation,* 50 (July/August 1998), 14–15.

Erickson, Kathy, ed. *Coos County: The Early Years* (Portland, 1998) [a pictorial history].

Griffith, John. "Nucor Offers Hope for Coos Bay," *Oregonian,* Feb.26, 1998, D1.

Griffith, John. "Hoping to Grow Money on Trees," *Oregonian,* Mar.27, 1998, D2.

Price, Nancy. "The Coos Bay Hotel Company and the Building of the Chandler Hotel," *Coos Historical Journal* (Autumn 1985), 1–8.

Robbins, William G. *Hard Times in Paradise: Coos Bay, Oregon, 1850–1986* (Seattle and London, 1988).

Sengstacken, Agnes Ruth. *Destination West* (Portland, 1942).

Wagner, Dick. *Louie Simpson's North Bend* (North Bend, 1986).

West, Victor. Logging Locomotive No. 104, Historical Series No. 2, Coos-Curry Museum (North Bend, 1980).

Coastal Beaches and Dunes (Coos Bay-Florence)

Alley, William. "Air Minded City: Commercial Aviation Comes to the Rogue Valley," *Southern Oregon Heritage,* 3, No.1 (1997), 24–29.

Final Environmental Statement. Oregon Dunes National Recreation Area. Management Plan. Dec. 8, 1978, Forest Service, U.S. Dept. of Agr., A History of the Siuslaw National Forest Oregon As of Dec. 31, 1939 (Washington, D. C. 1968).

Hill, Richard L. "Battle Launched to Reclaim Dunes," *Oregonian,* July 22, 1998, B14.

Newspapers: *Coos Bay World,* 6/17/68, 6/20/68; *Eugene Register-Guard,* 12/2/68, 8/18/70.

Overlook Dunes Restoration Project: Environmental Assessment, USDA Forest Service, Siuslaw National Forest, Oregon dunes National Recreation Area (1998?).

Siuslaw Pioneer, 1950, pp. 24, 28; 1959, pp. 14–16.

Thornton, Nancy. "The First Lighthouse at Umpqua and How It Slipped into the Sea," *Northwest Magazine* (June 22, 1969).

Wiedemann, Alfred M., LaRea J. Dennis, and Frank H. Smith. *Plants of the Oregon Coastal Dunes* (Corvallis, 1969).

Umpqua River

"A Guide to Historic Districts in Douglas County Oregon," [Promotional brochure prepared by the Douglas County Planning Department and Douglas County Museum, n.d.]

Beckham, Stephen Dow. "Lonely Outpost: The Army's Fort Umpqua," *Oregon Historical Quarterly,* 70 (Sept. 1969), 233–237.

Beckham, Stephen Dow. *Land of the Umpqua: A History of Douglas County,* Oregon (Roseburg, 1986).

Bensell, Royal A. *All Quiet on the Yamhill: The Civil War in Oregon, The Journal of Corporal Royal A. Bensell*, Edited by Gunther Barth (Eugene, 1959).

Bright, Verne. "The Lost County, Umpqua, Oregon, and Its Early Settlement," *Oregon Historical Quarterly*, XXI (June 1950), 111–126.

Douthit, Nathan. "The Hudson's Bay Company and the Indians of Southern Oregon," *Oregon Historical Quarterly*, 93 (Spring 1992), 25–64.

Lyman, Albert. The journal of Captain Albert Lyman, 1850–1851, Transcript from a microfilm of the original journal with Lyman's spelling and footnotes prepared by the Douglas County Museum Librarian, Douglas County Museum, Roseburg, Oregon.

Minter, Harold A. *Umpqua Valley Oregon and Its Pioneers* (Portland, 1967).

Pictorial History of the Lower Umpqua (Reedsport, 1976).

"Scenes and Incidents of Oregon Territory," *Frank Leslie's Illustrated Magazine*, Apr. 24, 1858, pp. 332–333.

Scholfield, Socrates. "The Klamath Exploring Expedition, 1850," *Oregon Historical Quarterly*, XVII (Dec. 1916), 341–357.

Winterbotham, Jerry. *Umpqua: The Lost County of Oregon* (Brownsville, OR, 1994).

Florence

Calder, Bill. "A Walking Tour of Old Town Florence," *Lane County Historian*, XXIX (Fall 1984), 59–67.

Cox, Thomas R. "William Kyle and the Pacific Lumber Trade," *Journal of Forest History*, 19 (Jan.1975), 4–14.

Lomax Alfred L. "Early Shipping and Industry in the Lower Siuslaw Valley," *Lane County Historian*, XVI (Summer 1971), 32–39.

Pursley, Ed. *Florence: A Diamond Set Among the Pearls* (Florence, 1989).

Shelton, Barb. "The Siuslaw Valley," Unpublished manuscript, Florence Public Library, 1974(?).

Siuslaw Pioneer, 1947.

Skinner, Mary Lou. "Florence, the "Fir-Clad' City," *Lane County Historian*, XVI (Summer 1971), 25–31.

Historical Societies, Museums, and Lighthouses

Chetco Valley Historical Museum. 15461 Museum Rd., Brookings, OR 97415. Telephone: 541-469-2753. Open: 1-5 pm, Fri.-Sun., Memorial Day through Labor Day..

Curry Historical Society Museum. Alice Wakeman Building, 29410 Ellensburg, Gold Beach, OR 97444. Telephone: 541-247-9396. Open: 10-4 pm, Tues.-Sat., except Jan. Web site: www.curryhistory.com.

Port Orford Lifeboat Station. Coast Guard Rd., Port Orford. Mail: Point Orford Heritage Society. P.O. Box 1132, Port Orford, OR 97476. Telephone: 541-332-0521. Open: 10-3:30 pm, Wed.-Mon., Apr.-Oct.

Historic Patrick Hughes House. 91814 Cape Blanco Rd., Sixes. Mail: Friends of Cape Blanco, P.O. Box 1178, Port Orford, OR 97465. Telephone: 541-332-0248. Open: 10-3:30 pm, Tues.-Sun., Apr.-Oct. Web site: www.hugheshouse.org.

Agness-Illahe Museum. 34470 Agness-Illahe Rd., Agness, OR 97406. Telephone 541-247-2014. Open: 11-2 pm, May-Sept.

Cape Blanco Lighthouse. Cape Blanco Rd., Sixes. Mail: Friends of Cape Blanco, P.O. Box 1178, Port Orford, OR 97465. Telephone: 541-332-2207. Web site: www.capeblancolighthouse.org.

Bandon Historical Society Museum. 270 Fillmore & US 101, Bandon. Mail: P.O. Box 737, Bandon, OR 97411. Telephone: 541-347-2164. Open: Winter, 10-4 pm, Mon.-Sat.; Summer, noon-3 pm, all days. Web site: www.bandonhistoricalmuseum.org

Coquille River Lighthouse. Bullards Beach State Park, north of Bandon. Open year-round, daylight hours.

Coos County Logging Museum. 705 Maple St., Myrtle Point, OR 97701. Telephone: 541-572-1014. Hours: 10-4 pm, Mon.–Sat.; 1–4 pm, Sun.; June-Septt. Web site: www.cooscountyloggingmuseum.4t.com.

Pioneer (Wagner) House and Railroad Museum. Powers. Open: summer weekends, holidays, and by appointment. Contact: 541-439-3811 or 541-439-3331 for information.

Cape Arago Lighthouse. Near Sunset Bay; reach through Charleston, off US 101 through Coos Bay. Closed to the public; views from Sunset Bay State Park.

South Slough National Estuarine Research Reserve. Seven Devils Rd., Charleston. Mail: P.O. Box 5417, Charlston, OR 97420. Telephone: 541-888-5558. Open: 10-4:30 pm. Web site: www.oregon.gov/DSL/SSNERR.

Marshfield Sun Printing Museum. 1049 Front St., Coos Bay. Mail: P.O. Box 783, Coos Bay, OR 97420. Telephone: 541-267-3762. Open: 1-4 pm, Tues.–Sat.; June-Aug.; rest of year by appointment.

Coos Historical and Maritime Museum. 1220 Sherman, North Bend, OR 97459. Telephone: 541-756-6320. Open: 10-4 pm, Tues.–Sat., except major holidays. Web site: www.cooshistory.org.

Coastal Visitor Center/Umpqua River Lighthouse. Lighthouse Road, west of Winchester Bay-Salmon Harbor. Telephone: 541-271-4631. Open: 10-4 pm, May-Oct.

Umpqua Discovery Center. 409 Riverside Way, Reedsport, OR 97467. Telephone: 541-271-4816. Open: 9-5 pm, June–Sept.; 10-4 pm, Oct.-May. Web site: www.umpquadiscoverycenter.com.

Siuslaw Pioneer Museum. 2nd and Maple Sts., Florence. Mail: P.O. Box 2637, Florence, OR 97439. Telephone: 541-997-7884. Open: 12-4 pm, Tues.-Sun., except Jan., holidays.

Heceta Head Lighthouse. 10 miles north of Florence at milepost 178.3; 13 miles south of Yachats. Tour times: May-Sept., 11-5 pm; Mar., Apr., Oct. 11-3 pm. For special tours call 541-547-3416. Heceta House B&B reservations: 1-866-547-3696.

Index

NATHAN DOUTHIT is professor emeritus of history and political science at Southwestern Oregon Community College in Coos Bay, where he taught from 1969 to 1997. He is the author of *Uncertain Encounters: Indians and Whites at Peace and War in Southern Oregon, 1820s-1860s* (Oregon State University Press, 2002) and *The Coos Bay Region 1890-1944: Life on a Coastal Frontier* (Coos County Historical Society, 2005). The author's interest in writing about the history of Oregon's South Coast grew out of his experience of living in the region for many years and teaching classes on local and Pacific Northwest history. A few years ago, he and his wife moved to Portland, Oregon; they return to the South Coast each year to visit friends and to renew their experience of the region's natural and human history.